pasta

pasta

Classic and Contemporary Pasta, Risotto, Crespelle, and Polenta Recipes

Gianni Scappin AND Alberto Vanoli

Photography AND Food Styling BY Francesco Tonelli

THE CULINARY INSTITUTE OF AMERICA®

WILEY

JOHN WILEY & SONS, INC.

Cover and interior design: Vertigo Design NYC

Cover and interior photography: copyright © 2013 by Francesco Tonelli

THE CULINARY INSTITUTE OF AMERICA

President	Dr. Tim Ryan '77
Provost	Mark Erickson '77
Director of Publishing	Nathalie Fischer
Editorial Project Manager	Mary Donovan '83
Editorial Assistant	Shelly Malgee '08

Published by John Wiley & Sons, Inc., Hoboken, New Jersey
Published simultaneously in Canada

For general information on our other products and services, or technical support, please contact our Customer Care Department within the United States at 800–762–2974, outside the United States at 317–572–3993 or fax 317–572–4002. Wiley publishes in a variety of print and electronic formats and by print-on-demand. Some material included with standard print versions of this book may not be included in e-books or in print-on-demand. If this book refers to media such as a CD or DVD that is not included in the version you purchased, you may download this material at http://booksupport.wiley.com. For more information about Wiley products, visit www.wiley.com.

LIBRARY OF CONGRESS CATALOGING-IN-PUBLICATION DATA

Scappin, Gianni.
Pasta: Classic and contemporary pasta, risotto, crespelle, and polenta recipes/
Gianni Scappin, Alberto Vanoli ; photographs by Francesco Tonelli.
p. cm.
Includes index.
ISBN 978-0-470-58779-9 (cloth : alk. paper) 1. Cooking (Pasta) 2. Noodles. I.
Vanoli, Alberto. II. Culinary Institute of America. III. Title.
TX809.M17S229 2013
641.82'2--dc23
2012013067

Printed in China

10 9 8 7 6 5 4 3 2 1

Summer 1

Autumn 57

Winter 113

Spring 173

BASICS 232

INDEX 261

Summer

Penne con pomodoro e basilico

Penne with fresh tomato and basil

Serves 4 to 6

Fresh tomato and basil sauce

6 lb ripe beefsteak tomatoes, peeled and halved (see page 248)

½ cup extra-virgin olive oil

1 large yellow onion, minced

¾ cup torn basil

Kosher salt, as needed

1 lb dried penne rigate

Grated Parmigiano-Reggiano, as needed for serving (optional)

Six pounds of beefsteak tomatoes, if properly ripe, will produce about 4 cups of finished tomato sauce, so you might have some tomato sauce left over. You can store it in the refrigerator in a covered container for up to 5 days.

1. Squeeze the tomatoes to remove the seeds and juices (the juices can be reserved for use in another dish). Cut into large chunks and let them drain in a colander until they are fairly dry, about 1 hour.

2. Heat the oil in a large, wide pan over medium-low heat. Add the onion and cook, stirring frequently, until tender, about 10 minutes. Add the tomatoes and bring to a simmer. Cook, stirring frequently, until the tomatoes are falling apart and most of the liquid has reduced, about 1 hour. (If the sauce still appears too watery, spoon off some of the excess liquid.) Add about half of the basil, taste, and adjust the seasoning with a pinch of salt, if needed. Set aside.

3. Bring a large pot of salted water to a boil over high heat. Add the penne all at once and stir a few times to separate and submerge the pieces. Cook, uncovered, until the pasta is almost cooked, 6 to 7 minutes (check the cooking time for your pasta and cook it 1 to 2 minutes less than the recommended time). Drain the pasta in a colander. Shake well to remove any water clinging to the pasta.

4. Reheat about 3 cups of the tomato sauce in a large pan, add the drained pasta, and cook over medium heat until the pasta is coated well and cooked through. Add the cheese, if using, and serve in a heated serving dish or in pasta plates, topped with the remaining basil.

Recipe notes *You can use canned tomatoes, if you prefer; use about 10 cups and reduce the cooking time to 30 minutes.*

Use a whisk or a potato masher to break up the tomatoes as the sauce cooks. If you want a smoother sauce, you can purée it through a food mill using the largest opening.

You can add garlic (about 4 cloves, minced or sliced) when cooking the onion in step 2. If you have any leftover Parmesan rind, you can add it to the tomato sauce while it is cooking.

You can also add 1 bay leaf to the sauce while it is cooking. Remove and discard before serving.

Pasta con polipi e mollica di pane

Pasta with octopus and bread crumbs

SERVES 4 TO 6

Octopus and tomato sauce

¼ cup extra-virgin olive oil

3 garlic cloves, thinly sliced

1 fresh red chile (peperoncino), seeded and, thinly sliced

2 lb cleaned octopus, cut into ½-inch pieces (see Recipe Note)

¼ cup chopped flat-leaf parsley

¾ cup dry white wine

2 cups canned whole San Marzano tomatoes, seeded, chopped, and juices reserved

1 bay leaf

1 pt ripe cherry tomatoes, halved

Kosher salt and freshly ground black pepper, as needed

1 lb dried spaghetti, bucatini, linguine, or other long pasta shapes

¼ cup chopped flat-leaf parsley

Toasted Bread Crumbs (page 247)

Extra-virgin olive oil, as needed for serving

For this dish, we suggest a long and thick dried pasta. Undercook the pasta so that it slightly firmer than al dente. It will finish cooking in the sauce.

1. Heat the oil in a wide saucepan over medium heat. Add the garlic and the chile and cook, stirring frequently, just until the garlic starts to get some color, about 1 minute.

2. Add the octopus and ¼ cup of the parsley and stir until the octopus is evenly coated with the oil. Add the wine, reduce the heat slightly, and cook until the wine has cooked away, about 3 minutes.

3. Add the canned tomatoes and the bay leaf. Season with salt and pepper. Simmer, partially covered, using a fork occasionally to help break down the tomatoes, until the octopus is very tender and the sauce is thick, 20 to 45 minutes. (The cooking time will vary depending on the size and the quality of the octopus.)

4. Remove the lid, add the cherry tomatoes, and simmer just long enough to heat the cherry tomatoes and they start to break up a bit, another 5 minutes. Remove and discard the bay leaf. Set aside.

5. Bring a large pot of salted water to a boil over high heat. Add the spaghetti and stir to submerge and separate the strands. Cook, uncovered, until the pasta is almost cooked, 6 to 7 minutes (check the cooking time for your pasta and cook it 1 or 2 minutes less than the recommended time).

6. Drain the pasta in a colander. Shake well to remove any water clinging to the pasta. Pour the drained pasta into the saucepan with the sauce. Toss the pasta and the sauce together over medium heat until thoroughly combined and the pasta is cooked. Stir in the ¼ cup parsley. Season with salt and pepper as needed.

7. Serve the spaghetti in a heated serving bowl or in pasta plates, topped with the bread crumbs and drizzled with oil.

Recipe note *We suggest that, if possible, you have your fishmonger clean the octopus for you; it can be a rather messy procedure. If you are using a whole octopus that hasn't been cleaned, you will need about 2¾ pounds, since the octopus loses about 30 percent of its weight once cleaned.*

Maccheroni alla chitarra ai frutti di mare e pomodoro

Maccheroni with seafood and fresh tomato

SERVES 6 TO 8

Seafood and fresh tomato sauce

One whole 2-lb lobster

¼ cup extra-virgin olive oil

1 medium shallot, thinly sliced

5 garlic cloves, thinly sliced

¼ cup chopped flat-leaf parsley

1 tsp red pepper flakes

16 mussels, scrubbed and debearded (about 1½ lb)

2 oz squid, cleaned and cut into rings

2 oz medium shrimp, peeled and deveined

2 oz scallops, muscle tabs removed

¾ cup dry white wine

2 cups peeled, seeded, chopped fresh or canned tomatoes (page 248)

Kosher salt, as needed

1 lb Maccheroni alla Chitarra (page 240) or 1 lb dried maccheroni alla chitarra

¼ cup extra-virgin olive oil

½ cup basil, torn in pieces

¼ cup chopped flat-leaf parsley

If you can find dried maccheroni alla chitarra, you can use that instead of making fresh pasta. Or, substitute any thick long dried pasta you like, as long as it is fairly substantial, such as spaghetti, bucatini, trenette, or linguine.

1. Bring a large pot of water to a boil over high heat. Add the lobster and cook until the shell changes color, 4 to 5 minutes. Remove the lobster from the water and cool in a large bowl of ice water. When cool enough to handle, pull away the tail. Using scissors, cut away the bottom side of the shell and cut the meat into slices about ½ inch thick, leaving them in the shell.

2. Heat the ¼ cup of oil in a wide deep pot over medium heat. Add the shallot and cook, stirring frequently, until the shallot sizzles, about 1 minute. Add the garlic and continue to cook, stirring, until the garlic is lightly browned, about 1 minute. Add ¼ cup of the parsley and the red pepper flakes and stir to combine.

3. Add the seafood at about 1-minute intervals: first the cooked lobster, then the mussels, squid, shrimp, and finally the scallops. Stir to coat the seafood with the hot oil. Add the wine and bring to a simmer, then add the tomatoes. Simmer until all of the seafood is cooked and the liquid is flavorful, about 8 minutes. Discard any mussels that do not open.

4. Bring a large pot of salted water to a boil over high heat. Add the maccheroni all at once and stir to submerge and separate the strands. Cook, uncovered, until tender but still al dente, 3 to 4 minutes for fresh pasta and 8 to 10 minutes for dried.

5. Drain the maccheroni in a colander. Shake well to remove any water clinging to the pasta. Pour the drained pasta into a bowl, add the seafood and tomato sauce, the ¼ cup of oil, the basil, and the ¼ cup parsley, and toss together until combined. Serve at once in heated pasta plates.

Recipe notes *If the sauce is too wet, remove the seafood from the sauce and add it to the hot pasta in step 8. Return the rest of the sauce to the heat and simmer to reduce slightly, and then pour it over the seafood and the pasta.*

Farfalle con cavolfiore, acciughe e uova sode

Farfalle with cauliflower, anchovy, and hard-cooked egg

SERVES 4 TO 6

Roasted cauliflower with
onions and capers

1 head cauliflower (28 to 30 oz)

1 medium red onion, cut into
¼-inch-thick slices

2 tsp capers, rinsed and coarsely
chopped

3 tbsp extra-virgin olive oil

Kosher salt and freshly ground
pepper, as needed

1 lb dried farfalle

5 tbsp extra-virgin olive oil

6 oil-packed anchovy fillets

3 garlic cloves, chopped

½ cup chopped flat-leaf parsley

½ cup grated Pecorino Romano
or Parmigiano-Reggiano

3 hard-cooked eggs, coarsely
chopped (see Recipe note)

A pinch of fresh marjoram or lemon zest combines well with the other flavors in dish. We like coarsely chopped eggs as a garnish for their great flavor and color.

1. Preheat the oven to 400°F. Trim away the leaves and cut out the core of the cauliflower with a paring knife. Cut and break the cauliflower into bite-size florets. Rinse thoroughly and drain.

2. Combine the onion and capers with the 3 tablespoons oil in a baking pan. Add the cauliflower and toss to coat evenly. Season generously with salt and pepper, and spread in an even layer. Roast until tender and lightly browned, about 20 minutes. This can be done up to 1 day in advance.

3. Bring a large pot of salted water to a boil over high heat. Add the farfalle and stir to submerge and separate the pieces. Cook, uncovered, until the pasta is just tender (al dente), about 8 minutes (check the cooking time for your pasta).

4. While the pasta is cooking, heat the 5 tablespoons oil in a large sauté pan over medium-high heat. Add the anchovies, stirring and smashing them in the hot oil, until they are almost melted. Add the garlic and cook, stirring constantly, until aromatic but still translucent, about 1 minute. Add the roasted cauliflower mixture and half of the parsley and toss until the cauliflower is well coated and heated through, 2 to 3 minutes.

5. Drain the pasta immediately in a colander. Shake well to remove any water clinging to the pasta. Add the drained pasta to the cauliflower mixture. Add the remaining parsley and the cheese. Toss until just combined and serve at once in a heated bowl, topped with the eggs, hot or at room temperature.

Hard-Cooked Eggs *We like to add coarsely chopped hard-cooked eggs to this recipe, and wanted to share our technique for making tender eggs with bright yellow yolks and no green rings:*

Place the eggs in a small pot and add enough cold water to cover them by at least an inch. Do not add salt to the water. Bring the water to a boil and let them cook for 3 minutes. Pull the pot off the heat and cover it tightly. Let the eggs stand in the water for 8 minutes. Drain the water from the eggs and let cold water from the tap run over the eggs until they are cool to the touch. Peel the eggs if you plan to use them right away. They will last for 2 or 3 days in their shells in the refrigerator.

Recipe note *Replace the farfalle with other pasta shapes: orecchiette, tubettini, short penne, or any type of short pasta would work well in this dish.*

Trenette con peperoni e cipollotti

Trenette with peppers and spring onions

SERVES 6

Kosher salt, as needed

1 lb dried trenette or linguine

½ cup extra-virgin olive oil

1 lb spring onions, trimmed, halved lengthwise, and cut into thin strips

1½ lb frying peppers, peeled, seeded, and cut into 3-inch long strips

1 fresh red chile (peperoncino), minced

½ cup chopped flat-leaf parsley

½ cup grated Pecorino Romano

Trenette is a pasta with a close association with Liguria. It is long and ribbon-shaped, similar to linguine but not as wide and often thicker. This means that the pasta has more surface area to hold the sauce you are using.

1. Bring a large pot of salted water to a boil over high heat. Add the pasta all at once and stir a few times to separate the pasta and submerge the strands. Cook, uncovered, until the pasta is almost cooked, 6 to 8 minutes (check the cooking time for your pasta and cook it 1 or 2 minutes less than the recommended time). Reserve about 1 cup of the pasta cooking water to finish the sauce in step 3.

2. While the pasta is cooking, heat the oil in a large sauté pan over medium-high heat. Add the onions, reduce the heat to low, and cook, stirring frequently, until the onions are tender, about 4 minutes. Add the frying peppers and the chile, season with salt, and continue to cook until the peppers are very soft, 4 to 5 minutes. Keep the heat at low to avoid browning the vegetables.

3. Drain the pasta in a colander. Add the drained pasta to the onions and peppers. Add the parsley and let the pasta and sauce cook together over low heat so the pasta can absorb the flavors. If the pasta seems too dry, add some of the reserved pasta cooking water. Stir in the cheese and then serve in a heated serving bowl or in pasta plates.

Insalata di pasta con arugula e pomodorini

Pasta salad with arugula and grape tomatoes

SERVES 4 TO 6

Kosher salt, as needed

1 lb dried short pasta, such as fusilli, rotini, short penne, or small conchiglie

½ cup extra-virgin olive oil

1 pt ripe yellow grape tomatoes, quartered

1 pt ripe red grape tomatoes, quartered

6 oz arugula (about 3 packed cups), stems removed if necessary

½ cup basil, torn in small pieces

3 tbsp lemon juice

½ cup grated Pecorino Romano or Parmigiano-Reggiano

Freshly ground black pepper, as needed

If you prefer to serve this pasta hot or warm, toss the pasta with the tomatoes and arugula while it is still very hot. The arugula and the tomato will wilt a little, so it may not look as pretty but it will still be delicious. Try adding some capers or olives for a little sharpness, or some good-quality oil-packed tuna and cubed mozzarella for a richer and more complex flavor.

1. Bring a large pot of salted water to a boil over high heat. Add the pasta and stir to submerge and separate the pieces. Cook, uncovered, until just tender (al dente), 7 to 8 minutes (check the cooking time for your pasta).

2. Drain the pasta in a colander. Rinse with cold water until it is cooled. Shake well to remove any water clinging to the pasta. Pour the drained pasta into a bowl and drizzle with 1 tablespoon of the oil. The pasta can be covered and stored in the refrigerator for up to 8 hours before finishing and serving.

3. When you are ready to serve the salad, combine the tomatoes, arugula, and basil. Add the remaining 7 tablespoons of oil and the lemon juice and toss to combine.

4. Toss the arugula and tomato mixture with the pasta. Add the cheese and toss together. Season with salt and pepper as needed. Serve the salad directly in the bowl or on chilled plates.

Orecchiette con cozze e broccoletti

Orecchiette with mussels and broccoli

SERVES 4 TO 6

1 lb broccoli

Kosher salt, as needed

1 lb dried orecchiette

½ cup extra-virgin olive oil

4 garlic cloves, thinly sliced

Red pepper flakes, as needed

2 lb mussels, scrubbed and debearded

¾ cup dry white wine

½ cup chopped flat-leaf parsley

Freshly ground black pepper, as needed

We like to include both the broccoli florets and the stems in this dish. Cooking the broccoli along with the pasta saves a step and cuts down on cleanup.

1. Cut the broccoli florets into small pieces. Peel the stems, slice them on the diagonal, and set aside.

2. Bring a large pot of salted water to a boil over high heat. Add the orecchiette all at once and stir to separate the pasta and submerge the pieces. Cook, uncovered, until the pasta is partially cooked, 5 to 6 minutes (check the cooking time for your pasta and cook it about 3 minutes less than the recommended time). Add the peeled broccoli stems, continue cooking for 1 minute, then add the florets and cook until the pasta is done and the broccoli is bright green and very hot, another 2 minutes.

3. While the pasta and broccoli are cooking, heat the oil in a large sauté pan over medium-high heat. Add the garlic and cook, stirring frequently, until it is golden brown, about 2 minutes. Add the red pepper flakes and mussels and toss to coat evenly with the oil. Add the wine, cover the pot, and let the mussels cook until they are completely open, 1 to 2 minutes. Transfer the mussels to a bowl with a slotted spoon, letting as much of the cooking liquid drain back into the pot as possible. Discard any unopened mussels. Strain the cooking liquid through a coffee filter into a clean pan. Add half of the parsley and stir to combine. Return the mussels to the pan.

4. Drain the pasta and broccoli in a colander. Shake well to remove any excess water clinging to the pasta. Add the drained pasta and broccoli to the mussels and toss over medium heat until combined and the pasta is fully cooked, 2 to 3 minutes. Season with salt and black pepper and add the remaining parsley. Serve in a heated serving bowl or in pasta plates.

Recipe notes *If you would rather not serve the pasta with the mussel's still in shells, cook them in advance and pull the meat from the shells. Discard the shells, return the shelled mussels to the sauce and then proceed as instructed in step 3.*

If desired, you can also add about ½ cup tomato sauce to the mussels when they open and then proceed with the recipe as instructed in step 3.

Linguine con vongole, cozze, e peperoni

Linguine with clams, mussels, and peppers

SERVES 6

Pan-steamed clams and mussels

2 tbsp extra-virgin olive oil

2 garlic cloves, smashed

2 slices fresh chile

½ lb clams, scrubbed

½ lb mussels, scrubbed and debearded

½ cup dry white wine

1 cup water

Kosher salt, as needed

1 lb dried linguine

¼ cup extra-virgin olive oil

2 garlic cloves, minced

4 ripe plum tomatoes, peeled, seeded, and diced (see page 248)

1 red pepper, roasted, peeled, seeded, and diced

1 small yellow pepper, roasted, peeled, seeded, and diced

¼ cup chopped flat-leaf parsley

This dish cooks very quickly, so you'll need to have a pot of water coming to a boil while you cook the clams and mussels. Then, once the mussels and clams are cooked and the pasta is submerged in the water, start sautéing the garlic and peppers to complete the dish.

1. To pan steam the clams and mussels: Heat 1 tablespoon of oil in each of two deep wide pots over medium heat. Add a smashed garlic clove and a piece of the chile to each pot and cook just until the garlic is aromatic, about 2 minutes. Add the clams to one pot and the mussels to the other. Divide the wine and the water between the pots, cover tightly, and pan steam until the shells open completely, 7 to 8 minutes. Discard any unopened clams or mussels.

2. Transfer the clams and mussels to a bowl and let them cool until you can handle them. Pull the meat from the shells and place in a bowl. Strain the cooking liquid from the shellfish through a coffee filter and reserve separately.

3. Bring a large pot of salted water to a boil over high heat. Add the linguine and stir to submerge and separate the strands. Cook, uncovered, until the pasta is almost cooked, 6 to 7 minutes (check the cooking time for your pasta and cook it 1 or 2 minutes less than the recommended time). Reserve about ½ cup of the pasta cooking water to adjust the sauce.

4. While the pasta is cooking, heat ¼ cup oil in a wide saucepan or sauté pan over medium heat. Add the minced garlic and sauté just until aromatic, about 1 minute. Add the tomatoes and bell peppers and season with a pinch of salt. Cook, stirring frequently, until the tomatoes are heated through. Add the reserved cooking liquid from the clams and mussels and simmer until everything is very hot and the liquid is reduced, about 3 minutes.

5. Drain the pasta in a colander. Pour the drained pasta into the saucepan with the peppers and tomatoes. Continue to cook until the linguine has absorbed the liquid, 2 to 3 minutes. Add the steamed clams and mussels and the parsley. If the dish appears too dry, add a bit of the reserved cooking water.

6. Serve the linguine at once in a heated serving bowl or in pasta plates.

Paccheri con ragù di scorfano, zafferano e pomodorini

Paccheri with rockfish, saffron, and grape tomatoes

SERVES 6

1 whole rockfish (about 1½ lb) (see Recipe note)

2 tbsp extra-virgin olive oil

1 tbsp chopped chervil

Kosher salt and freshly ground black pepper, as needed

6 basil leaves, shredded or torn

Saffron-tomato sauce

6 tbsp extra-virgin olive oil

3 garlic cloves, smashed

Bones reserved from filleted rockfish

¾ cup minced yellow onion

6 tbsp dry white wine

1 pt ripe grape tomatoes, halved

1 fresh red chile (peperoncino), seeded and thinly sliced

2 bay leaves

1 tsp lightly crushed saffron threads

1 lb dried paccheri

Recipe note *To prepare a whole rockfish, scale the fish, open it flat, rinse the inside and outside, and pat dry. Cut down the backbone with a filleting knife between the flesh and bones on the first side. Repeat on the second. Remove the skin and check the fillets for bones.*

Rockfish is a white-fleshed fish with a firm texture. Farmed striped sea bass or trout may be a good substitute for rockfish if it isn't available in your area. If you have a fishmonger fillet the fish for you, ask for the bones.

1. Reserve the fish bones for the sauce in step 2. Cut the fillets into ½-inch cubes, place in a bowl and combine with the 2 tablespoons oil, the chervil, a pinch of salt and pepper, and the basil. Cover the bowl and set aside in the refrigerator.

2. Heat 4 tablespoons of the oil in a wide saucepan over medium heat. Add the garlic and cook, stirring, until the garlic is aromatic, about 1 minute. Add the fish bones and sauté until heated and any flesh on the bones has changed color, about 5 minutes.

3. Add the onion and sauté, stirring frequently, until the onions are tender and translucent, about 5 minutes. Add the wine, tomatoes, chile, bay leaves, and saffron. Simmer, covered, until the tomatoes have started to fall apart, about 10 minutes. If the sauce seems too dry, add a bit of water to keep it moistened.

4. Remove the pan from the heat and let the sauce cool for about 10 minutes, and then remove the bones. Pick any meat from the bones and return it to the sauce. Discard the bones. Remove and discard the bay leaves. Set the sauce aside. (If made in advance, reheat the sauce before combining it with the paccheri.)

5. Bring a large pot of salted water to a boil over high heat. Add the paccheri and stir to submerge and separate the pieces. Cook, uncovered, until the pasta is just tender (al dente), 10 to 14 minutes (check the cooking time for your pasta).

6. While the pasta is cooking, heat the remaining 2 tablespoons oil in a sauté pan over medium heat. Add the cubed fish and cook, turning as necessary, until the fish is golden brown on all sides, about 5 minutes.

7. Drain the pasta in a colander. Shake well to remove any water clinging to the pasta. Pour the drained pasta into a heated bowl, add the saffron-tomato sauce, and toss together until thoroughly combined. Fold in the fish and the basil and toss to distribute the fish evenly. Serve in a heated bowl or in pasta plates.

Spaghetti al nero di seppia

Spaghetti with squid ink

SERVES 6

½ cup extra-virgin olive oil

3 garlic cloves, minced

2 shallots, minced

¼ cup chopped flat-leaf parsley

¼ cup chopped fennel or dill fronds

1 lb whole cuttlefish, cleaned and cut into strips, ink sac reserved (see sidebar below)

1 cup canned whole San Marzano tomatoes, crushed through a food mill or sieve

¼ cup dry white wine

Kosher salt, as needed

1 lb dried spaghetti

1. Heat the oil in a wide saucepan over medium-high heat. Add the garlic and shallots and cook, stirring, until the garlic is aromatic and the shallots are tender, about 2 minutes. Add the parsley and fennel or dill fronds and sauté for 1 minute.

2. Add the cuttlefish and sauté, stirring, until it has changed color, about 3 minutes. Add the tomatoes, wine, and the reserved ink sac from the cuttlefish. Simmer the sauce over low heat, covered, until the cuttlefish is tender and the sauce is very flavorful, about 10 minutes. If the sauce seems too dry, add a bit of water to keep it moistened.

3. Bring a large pot of salted water to a boil over high heat. Add the spaghetti and stir to submerge and separate the strands. Cook, uncovered, until just tender (al dente), 6 to 8 minutes.

4. Drain the spaghetti in a colander. Shake well to remove any water clinging to the pasta. Pour the drained pasta into a heated bowl, add the sauce, and toss together until thoroughly combined.

5. Serve the spaghetti at once in a heated bowl or in pasta plates.

Cuttlefish *Clean the cuttlefish by removing first the head and the backbone. Remove the interior and look for the ink sac. The main part of the sac is located at the end of the body. Carefully remove it and set aside. Peel the skin from the outer body and wings and any thin membranes that cover the inside of the body. Open the head in half and remove the mouth and the eye. Wash and dry all the parts of the cuttlefish.*

Vermicelli con le cozze e pecorino

Vermicelli with mussels and pecorino romano

SERVES 6

Pan-steamed mussels and tomato sauce

¼ cup extra-virgin olive oil

4 garlic cloves, 2 smashed and 2 minced

½ lb mussels, scrubbed and debearded

½ cup dry white wine

1 fresh red chile (peperoncino), thinly sliced

1 pt ripe cherry tomatoes, halved or quartered, depending on their size

Kosher salt, as needed

1 lb dried vermicelli

½ cup chopped flat-leaf parsley

½ cup grated Pecorino Romano

You can choose any red chile you like or that is available at your market. Take a taste of the chile before you use it. Add as much of the red chile as you like, but remember that there should be more flavors in the dish than simply heat. If you can't locate a fresh chile at your market, use red pepper flakes.

1. Heat 2 tablespoons of the oil in a wide deep pot over medium heat. Add the smashed garlic and cook just until aromatic, about 1 minute. Add the mussels and the wine, cover the pot tightly, and pan-steam until the shells are completely open, 7 to 8 minutes. Discard any unopened mussels.

2. Transfer the mussels to a bowl and let them cool until you can handle them. Pull the meat from the shells and place in a bowl. Strain the cooking liquid through a coffee filter over the shelled mussels and set aside.

3. Heat the remaining 2 tablespoons oil in a wide saucepan over medium-high heat. Add the minced garlic and chile and cook, stirring, until the garlic is aromatic, about 2 minutes.

4. Add the tomatoes and cook, stirring frequently, until the tomatoes begin to break apart, about 3 minutes. Add the shelled mussels and their cooking liquid and set aside.

5. Bring a large pot of salted water to a boil over high heat. Add the vermicelli and stir to submerge and separate the strands. Cook, uncovered, until just tender (al dente), 5 to 7 minutes (check the cooking time for your pasta).

6. Drain the vermicelli immediately through a colander. Shake well to remove any water clinging to the pasta. Pour the drained pasta into the pan with the tomato-mussel sauce and toss together until thoroughly combined. Add the parsley, and cook over low heat until the sauce clings to the vermicelli, about 2 minutes. Add the cheese and stir to combine.

7. Serve the vermicelli at once in a heated serving bowl or in pasta plates.

Spaghetti con aglio, pomodoro, menta e tonno fresco

Spaghetti with garlic, tomato, mint, and fresh tuna

SERVES 4 TO 6

⅓ cup extra-virgin olive oil

3 garlic cloves, crushed

10 oz fresh tuna, cut into ¼-inch cubes

2 tsp minced garlic

2 tbsp chopped flat-leaf parsley

⅓ cup dry white wine

2 cups peeled seeded, diced fresh or canned tomatoes (see page 248)

Kosher salt, as needed

1 lb dried spaghetti

1 tbsp thinly sliced or chopped mint

You can add more ingredients to this dish, such as capers, olives, some fresh or dry oregano, and a sprinkling of Toasted Bread Crumbs (page 247).

1. Heat the oil in a wide saucepan over medium-high heat. Add the crushed garlic cloves and sauté until the garlic is aromatic and just starting to turn brown. Remove and discard the garlic. Add the tuna and cook, stirring as necessary, until the tuna is seared on all sides, about 1 minute.

2. Add the minced garlic and the parsley and stir to combine. Add the wine and once the wine is simmering, about 1 minute, add the tomatoes. Cook, stirring frequently, until the tuna is fully cooked, about 5 minutes. Set aside.

3. While the tuna is cooking, bring a large pot of salted water to a boil over high heat. Add the spaghetti and stir to submerge and separate the strands. Cook, uncovered, until the pasta is almost fully cooked, 5 to 7 minutes (check the cooking time for your pasta and cook 1 to 2 minutes less than the recommended time).

4. Drain the spaghetti in a colander. Shake well to remove any water clinging to the pasta. Pour the drained pasta into the pan with the tuna and sauce and toss together over medium heat until evenly combined. Add the mint and cook over low heat until the spaghetti is fully cooked and the sauce thickens and clings to the spaghetti, about 2 minutes.

5. Serve at once in a heated serving bowl or in pasta plates.

Troccoli al ragù d'agnello e peperoni

Troccoli with lamb and pepper sauce

SERVES 6

Lamb and pepper ragù

¼ cup extra-virgin olive oil

1 lb boneless lamb shoulder, cut in 1-inch cubes

½ cup minced onion

1 tsp red pepper flakes

¼ cup dry red wine

3 cups canned whole San Marzano tomatoes, crushed through a food mill or sieve

1 bay leaf

½ red pepper, cut in half and seeded

Meat Broth (page 251), as needed

Kosher salt, as needed

1 lb Troccoli (page 240)

1. Heat the oil in a 4-quart Dutch oven over medium heat. Add the lamb and cook, stirring, until browned on all sides. Transfer to a plate.

2. Add the onion and red pepper flakes to the same pot and cook, stirring frequently, until the onion is tender, about 2 minutes. Return the lamb to the pot with any accumulated juices and add the wine, tomatoes, and bay leaf and cook over low heat, stirring gently, until the meat is partially cooked, about 2½ hours. Add the red pepper and continue to cook until the lamb is extremely tender, another 1½ to 2 hours. Add a bit of broth if the ragù looks too dry as it cooks. Remove and discard the bay leaf and the red pepper.

3. Remove the ragù from the heat and let sit for about 15 minutes, then pull the lamb apart into smaller pieces, but do not shred it completely. Season with salt, as needed.

4. Bring a large pot of salted water to a boil over high heat. Add the troccoli all at once and stir to submerge and separate the strands. Cook, uncovered, until just tender (al dente), 3 to 4 minutes.

5. Drain the troccoli in a colander. Shake well to remove any water clinging to the pasta. Pour the drained pasta into a bowl, add the ragù, and toss together until well combined. Serve at once in heated pasta plates.

Maccheroncini al pesto trapanese

Maccheroncini with almond-tomato pesto

SERVES 6

Almond-tomato pesto

2 garlic cloves, crushed

14 large basil leaves

½ cup whole almonds, lightly toasted

6 ripe plum tomatoes, peeled, seeded, and chopped (see page 248)

6 tbsp extra-virgin olive oil

½ cup grated Pecorino Siciliano

Kosher salt, as needed

1 lb dried maccheroncini

Grated Pecorino Siciliano, as needed for serving

This dish comes from the city of Trapani on Sicily's westernmost coast. It features almonds and tomatoes for a pesto that looks and tastes quite different than the more familiar pesto from Liguria.

1. Combine the garlic, basil, and almonds in a large mortar and pestle and pound until coarsely crushed. Add the tomatoes, a little at a time, continuing to pound the ingredients together. Once the tomatoes are incorporated, add the oil a little at a time. Add the cheese last. (You may also grind the ingredients together in a food processor.) Set aside.

2. Bring a large pot of salted water to a boil over high heat. Add the maccheroncini and stir a few times to separate the pasta and submerge the pieces. Cook, uncovered, until the pasta is just tender but still al dente, 8 to 10 minutes (check the cooking time for your pasta).

3. Drain the pasta in a colander. Shake well to remove any water clinging to the pasta. Pour the drained pasta into a large heated serving bowl, add the pesto, and toss together to coat evenly.

4. Serve at once and pass with cheese on the side, if desired.

Scialatielli con calamari e filetti di pomodoro

Scialatielli with baby squid and fresh tomatoes

SERVES 4 TO 6

Baby squid and fresh tomato sauce

1 lb baby squid, cleaned (see headnote)

3 tbsp extra-virgin olive oil

2 garlic cloves, thinly sliced

½ tsp red pepper flakes or minced fresh chile (peperoncini)

⅓ cup chopped flat-leaf parsley

1 qt canned whole San Marzano tomatoes, seeded and sliced

Kosher salt, as needed

1¼ lb Scialatielli (page 240)

Choose the smallest squid you can find so that it will cook quickly. That is the essence of this dish and why it is sometimes known as the "two-minute calamari sauce." As long as the squid are not overcooked, they stay tender to the bite.

1. Cut the squid into ¼-inch rings, tentacles included, and set aside.

2. Heat the oil in a large wide pan over medium-low heat. Add the garlic and cook, stirring frequently, until just starting to turn golden, about 1 minute. Add the pepper flakes or chile and half of the parsley and stir to combine. Add the tomatoes and bring to a simmer. Cook, stirring frequently, until the sauce has reduced by half, about 15 minutes. Add the sliced squid and cook until just cooked through and still very tender, about 2 minutes.

3. Bring a large pot of salted water to a boil over high heat. Add the scialatielli and stir a few times to separate the pasta and submerge the strands. Cook, uncovered, until the pasta is almost cooked, 3 to 4 minutes.

4. Drain the pasta in a colander, shaking to remove the excess water, and then add the drained scialatielli to the sauce. Stir the pasta and sauce together over medium heat until the scialatielli is evenly coated. Add the remaining parsley. Serve at once in a heated bowl or in individual pasta plates.

Recipe note *Dried scialatielli can be found in Italian specialty food stores. You could also use any thick spaghetti or even a short pasta, such as orecchiette or farfalle.*

Ravioli ai formaggi freschi con pesto e pignoli

Fresh cheese ravioli with pesto and pine nuts

SERVES 6 TO 8

Cheese filling

6 oz Robiola

4 oz mascarpone

6 oz ricotta

1 lb Pasta Sheets (page 235)

Egg wash: 1 large egg blended with 2 tbsp water

Kosher salt, as needed

2 tbsp extra-virgin olive oil

½ cup Pesto (page 247)

½ cup pine nuts, lightly toasted

Freshly ground black pepper, as needed

1. In a small bowl, stir together the Robiola, mascarpone, and ricotta for the filling in a small bowl. Set aside.

2. Brush one pasta sheet with egg wash. Spoon the filling in mounds (about 2 teaspoons each) down the center of the dough. Cover with a second pasta sheet and press the dough together around the filling to seal the sheets together and to remove any air pockets. Using a 2-inch round cutter, cut out the ravioli.

3. Bring a large pot of salted water to a boil over high heat. Add the ravioli all at once and stir a few times to separate them. Cook, uncovered, at a gentle boil until just tender to the bite, 8 to 10 minutes. Drain the ravioli in a colander. Shake well to remove excess water. Transfer to a heated serving bowl, add the olive oil and pesto, and toss to coat evenly. Or, spoon the pesto into warmed pasta plates, top with ravioli, and drizzle with olive oil.

4. Serve the ravioli in a heated serving bowl or pasta plates, topped with the pine nuts and seasoned with salt and pepper.

Ravioli di melanzane con pomodoro e olive

Eggplant ravioli with candied tomatoes and olives

SERVES 8

Candied tomatoes

1 pt ripe cherry tomatoes

¼ cup extra-virgin olive oil

Kosher salt, as needed

Sugar, as needed

2 thyme sprigs, plus additional leaves as needed

4 garlic cloves

Eggplant filling

1 globe eggplant (about 2½ lb)

¼ cup extra-virgin olive oil

1 garlic clove, smashed

8 basil leaves, thinly sliced

1 lb Pasta Sheets (page 235)

Egg wash: 1 large egg blended with 1 tbsp water

Flour, as needed

¼ cup extra-virgin olive oil

40 whole small olives, such as Taggiasche or Niçoise, pitted (about 3½ oz)

16 whole small basil leaves

The slow-roasted candied tomatoes in this dish add a complex flavor note. They are a great way to prepare a large supply of cherry tomatoes and will last up to 4 weeks in the refrigerator. However, diced fresh tomatoes are also an excellent condiment in this recipe if don't have the time to roast them.

1. Preheat the oven to 250°F.

2. Bring a large pot of water to a boil. Add the cherry tomatoes (working in batches) and blanch for no more than 10 seconds, just long enough to loosen the skin. Transfer to a bowl of ice water.

3. Peel the tomatoes and combine them with 2 tablespoons of the oil, a pinch of salt, and a pinch of sugar. Line a baking sheet with parchment paper or foil. Pour the oiled tomatoes onto the baking sheet and add the thyme sprigs and the whole garlic cloves. Bake until the tomatoes have browned and shriveled, about 2 hours. Remove and discard the thyme sprigs. Transfer the tomatoes to a bowl and add the remaining 2 tablespoons oil and fresh thyme leaves. Toss together and set aside.

4. Preheat the oven to 400°F.

5. Wash and dry the eggplant and brush with 1 tablespoon of the oil. Place it on a rack in a baking sheet or roasting pan and bake until fully cooked, 30 to 40 minutes.

6. Remove the eggplant from the oven and let it cool until it can be handled. Cut the eggplant in half lengthwise and scoop out and chop the pulp. Transfer the eggplant to a wire-mesh sieve and salt it lightly. Let the eggplant drain to lose some of the excess moisture, about 30 minutes.

7. Combine the drained eggplant with the smashed garlic clove, the sliced basil, and the remaining 3 tablespoons of oil. Season with salt as needed. Set aside.

Continued

8. Brush one pasta sheet with some of the egg wash. Remove and discard the garlic from the eggplant filling. Spoon the filling in mounds (about 2 teaspoons each) down the center of the dough, about ¾ inch apart. Cover with the second pasta sheet and press the dough together around the filling to seal the sheets together and to remove any air pockets. Using a 2-inch round cutter, cut out the ravioli. Transfer to a lightly floured baking sheet as they are completed.

9. Bring a large pot of salted water to a boil over high heat. Add the ravioli and stir to submerge and separate them. Reduce the heat and cook, uncovered, at a gentle boil until just tender to the bite (al dente), 4 to 5 minutes. Drain the ravioli in a colander. Shake well to remove excess water. Transfer to a heated serving bowl, add ¼ cup oil, and toss to coat evenly.

10. Serve at once, topped with the candied tomatoes, olives, and whole basil leaves.

Ravioli di mozzarella con pomodoro crudo, capperi, olive e acciughe

Ravioli with mozzarella, raw tomato, capers, olives, and anchovies

SERVES 6 TO 8

Mozzarella and anchovy filling

2 lb mozzarella, small dice

4 oz (½ cup) ricotta

⅔ cup grated Parmigiano-Reggiano

2 tbsp salted capers, rinsed and drained

2 tsp chopped salted anchovies, rinsed and drained

1 tbsp chopped basil

½ tsp minced oregano

1 large egg

Kosher salt and freshly ground black pepper, as needed

1 lb Pasta Sheets (page 235)

Egg wash: 1 large egg mixed with 1 tbsp water

Flour, as needed

½ cup extra-virgin olive oil

2 tsp salted anchovies, rinsed and chopped

2 tbsp salted capers, rinsed and drained

2 tbsp pitted and sliced black olives

2 ripe plum tomatoes, peeled, seeded, cut into small dice (page 248)

2 tbsp thinly sliced basil

If your mozzarella or ricotta is extremely wet, squeeze out any excess water by wrapping the cheese in a clean towel or cheesecloth and twisting before you proceed with the recipe. You may like to add some crushed red pepper flakes or adjust the amount of anchovies and capers.

1. Mix together all the ingredients for the filling except the salt and pepper. Taste and season only if needed (the capers and anchovies are already fairly salty). Set aside.

2. Brush one pasta sheet with egg wash. Spoon the mozzarella filing in mounds (about 2 teaspoons each) down the center of the dough, about ¾ inch apart. Cover with the second pasta sheet and press the dough together around the filling to seal the sheets together and to remove any air pockets. Using a knife or a 2-inch fluted pasta cutter, cut out the ravioli. Transfer to a lightly floured baking sheet as the ravioli are completed.

3. Bring a large pot of salted water to a boil over high heat. Add the ravioli all at once to the boiling water and stir a few times to separate them. Cook, uncovered, at a gentle boil until just tender to the bite, 4 to 5 minutes. Drain the ravioli in a colander. Shake well to remove excess water.

4. Heat the olive oil in a sauté pan over medium heat. Add the anchovies and cook, stirring, until they are melted into the oil. Add the capers and the olives and cook just long enough to warm them, about 1 minute. Add the tomatoes. Toss together and cook just long enough to warm the tomatoes, about 30 seconds. Remove the pan from the heat and set aside.

5. Transfer the ravioli to a heated serving bowl, pour the tomato mixture over them, and serve.

Ravioli alle ortiche con burro e salvia

Ravioli with nettles, butter, and sage

SERVES 6 TO 8

Nettle stuffing

8 oz nettle leaves (about 3 packed cups)

Kosher salt, as needed

1 oz (2 tbsp) unsalted butter

1 small shallot, minced

Freshly ground black pepper, as needed

½ cup fresh ricotta

⅔ cup grated Parmigiano-Reggiano

1 large egg

1 lb Pasta Sheets (page 235)

Egg wash: 1 large egg blended with 1 tbsp water

Flour, as needed

4 oz (½ cup) unsalted butter

6 sage leaves

Nettles are not always easy to come by unless you forage for them yourself. However, you may substitute other types of greens for the nettles, including dandelion or mustard greens, chicory, or escarole.

1. If the nettles are not cleaned already, wear gloves to pull the leaves from stems. Wash the leaves gently in plenty of cold water. Bring a large pot of salted water to a boil and add the nettle leaves all at once, stirring to submerge them completely. Cook the leaves for 2 minutes. Drain the nettles in a colander and then transfer them to a bowl of ice water to stop the cooking. Once the leaves are cool, drain them in a colander and squeeze dry. Chop the nettles and set aside.

2. Heat the butter in a sauté pan over medium heat. Add the shallot and cook, stirring, until softened, about 2 minutes. Add the chopped nettles and sauté until they are hot and flavored with the butter and shallot. Season with a pinch of salt and pepper. Transfer to a mixing bowl and let the mixture cool to room temperature.

3. Add the ricotta and Parmigiano-Reggiano and stir to combine. Season with salt and pepper, as needed. Stir in the 1 large egg until blended. Let the filling mixture firm in the refrigerator, covered, for at least 1 hour before filling the ravioli.

4. Brush one pasta sheet with some of the egg wash. Spoon the nettle stuffing in mounds (about 2 teaspoons each) down the center of the dough, about ¾ inch apart. Cover with the second pasta sheet and press the dough together around the filling to seal the sheets together and to remove any air pockets. Using a knife or a fluted pasta cutter, cut out the ravioli. Transfer to a lightly floured baking sheet as they are completed.

5. Bring a large pot of salted water to a boil over high heat. Add the ravioli all at once to the boiling water and stir a few times to separate them. Cook, uncovered, at a gentle boil until just tender to the bite, 4 to 5 minutes. Drain the ravioli in a colander. Shake well to remove excess water.

6. While the ravioli is cooking, heat the ½ cup butter in a skillet over medium-low heat with the sage leaves. Cook until the sage leaves are crisp and the butter is brown with a nutty aroma.

7. Transfer the ravioli to a heated serving bowl, add the brown butter and sage leaves, toss to coat evenly, and serve.

Rotolini di pasta con pesce, broccoletti, capperi e acciughe

Pasta rolls with fish, broccoli, capers, and anchovies

SERVES 6 TO 8

Broccoli filling

Kosher salt, as needed

1 lb broccoli, cut into small pieces, stems peeled if tough

3 tbsp extra-virgin olive oil

2 garlic gloves thinly sliced

3 salted anchovy fillets, rinsed and drained

1 tbsp salted capers, rinsed and drained

1 lb Squid Ink Pasta Sheets (page 236)

1 lb sea bass fillets, cut lengthwise into strips

1 tbsp extra-virgin olive oil, plus more as needed for baking

Kosher salt and freshly ground black pepper, as needed

6 ripe plum tomatoes, peeled, seeded, and diced (see page 248)

1 cup plain dry bread crumbs

2 tbsp grated Pecorino Romano

6 basil leaves, chopped

1 tbsp dried oregano

1. Bring a large pot of salted water to a boil over high heat. Add the broccoli and cook, uncovered, until bright green and very tender, about 8 minutes. Drain well.

2. Heat the 3 tablespoons of oil in a sauté pan over medium heat. Add the garlic and sauté until just golden, about 2 minutes. Add the anchovies and capers and cook until hot, about 2 minutes. Add the broccoli and continue to cook until the broccoli is well flavored and hot. Transfer to a food processor and let cool for several minutes. Purée the broccoli mixture, pulsing the machine on and off, until it is finely chopped. Set aside.

3. Bring another large pot of salted water to a boil over high heat. Add the pasta sheets and cook for 1 minute, then remove the pasta sheets from the water, drain well, and lay them on a flat surface to cool.

4. Toss the sea bass fillets together with the 1 tablespoon of olive oil to coat them lightly and season with salt and pepper.

5. Lay a sheet of cooked pasta on a flat surface and spoon or pipe some of the broccoli filling down the center of the pasta. Place a piece of the fish on the pasta, running the length of the sheet. Roll the pasta sheet up on the long side to form a log. Cool the roll of pasta for few hours in the refrigerator to let the filling firm up and then cut the logs into 1½-inch-thick pieces.

6. Preheat the oven to 325°F. Place the diced tomatoes in an even layer in the bottom of an oiled baking dish and season them with olive oil, salt, and pepper. Place the pasta slices on top of the tomatoes, cut side down.

7. Mix the bread crumbs with the cheese, basil, and oregano. Sprinkle in an even layer over the rolls. Drizzle with additional olive oil and bake until the top of the pasta has a golden color and the fish is cooked through, 15 to 20 minutes.

Cannelloni con erbette e caprino fresco

Cannelloni with swiss chard and fresh goat cheese

SERVES 6

Swiss chard and goat cheese filling

1 lb green Swiss chard

Kosher salt, as needed

¼ cup extra-virgin olive oil

¾ cup minced yellow onion

6 oz fresh goat cheese, crumbled

¼ cup grated Pecorino Romano

1¼ cups fresh soft bread crumbs

Freshly ground pepper, as needed

2 tbsp extra-virgin olive oil, plus more as needed for baking dish

1 lb Cannelloni Sheets (page 235), cooked and cooled

2 cups Tomato Sauce (page 248)

½ cup plain dry bread crumbs, as needed

¼ cup grated Pecorino Romano

1. Cut the green leaves from the stems of the Swiss chard and keep them separate.

2. Bring a large pot of salted water to a boil over high heat. Add the chard leaves and stir to submerge the leaves. Cook, uncovered, until tender and a deep color, 3 to 4 minutes. Lift the leaves out of the water with a sieve or slotted spoon and transfer to a bowl of ice water. After the leaves have cooked, add the white stems, and cook uncovered until tender, about 5 minutes. Lift the stems out of the water and transfer to the bowl of ice water. After the leaves and stems are chilled, drain in a colander for several minutes and then squeeze dry. Finely chop the chard and set aside.

3. Heat the ¼ cup oil in a medium sauté pan over medium heat. Add the onion and cook over low heat, stirring frequently, until very translucent, about 3 minutes. Add the chopped chard, stir well, and cook, covered, over low heat, stirring occasionally, until the greens are soft, about 2 minutes. Transfer to a bowl and let cool.

4. Add the goat cheese, ¼ cup of the Pecorino Romano, and the fresh bread crumbs and stir well. Season with salt and pepper, as needed. Set aside.

5. Preheat the oven to 350°F. Brush a baking dish or casserole with oil. Add the tomato sauce to the dish.

6. To assemble the cannelloni: Divide the chard filling between the sheets of cooked pasta. Roll the pasta around the filling into logs about 3 inches in diameter and then cut them into cannelloni about 4 inches long. Set them into the sauce in baking dish, seam side down, and brush the tops with the 2 tablespoons olive oil.

7. Combine the dry bread crumbs and the ¼ cup Pecorino Romano in a small bowl and scatter in a thin, even layer over the cannelloni. (You may bake the dish now, or cover the dish and keep refrigerated for up to 2 days.)

8. Bake until the cannelloni are very hot, 15 to 20 minutes (or longer if they were held in the refrigerator). Serve directly from the baking dish or on heated serving plates.

Lasagna con melanzane, pomodoro e mozzarella

Lasagna with eggplant, tomato, and mozzarella

SERVES 6 TO 8

Fried eggplant

2 lb eggplant

Kosher salt, as needed

Extra-virgin olive oil, as needed
for frying

Tomato-basil sauce

¼ cup extra-virgin olive oil

½ cup chopped yellow onion

2 garlic cloves, minced

2 qt canned whole San Marzano
tomatoes with their juices

Kosher salt, as needed

5 or 6 large basil leaves

Extra-virgin olive oil, as needed for
the baking pan

1 lb Lasagna Sheets (page 235),
cooked and cooled

20 basil leaves

12 oz mozzarella, thinly sliced

1 cup grated Parmigiano-Reggiano

1. Rinse the eggplant, trim the ends, and then slice crosswise, about ¼ inch thick. Lay them on a baking sheet and season lightly with salt. Let the eggplant rest for about 2 hours; this will draw out the excess liquid. Rinse the eggplant and blot it dry with paper towels.

2. Heat about ½ inch of olive oil in a deep sauté pan over medium heat. When hot, but not smoking, add the eggplant slices, working in batches to avoid crowding the pan. Fry until golden brown on both sides, turning the eggplant once as it cooks, about 5 minutes total cooking time. Transfer the fried eggplant to a paper towel–lined plate to drain. Set aside.

3. Heat the ¼ cup oil in a saucepan over low heat. Add the onion and garlic and cook, stirring frequently, until tender and translucent, and then add tomatoes. Season the sauce lightly with salt, add the basil leaves, and simmer the sauce until it is thickened and flavorful, 20 to 30 minutes. When the sauce is cooked, remove and discard the basil leaves, pass the sauce through a food mill and set aside.

4. Preheat the oven to 350°F. Brush a baking pan with olive oil.

5. Scoop about ¾ cup of the tomato-basil sauce on the bottom, then add a layer of lasagna sheets. Top with one-third of the eggplant, and spread about ¾ cup of the tomato basil sauce over the eggplant. Top with 6 or 7 of the basil leaves. Add one-third of the mozzarella and sprinkle with 3 tablespoons of the Parmigiano-Reggiano.

6. Repeat this layering sequence twice. Finish the lasagna with a layer of lasagna sheets, the remaining tomato-basil sauce, and the remaining Parmigiano-Reggiano.

7. Bake the lasagna until it is very hot all the way through and the cheese is browned on top. Let the lasagna rest for about 45 minutes before cutting and serving.

Lasagnetta alle verdure con salsa di pomodoro fresco

Vegetable lasagna with fresh tomato sauce

SERVES 6 TO 8

Roasted vegetables

1 large eggplant (about 2 lb)

4 medium zucchini (about 1½ lb)

2 large ripe yellow tomatoes

Kosher salt, as needed

3 garlic cloves, thinly sliced

Leaves from 6 thyme sprigs

3 red peppers

Extra-virgin olive oil, as needed

Extra-virgin olive oil, as needed

3 cups Fresh Tomato Sauce (page 249), plus as needed

1 lb Lasagna Sheets (page 235), cooked and cooled

20 basil leaves

¾ cup grated Parmigiano-Reggiano

1½ cups steamed broccoli florets

1. Preheat the oven to 400°F.

2. Trim the stem and blossom ends from the eggplant and zucchini. Slice them about ¼ inch thick. Remove the core from the tomatoes and slice them ¼ inch thick. Place the vegetables on three separate baking sheets (they should be in a single layer) and season with a little salt, the garlic, and the thyme. Drizzle with oil and roast until the vegetables are tender, about 20 minutes. Remove and set aside, keeping the vegetables separate.

3. Rub the peppers with oil and place them in a baking dish. Roast the peppers until they are tender enough to collapse and the skin is wrinkled and starting to pull away, about 20 minutes. Place the peppers in a bowl and cover them to help loosen the skin. When they are cool enough to handle, cut around the stem and pull out the seeds and ribs. Make a cut through one side of the pepper and open it flat to scrape out any remaining seeds or ribs. Set aside.

4. Preheat the oven to 350°F. Brush a lasagna pan with oil.

5. Spread about 1 cup of the tomato sauce in the bottom of the pan, then add a layer of the lasagna sheets. Top with a layer of roasted eggplant. Sprinkle with a few basil leaves and about ¼ cup of the cheese. Add another layer of lasagna sheets, then a layer of the roasted peppers. Add another layer of lasagna sheets and top with the roasted yellow tomatoes, a few basil leaves, and ¼ cup of the cheese. Add another layer of sheets and top with the roasted zucchini and the remaining ½ cup cheese. Add another layer of and top with ¾ cup of the tomato sauce and the broccoli.

6. Cover the pan with aluminum foil and bake the lasagna until it is very hot all the way through, about 45 minutes. Let the lasagna rest for about 15 minutes before cutting and serving. Serve the lasagna with additional tomato sauce.

Stracci con pesto, fagiolini e patate

Pasta with pesto, green beans, and potatoes

SERVES 6 TO 8

Kosher salt, as needed

1 lb white waxy potatoes, peeled and cut into ½-inch dice

1 lb green beans, trimmed and cut into 1-inch lengths

1½ lb Stracci (page 237)

1 cup Pesto (page 247)

2 tbsp pine nuts, lightly toasted

1. Bring a large pot of salted water to a boil over high heat. Add the potatoes and green beans and cook, uncovered, until they are nearly tender, about 5 minutes.

2. Add the stracci and continue to cook until the potatoes are tender and the pasta is cooked, about 3 minutes more. Drain and transfer to a heated bowl.

3. Add the pesto and toss together until evenly coated. Serve at once, garnished with the pine nuts.

Crespelle con melanzane, pomodoro fresco e ricotta

Crespelle stuffed with eggplant and topped with fresh tomatoes and ricotta

SERVES 6 TO 8

Eggplant filling

2 large globe eggplants (about 2½ lb)

¼ cup extra-virgin olive oil

Kosher salt, as needed

2 marjoram sprigs

2 garlic cloves, smashed

6 to 8 Crespelle (page 242)

6 tbsp extra-virgin olive oil, plus as needed for serving

12 ripe plum tomatoes (about 1½ lb), peeled, seeded, diced, and drained (see page 248)

3 whole garlic cloves

1 small dried red chile, crushed

4 thyme sprigs

1 lb (2 cups) fresh ricotta, at room temperature

12 to 16 small basil leaves

1. Preheat the oven to 400°F.

2. Wash and dry the eggplants, and brush with 1 tablespoon of the oil. Place them on a rack in a baking sheet or roasting pan and bake until fully cooked, 30 to 40 minutes.

3. Remove the eggplants from the oven and let them cool until they can be handled. Cut the eggplants in half lengthwise, scoop out and chop the pulp. Transfer the pulp to a wire-mesh sieve and salt it lightly. Let drain to lose some of the excess moisture, about 30 minutes.

4. Combine the drained eggplant with the marjoram, the smashed garlic cloves, and the remaining 3 tablespoons of oil. Season with salt as needed. Let the filling rest at room temperature for up to 1 hour, or in the refrigerator for up to 12 hours. Remove and discard the garlic and marjoram just before using it to fill the crespelle.

5. Mound the filling mixture near the center of 1 crespella. Fold in each side about 1 inch and then fold the bottom of the crespella up and over the filling. Roll the crespelle up until you have the filling completely enclosed.

6. Place the stuffed crespelle in a ceramic dish and reheat in a microwave or in a steamer until very hot. Allow 4 to 6 minutes in the microwave or 12 minutes in a steamer. Reheating times will vary depending upon the power of your microwave.

7. While the crespelle are heating up, heat the 6 tablespoons oil in a sauté pan over medium-low heat. Add the tomatoes, whole garlic cloves, crushed dried chile, and the thyme. Heat this mixture just long enough to warm the tomatoes and make the garlic aromatic, about 1 minute; it is not really cooked. As soon as it is warm, turn the heat off and remove and discard the garlic, thyme sprigs, and chile.

8. Serve the crespelle at once on a heated platter or serving plates, topped with a scoop of the ricotta and the warmed tomatoes. Drizzle with oil and garnish with the basil leaves.

Gnocchi di melanzane con pomodoro fresco e ricotta salata

Eggplant gnocchi with fresh tomato sauce and ricotta salata

SERVES 4 TO 6

Roasted eggplant gnocchi

1 lb Italian or Japanese eggplant

2 tbsp extra-virgin olive oil

2 garlic cloves, lightly smashed

1 cup all-purpose or 00 flour

½ cup basil leaves, torn into very small pieces or chopped

½ cup grated Parmigiano-Reggiano cheese

1 large egg

Kosher salt and freshly ground black pepper, as needed

3 cups Fresh Tomato Sauce (page 249)

¾ cup grated ricotta salata

Choosing the eggplant is the secret here. Small eggplants will have smaller seeds. If your eggplant is large, it may have larger seeds that you'll need to strain out of the purée and it may be somewhat spongy. In that case, buy enough eggplant to compensate for the loss when you strain out the seeds and drain the cooked eggplant. If the eggplant is still a bit wet, even after draining, you might have to adjust the recipe a little by adding an additional egg or a bit more flour to hold the gnocchi together.

1. Preheat the oven to 350°F.

2. Wash the eggplant and cut them lengthwise in half, or quarters depending on their size. Lay them in a sheet pan, cut side up, and poke them with a fork. Bake until completely soft, 30 to 45 minutes. Remove, let cool a little, and using a spoon, scoop the pulp from the skin. Chop the eggplant pulp and squeeze to remove as much liquid as possible.

3. Heat the oil in a saucepan over medium heat. Add the garlic, swirling them in the oil as they cook, until they take on a light golden color, about 3 minutes. Remove the garlic and add the roasted eggplant. Lower the heat and continue to cook long enough to dry out the eggplant a bit more, about 6 minutes. Transfer the eggplant to a bowl and let cool.

4. Add the flour, half of the basil, the Parmigiano-Reggiano, egg, and salt and pepper to the eggplant and mix with your hands until evenly blended.

5. Place the dough on a floured work surface and pinch off pieces, about 1 tablespoon each, and roll each into a log; use flour, as necessary, to keep them from sticking. Gently roll the gnocchi over the back of a fork to give them a slight indentation. Set them aside on a lightly floured baking sheet.

6. Bring a large pot of salted water to a boil over high heat. Add the gnocchi, and cook, uncovered, at a gentle boil. Cook until the gnocchi float to the surface, about 1 minute. Using a slotted spoon, lift them from the water and transfer to a colander to drain.

7. Add the gnocchi to the tomato sauce and simmer just long enough to combine the flavors. Taste and season with salt and pepper, as needed. Serve in a heated serving bowl or in pasta plates topped with the ricotta salata and the remaining basil.

Gnocchi alla fiorentina (gnudi)

Ricotta and spinach dumplings

SERVES 4 TO 6

1 lb fresh spinach, blanched, squeezed dry, and chopped (page 250)

12 oz (1½ cups) fresh ricotta, drained if necessary (see Recipe note)

½ cup all-purpose flour

1 cup fine semolina flour

¾ cup grated Parmigiano-Reggiano or aged Pecorino Toscano

2 egg yolks

Freshly grated nutmeg, as needed

Kosher salt and freshly ground pepper, as needed

4 oz (½ cup) unsalted butter

6 sage leaves, whole or thinly sliced

We like these gnocchi with a simple butter-and-sage sauce, but you might like to replace it with one of the tomato sauces in the Basics chapter (pages 248–249).

1. Combine the spinach, ricotta, all-purpose flour, ½ cup of the semolina flour, ½ cup of the Parmigiano-Reggiano or Pecorino Toscano, the egg yolks, a few grains of nutmeg, and a pinch of salt and pepper. Stir together until evenly combined. Cover the bowl and let this mixture rest in the refrigerator for about 1 hour to firm up.

2. To shape the gnocchi: Place the remaining semolina in a mound on a work surface or in a bowl. Lightly dust your hands with the semolina, and then pinch off a piece of the ricotta mixture (about 1 tablespoon) and roll it into a little ball. Dredge the gnocchi in the semolina and place them on a lightly floured baking sheet or platter. (The gnocchi are ready to cook now, or you may keep them, covered, in the refrigerator for up to 8 hours.)

3. Bring a large pot of salted water to a boil over high heat. Add the gnocchi and stir to submerge and separate them. Cook, uncovered, at a gentle boil until they rise to the surface and are cooked through, 2 to 4 minutes depending on their size. (To be certain, taste one of the gnocchi.)

4. While the gnocchi are cooking, heat the butter in a saucepan over medium heat until it starts to brown, about 2 minutes. Add the sage leaves and continue to cook until crispy, about 1 minute.

5. Serve the gnocchi at once on heated plates topped with the brown butter and sage leaves, and sprinkle with the remaining Parmigiano-Reggiano.

Recipe note *If the ricotta seems grainy, you might want to push it through a sieve to make it smoother. If the ricotta is wet, allow enough time for it to drain in a colander or use cheesecloth. Usually 4 hours is enough, but it is fine to let it drain overnight, as long as you keep it in the refrigerator.*

Gnocchi infornati con pomodoro, scamorza e oregano

Baked potato gnocchi with tomato, scamorza, and oregano

SERVES 6 TO 8

1½ cups Herbed Fresh Tomato Sauce (page 249)

Kosher salt, as needed

2½ lb Potato Gnocchi (page 243)

½ lb scamorza, diced

1 tsp minced oregano

⅔ cup grated Parmigiano-Reggiano

¼ cup extra-virgin olive oil

1. Preheat the oven to 350°F. Spread ¾ cup of the tomato sauce in a large baking dish.

2. Bring a large pot of salted water to a boil over high heat. Add the gnocchi and cook, uncovered, at a gentle boil until they rise to the surface and are cooked through, 2 to 4 minutes depending on their size. (To be certain, taste one of the gnocchi.) Using a slotted spoon, lift the cooked gnocchi out of the water and transfer them to the baking dish on top of the tomato sauce.

3. Top the gnocchi with the remaining sauce and sprinkle the scamorza evenly over the surface. Sprinkle with the oregano and the Parmigiano-Reggiano, then drizzle with the olive oil.

4. Bake the gnocchi until they are very hot and the cheese is melted. Serve at once directly from the baking dish.

Risotto al limone

Lemon risotto

SERVES 6

10 cups Meat Broth (page 251), or as needed

2 tbsp olive oil

4 oz (½ cup) unsalted butter

¾ cup minced yellow onion

1 lb (2⅔ cups) Carnaroli rice

½ cup dry white wine

Zest from 3 lemons

¼ cup lemon juice

8 mint leaves, cut into slivers

2 tbsp honey

½ cup grated Parmigiano-Reggiano

Kosher salt and freshly ground black pepper, as needed

1. Heat the broth in a pot over low heat; keep warm.

2. Heat the oil and 1 tablespoon of the butter in a large pot over low heat. Add the onion and cook, stirring frequently, until the onion is tender and translucent, about 4 minutes. Add the rice and toast lightly, stirring frequently, about 2 minutes.

3. Add the wine and cook until almost dry. Add enough of the broth to cover the rice by ½ inch, and cook, stirring frequently, to be sure the rice doesn't stick to the bottom. As the rice absorbs the broth, keep adding more, ½ cup at a time.

4. Once the rice has absorbed almost all the broth, and the grains are still al dente (about 18 minutes total cooking time), stir in the lemon zest, lemon juice, mint, and honey. Remove the pot from the heat. Add the remaining butter and the cheese and stir vigorously until the risotto is creamy. Taste and season with salt and pepper. Serve at once on heated plates.

Risotto ai frutti di mare

Risotto with seafood

SERVES 6

2 qt Shellfish Broth (page 252)

4 oz (½ cup) unsalted butter

¾ cup minced yellow onion

1 lb (2⅔ cups) Carnaroli rice

2 lb mixed seafood, such as mussels, shrimp, scallops, and squid

¼ cup chopped flat-leaf parsley

2 tbsp grated Parmigiano-Reggiano (optional)

1 tbsp brandy (optional)

Kosher salt and freshly ground black pepper, as needed

We like a combination of seafood in this dish—the more variety the better. A good starting point is to have 2 mussels, 3 pieces of medium shrimp, 2 medium scallops, and 1 small squid for every person. You can adjust the quantities and the number of varieties depending upon what you find in the market and what you'd like to spend, of course. Letting the mussels and clams cook in their own shells gives the dish more flavor, but it is very important that you clean them very well so there is no sand or grit remaining, and that you debeard the mussels.

1. Heat the broth in a pot over low heat; keep warm.

2. Heat 3 tablespoons of the butter in a large pot over low heat. Add the onion and cook, stirring frequently, until the onion is tender and translucent, about 4 minutes. Add the rice and toast lightly, stirring frequently, about 2 minutes.

3. Add enough of the broth to cover the rice by ½ inch, and cook, stirring frequently to be sure the rice doesn't stick to the bottom. As the rice absorbs the broth, keep adding more, ½ cup at a time. Add the seafood to the rice after it has cooked for about 12 minutes.

4. Once the rice has absorbed almost all the broth and the seafood is cooked, about 18 minutes total cooking time, remove the pot from the heat. Add the remaining 5 tablespoons butter, the parsley, cheese, and brandy, if using, and stir vigorously until the risotto is creamy. Taste and season with salt and pepper. Serve the risotto at once on warmed plates, dividing the seafood evenly among the plates.

Risotto ai peperoni dolci e capesante

Risotto with sweet peppers and scallops

SERVES 6

1½ lb red and/or yellow peppers (about 4 medium)

½ cup extra-virgin olive oil

6 cups vegetable or chicken broth

3 oz (6 tbsp) unsalted butter, cubed

¾ cup minced yellow onion

1 lb (2⅔ cups) Carnaroli rice

1 lb scallops, muscle tabs removed

¼ cup chopped flat-leaf parsley

3 or 4 large basil leaves, torn into small pieces or chopped

2 tbsp grated Parmigiano-Reggiano (optional)

1 tsp chopped garlic

Kosher salt, as needed

If you can find bay scallops, they are perfect for this dish. If not, sea scallops are still good. If your sea scallops are extremely large, you can cut them in half.

1. Preheat the oven to 400°F.

2. Rub the peppers with oil and place them in a baking dish. Roast the peppers until they are tender enough to collapse and the skin is wrinkled and starting to pull away, about 20 minutes. Place the peppers in a bowl and cover them to help loosen the skin. When they are cool enough to handle, cut around the stem and pull out the seeds and ribs. Make a cut through one side of the pepper and open it flat to scrape out any remaining seeds or ribs. Cut the peppers into medium dice and set aside.

3. Heat the broth in a pot over low heat; keep warm.

4. Heat 3 tablespoons of the butter in a large pot over low heat. Add the onion and cook, stirring frequently, until the onion is tender and translucent, about 4 minutes. Add the rice and toast lightly, stirring frequently, about 2 minutes.

5. Add enough of the broth to cover the rice by ½ inch, and cook, stirring frequently to be sure the rice doesn't stick to the bottom. As the rice absorbs the broth, keep adding more, ½ cup at a time. Add the diced peppers and the scallops to the rice after it has cooked for 10 minutes. Continue adding broth and stirring until the rice is tender and creamy and the scallops are cooked, 6 to 8 minutes more.

6. Remove the pot from the heat. Add the remaining 3 tablespoons butter, the parsley, basil, cheese, if using, and garlic and stir vigorously until the risotto is creamy. Taste and season with salt, if needed. Serve at once on heated plates.

Recipe notes *If you are in a hurry and don't have time to heat up the oven to roast the peppers, you may place them directly on an open flame for few minutes, making sure you rotate the peppers once each side is well charred, then place under cold water and quickly peel them or let them cool and then peel them. You may peel the peppers in advance and if you have a lot of them you may use them for other different preparations, such as on pasta, as an appetizer, or even in any type of meat preparation or with fish. If you don't want to use any butter in your recipe, you may also purée the peppers separately and add them during cooking. This will still give you a somewhat creamy consistency without adding butter.*

Fregola con seppioline e zafferano

Saffron-scented fregola with marinated cuttlefish

SERVES 6 TO 8

Marinated cuttlefish

1 lb fresh whole cuttlefish, cleaned (page 16)

¼ cup chopped fennel or dill fronds

¼ cup extra-virgin olive oil

½ tsp kosher salt

Saffron broth

2 qt Meat or Shellfish broth (page 251–252), plus more as needed

1 tsp saffron threads

¼ cup extra-virgin olive oil

¼ cup minced shallot

3 garlic cloves, minced

1 lb fregola

5 to 6 ripe plum tomatoes, peeled, seeded, and diced (page 248)

¼ cup minced flat-leaf parsley

Freshly ground pepper, as needed

1. Cut the cuttlefish in strips. Toss the cuttlefish together with the fennel or dill fronds, olive oil, and salt. Let the cuttlefish marinate at room temperature for 20 to 30 minutes.

2. Bring the broth to a simmer over medium heat in a saucepan. Add the saffron and let it steep until the broth is a rich golden yellow color. Keep the broth hot.

3. Heat the oil in a large pot over low heat. Add the shallot and garlic and cook, stirring frequently, until the onion is tender and translucent, about 4 minutes. Add the fregola and the tomatoes and stir to coat evenly with the oil.

4. Add enough of the broth to cover the fregola by ½ inch, and cook, stirring occasionally. As the fregola absorb the broth, keep adding more, and cook until the fregola are tender but still have a bit of bite, about 12 minutes. They should be quite moist, with a loose but not soupy consistency. Add the cuttlefish and the parsley and continue to cook for 2 minutes more, just until the cuttlefish is cooked. Taste and season with pepper. Serve at once on heated plates.

Insalata di riso

Rice salad

SERVES 8 TO 10

Kosher salt, as needed

1 lb (2⅔ cups) Carnaroli or Arborio rice

½ cup extra-virgin olive oil

¼ cup lemon juice, plus more as needed

6 oz cooked ham, diced (see Recipe note)

6 oz Emmentaler cheese, diced

¼ cup diced marinated red or yellow peppers

8 oil-packed artichoke hearts, drained and sliced

4 tbsp diced marinated mushrooms

2 tbsp thinly sliced cornichons

2 tbsp salted capers, rinsed and drained

3 tbsp slivered pitted black olives, such as Taggiasche or Niçoise

3 tbsp slivered pitted green olives, such as Picholine or Sicilian

8 brined pearl onions, drained and cut in half (or quarters, if large)

3 hard-cooked eggs (page 6), chopped

Make this with whole grains such as brown rice, spelt, or barley for a healthier salad. Increase the cooking time for these grains and cook them long enough to be tender to the bite.

1. Bring a large pot of salted water to a boil over high heat. Add the rice all at once and stir well to separate the grains. Continue to cook the rice, stirring occasionally, until it is tender to the bite, about 12 minutes for Carnaroli rice and 14 minutes for Arborio rice. Drain the rice through a wire-mesh sieve and spread it out in an even layer in a baking dish to cool to room temperature.

2. Combine the olive oil, lemon juice, and ½ teaspoon salt in a large mixing bowl. Add the rice and toss to coat evenly. Add the ham, cheese, peppers, artichokes, mushrooms, cornichons, capers, olives, and onions. Toss to distribute the ingredients evenly. The salad can be made ahead to this point and stored in a covered container in the refrigerator for up to 2 days.

3. Just before serving, taste the salad and season with additional lemon juice or salt, if needed. Top with chopped eggs and serve.

Recipe note *You can replace the ham we suggest here with 6 ounces of oil-packed tuna that you've drained and flaked.*

Autumn

Bavette alle noci

Bavette with walnut sauce

SERVES 6

Walnut sauce

2 oz peasant-style bread, crust removed (about 2 thick slices)

¾ cup water

1¼ cups chopped walnuts

1 garlic glove, minced and rinsed under cold water

6 tbsp extra-virgin olive oil

2 tbsp walnut oil

¼ cup sour cream

Kosher salt, as needed

1 lb dried bavette or linguine

¼ cup extra-virgin olive oil

Leaves from 3 or 4 marjoram sprigs, torn into pieces

5 tbsp grated Pecorino Romano, or more as needed

5 tbsp chopped walnuts (optional)

You can use a mortar and pestle to make the sauce, as we do here, or make it in a food processor. If you use a food processor, simply combine all the ingredients at once in the bowl of the processor and pulse the machine on and off until you have a smooth sauce.

1. Shred the bread into small pieces with your fingers and place in a small bowl with the water. Let the bread absorb the water until it is soft.

2. Place the walnuts and garlic in a mortar and crush them with the pestle until they are ground fine. Add the softened bread and the oils a little at a time, and continue to crush and pound until they are all incorporated and the sauce has a fine, mush-like texture. Blend in the sour cream and set the sauce aside.

3. Bring a large pot of salted water to a rolling boil over high heat. Add the bavette or linguine all at once and stir a few times to separate the pasta and submerge the strands. Cook, uncovered, until the pasta is almost cooked, 8 to 10 minutes (check the cooking time for your pasta).

4. Drain the pasta in a colander. Shake well to remove any water clinging to the pasta. Pour the drained pasta into a large serving bowl. Dress first with the oil and marjoram leaves and then pour the walnut sauce over the pasta and toss to coat evenly. Serve the pasta with the freshly grated cheese and some chopped walnuts, if desired.

Bucatini all'amatriciana

Bucatini with cured pork, onions, and tomato

SERVES 4 TO 6

Amatriciana sauce

6 oz guanciale (cured pork jowl), sliced ⅛ inch thick and cut into ½-inch pieces

Extra-virgin olive oil, as needed

2 medium sweet onions, thinly sliced

½ cup dry white wine

8 canned whole San Marzano tomatoes, seeded and chopped, juices reserved

Kosher salt, as needed

Red pepper flakes, as needed

1 lb dried bucatini

⅔ cup grated Pecorino Romano

1. Heat a sauté pan over medium-low heat. Add the guanicale and cook, stirring from time to time, until it is browned and lightly crispy, about 4 minutes. Lift the guanciale from the pan with a slotted spoon and drain on paper towels. Set aside. There should be about 3 tablespoons of rendered fat in the pan. Add oil as needed or, if you prefer, pour out the fat and replace it with 3 tablespoons oil.

2. In the same pan, cook the sliced onions over medium heat, stirring as necessary to cook evenly, until the onions are very tender and a deep golden brown, 20 to 30 minutes. Keep a close eye on the onions as they cook and reduce the heat, if necessary. Add the wine and tomatoes, and season with salt and hot pepper flakes. Simmer over low heat until flavorful, 3 to 4 minutes. Taste the sauce and adjust the seasoning with salt and hot pepper flakes, if needed.

3. Bring a large pot of salted water to a boil over high heat. Add the bucatini and stir a few times to submerge and separate the strands. Cook, uncovered, until the pasta is just tender (al dente), 8 to 10 minutes (check the cooking time for your pasta).

4. Drain the pasta in a colander. Shake well to remove any water clinging to the pasta. Pour the drained pasta into the large sauté pan with the sauce and toss well over medium heat until the pasta is evenly coated.

5. Garnish the dish with the reserved guanciale and cheese and serve at once.

Bucatini alla gricia

Bucatini with cured pork, onions, and black pepper

SERVES 4 TO 6

8 oz guanciale (cured pork jowl), sliced ⅛ inch thick and cut into ½-inch pieces

Extra-virgin olive oil, as needed

2 sweet onions, thinly sliced

½ cup dry white wine

Kosher salt, as needed

1 or 2 dried red chiles (peperoncini), cracked or crushed

1 lb dried bucatini

⅔ cup grated Pecorino Romano

Freshly ground black pepper, as needed

Guanciale is the cheek of the pig, cured with salt and spices and air-dried. If it is hard to find. You can replace it with a good-quality pancetta, which is from the belly of the pig and cured in the same way as guanciale.

1. Heat a sauté pan over medium-low heat. Add the guanciale and cook, stirring from time to time, until it is browned and lightly crispy, about 4 minutes. Lift the guanciale from the pan with a slotted spoon and drain on paper towels. Set aside. There should be about ¼ cup of rendered fat in the pan. Add a bit of oil if needed or, if you prefer, pour out the fat and replace it with ¼ cup oil.

2. In the same pan, cook the sliced onions over medium heat, stirring as necessary to cook evenly, until the onions are very tender and a deep golden brown, 20 to 30 minutes. Keep a close eye on the onions as they cook and reduce the heat, if necessary. Add the wine and the chiles. Simmer over low heat until flavorful, 3 to 4 minutes. Add half of the reserved guanciale to the sauce and set the remainder aside to use as a garnish. Taste and adjust the seasoning with salt and chiles, if needed; set aside.

3. Bring a large pot of salted water to a boil over high heat. Add the bucatini all at once and stir a few times to separate the pasta and submerge the strands. Cook, uncovered, at a boil until the pasta is almost cooked, 8 to 10 minutes (check the cooking time for your pasta). Reserve a few ladlefuls of the pasta cooking to finish the sauce (you will need about ½ cup).

4. Drain the pasta in a colander. Pour the drained pasta into a large serving bowl. Add the reserved sauce and toss together, then add the cheese and mix well until the pasta is evenly coated. The dish should appear creamy, not oily. If necessary, add a few tablespoons of the reserved pasta cooking water.

5. Garnish the dish with the remaining guanciale. Season generously with pepper. Serve at once.

Pennette con la zucca, parmigiano e balsamico

Pennette tossed with pumpkin, parmigiano, and aged balsamic vinegar

SERVES 6

Pumpkin sauce

One 3-lb pumpkin or butternut squash

3 oz (6 tbsp) unsalted butter

6 large sage leaves, coarsely chopped

3 garlic cloves

Kosher salt and freshly ground pepper, as needed

Chicken or vegetable broth, as needed

1 lb dried penne

¾ cup grated Parmigiano-Reggiano

2 tbsp aged balsamic vinegar

1. Cut the pumpkin in half and scoop out the seeds. Use a chef's knife to cut away the peel and cut the pumpkin flesh into ½-inch dice.

2. Heat the butter in a Dutch oven or casserole over medium-high heat. When the foaming subsides, add the sage leaves and garlic. Cook until the sage is crisp, the garlic is lightly colored, and the butter has a light brown color and a nutty aroma. Adjust the heat as the mixture cooks, if necessary, so you do not burn the butter.

3. Add the diced pumpkin and toss to coat with the butter. Season with a pinch of salt and pepper and add enough broth to just barely cover the pumpkin. Bring to a simmer over medium heat, cover with a lid, and cook until the pumpkin is soft enough to crush with a fork, about 30 minutes. Stir from time to time, and add more broth to keep the pumpkin moistened. Remove and discard the garlic. Set aside.

4. Bring a large pot of salted water to a boil over high heat. Add the penne and stir to submerge the pasta and separate the pieces. Cook, uncovered, until the pasta is just tender (al dente), 8 to 10 minutes (check the cooking time for your pasta).

5. Drain the penne in a colander. Shake well to remove any water clinging to the pasta. Pour the drained pasta into a large heated serving bowl and stir together with the pumpkin until the pumpkin breaks up and forms a creamy sauce. Add the cheese, a little at the time, continuing to stir until it is all incorporated. Stir in the vinegar and serve at once.

Tajarin al tartufo bianco

Tajarin with white truffle

SERVES 4 TO 6

Kosher salt, as needed

1¼ lb Tajarin (page 239)

½ cup unsalted butter

1 cup grated Parmigiano-Reggiano

Freshly ground pepper, as needed

2½ oz white truffle

In Piedmont, tajarin noodles are a brilliant, almost saffron-yellow color, due to the use of fresh farmhouse egg yolks. Making these noodles strictly by hand is a commitment, but with freshly shaved truffles on top, it is worth the effort.

1. Bring a large pot of salted water to a boil over high heat. Add the tajarin and stir a few times to separate the strands. Cook, uncovered, until the pasta is just tender (al dente), 2 to 3 minutes. Reserve a few ladlefuls of the pasta cooking water for finishing the sauce (you will need about ½ cup).

2. Stir together half of the butter with ¼ cup of the reserved pasta cooking water in a serving bowl.

3. Drain the tajarin in a colander. Shake well to remove any water clinging to the pasta. Pour the drained pasta into a bowl. Add the remaining butter and the cheese and toss together until the pasta is evenly coated. The dish should appear creamy, not oily. If necessary, add a bit more of the pasta cooking water.

4. Season the tajarin with salt and pepper and serve at once, topped with shaved truffle.

Recipe note *The average quantity used in most restaurants is 15 to 20 grams of fresh white truffle per person, but more is better, of course, if your pockets are deep enough.*

Linguine con sugo di tonno e alici

Linguine with tuna and anchovies

SERVES 4 TO 6

Tuna and anchovy sauce

½ cup extra-virgin olive oil, plus
more as needed

One 2-oz can oil-packed anchovies,
drained

4 garlic cloves, minced

½ cup chopped flat-leaf parsley

Two 5-oz cans oil-packed tuna,
drained and flaked

½ cup dry white wine

One 6-oz can tomato paste

Kosher salt, as needed

Red pepper flakes, as needed

1 lb dried linguine

1. Heat the oil in a medium sauté pan over medium heat. Add the anchovies and cook, stirring and mashing them, until they melt. Add the garlic and continue to cook, stirring frequently, until the aroma is released, about 2 minutes. Stir in the parsley and cook another 1 or 2 minutes. Add the tuna and the wine and cook until the wine has nearly cooked away. Add the tomato paste, stirring well, and cook until it has a sweet aroma and a rich rusty color, another 2 minutes.

2. Add 6 cups of water and bring to a simmer. Reduce the heat to low and continue to cook, covered, until the sauce is reduced, thick, and rich, 45 to 60 minutes. Taste the sauce and season, as necessary, with salt and some red pepper flakes.

3. Bring a large pot of salted water to a boil over high heat. Add the linguine and stir to submerge the pasta and separate the strands. Cook, uncovered, until the pasta is just tender (al dente), 8 to 10 minutes (check the cooking time for your pasta). Reserve a few ladlefuls of the pasta cooking water for finishing the sauce (you will need about ½ cup).

4. Drain the pasta in a colander. Shake well to remove any water clinging to the pasta. Pour the drained pasta into a large heated serving bowl. Add the tuna and anchovy sauce and ¼ cup of the reserved pasta cooking water and toss together until the pasta is evenly coated.

5. Drizzle with oil and serve at once.

Tagliolini neri con astice e cavolfiore

Squid ink pasta with lobster and cauliflower

SERVES 6

Lobster and cauliflower sauce

½ cup extra-virgin olive oil

2 tbsp minced shallot

4 garlic cloves, thinly sliced

½ cup chopped flat-leaf parsley

Red pepper flakes, as needed

One 2-lb lobster, meat removed from shell and diced

½ cup dry white wine

2 tbsp brandy

2 cups roasted cauliflower florets (see Recipe note)

Kosher salt and freshly ground black pepper, as needed

1¼ lb Squid Ink Tagliolini (page 236)

Replace the lobster in this dish with any seafood you like or that is available, such as shrimp, scallops, mussels, clams, or crabmeat.

1. Heat a large sauté pan over medium heat. Add the ½ cup oil, and when it is hot, add the shallots and garlic. Sauté, stirring often, until the garlic is aromatic, about 1 minute. Add half of the parsley and the red pepper flakes and stir to combine. Add the lobster meat and stir to coat it with the oil, then add the wine and brandy. Cover the pan and let the lobster finish cooking, about 2 minutes. Remove the cover, stir in the cauliflower, and cook just long enough for the cauliflower to heat through, another 1 to 2 minutes more.

2. Bring a large pot of salted water to a boil over high heat. Add the tagliolini and stir to submerge the pasta and separate the strands. Cook, uncovered, until the pasta is just tender (al dente), 2 to 3 minutes (depending upon how dry your pasta is). Reserve a few ladlefuls of the pasta cooking water for finishing the sauce (you will need about ½ cup).

3. Drain the pasta in a colander. Shake well to remove any water clinging to the pasta. Pour the drained pasta into a large heated serving bowl. Add the lobster-cauliflower mixture, the remaining parsley, and a few tablespoons of the reserved pasta cooking water and toss together until the pasta is evenly coated. The dish should appear creamy, not oily. If necessary, add a bit more of the pasta water. Taste and season with slat and pepper. Serve at once.

Recipe note To roast the cauliflower: Preheat the oven to 400°F. Separate a head of cauliflower into florets. Place the florets in a bowl and toss with enough olive oil to coat them lightly. Season with salt and pepper and transfer to a baking sheet and roast them until lightly colored, about 10 minutes. Remove and set aside. If you have more roasted cauliflower than you need for this recipe, you can use it in salads or serve it as a side dish.

Tagliatelle con porcini
e gamberi

Tagliatelle with porcini and shrimp

SERVES 6 TO 8

Porcini and shrimp sauce

2 lb porcini mushrooms

3 oz (6 tbsp) unsalted butter or
3 tbsp extra-virgin olive oil

2 medium shallots, thinly sliced
or minced

2 garlic cloves, thinly sliced
or minced

¾ cup chopped flat-leaf parsley

1 cup dry white wine

Kosher salt and freshly ground
black pepper, as needed

1¼ lb Tagliatelle (page 237)

1. Wipe the porcini clean, removing any dirt; if necessary, wash them well. Separate the stems and caps and slice them. (Keep the stems and caps separated as the stems require a longer cooking time than the caps.)

2. Heat a sauté pan over medium heat. Add 3 tablespoons of the butter or oil and when it is hot but not smoking, add the shallots and garlic. Sauté, stirring often, until the shallots are tender, about 3 minutes. Add half of the parsley and the sliced porcini stems and stir to coat with the butter or oil. Continue to cook for 2 or 3 minutes, and then add the sliced porcini caps. Continue to cook until the mushrooms start to release their moisture, about 3 minutes.

3. Add the wine and stir well. Continue to cook until the wine is almost completely cooked away, about 5 minutes. Season with salt and pepper, if necessary. Reserve in the pan while cooking the pasta.

4. In a separate sauté pan, heat the remaining 3 tablespoons butter or oil over medium heat. Once it is hot, add the shrimp, stir to coat evenly and cook, turning or stirring the shrimp, as necessary, to cook them evenly, until they are just cooked through. Reserve the shrimp in the pan while cooking the pasta.

5. Bring a large pot of salted water to a boil over high heat. Add the tagliatelle and stir a few times to separate the pasta and submerge the strands. Cook, uncovered, until the pasta is just tender (al dente), 2 to 3 minutes (depending upon how dry the pasta is).

6. Drain the pasta in a colander. Shake well to remove any water clinging to the pasta. Pour the drained pasta into a large serving bowl. Add the porcini and the shrimp mixture and the remaining parsley and toss together until the pasta is evenly coated. The dish should appear creamy, not oily. If necessary, add a bit of the reserved pasta cooking water. Season with salt and pepper, as needed, and serve at once.

Pappardelle con ragù d'anatra

Pappardelle with duck ragù

SERVES 6 TO 8

Duck ragù

4 tsp golden raisins

¼ cup extra-virgin olive oil

1 cup minced yellow onion

½ cup minced celery

4 oz duck or chicken livers, chopped

2 tbsp chopped sage

½ cup chopped flat-leaf parsley

2 lb coarsely ground duck leg meat

3 cups dry white wine

Duck or chicken broth, as needed

3 bay leaves

½ stick cinnamon

Kosher salt and freshly ground black pepper, as needed

1¼ lb Pappardelle (page 237)

Zest from ½ orange or lemon

As you can see, this ragù does not contain any tomatoes, which is typical of some North Italian ragùs. You may also use this recipe to prepare a chicken ragù.

1. Place the raisins in a small bowl and add enough warm water to cover them. Let the raisins soak in the water until they are plump. Drain the raisins, chop them coarsely, and set aside.

2. Heat the oil in a 4-quart Dutch oven over medium heat. Add the onion and celery and cook, stirring frequently, until the vegetables are soft and well cooked, about 10 minutes. Add the liver and cook until it loses its raw appearance, 2 to 3 minutes. Add the sage, half of the parsley, the raisins, and the ground duck meat. Cook, stirring frequently, until the meat changes color and is well combined with the vegetables, about 5 minutes.

3. Stir in the wine and then add just enough broth to cover the meat. Add the bay leaves and cinnamon stick. Bring the ragù to a very slow simmer and cook, covered, until the ragù is very rich and thick, about 1½ hours. Remove and discard the bay leaves and cinnamon stick. Taste the ragù and season with salt and pepper, if needed. Remove and discard the bay leaves and cinnamon stick.

4. Bring a large pot of salted water to a boil over high heat. Add the pappardelle and stir to submerge the pasta and separate the noodles. Cook, uncovered, until the pasta is just tender (al dente), 3 to 4 minutes.

5. Drain the pasta in a colander. Shake well to remove any water clinging to the pasta. Pour the drained pasta into a large heated serving bowl. Add the ragù and toss the noodles and sauce together. Top with the orange or lemon zest and serve at once.

Pappardelle di castagne con cime di rapa e ricotta

Chestnut pappardelle with broccoli rabe and ricotta

SERVES 6 TO 8

Broccoli rabe and ricotta

2 lb broccoli rabe

Kosher salt, as needed

10 tbsp extra-virgin olive oil

2 garlic cloves, thinly sliced

1 dried red chile (peperoncino)

1¼ cups fresh ricotta

Freshly ground black pepper, as needed

1¼ lb Chestnut Pappardelle (page 239)

Grated Pecorino Romano, as needed for serving

1. Trim all the leaves from the broccoli rabe, and remove the central core from each leaf. Remove the bottom 3 inches of the stem and peel the rest up to the flower buds. Rinse well under cold running water. Bring a large pot of salted water to a boil. Add the broccoli rabe and stir to submerge. Cook, uncovered, until tender and a deep green color, 3 to 4 minutes. Lift the greens out of the water with a sieve or slotted spoon and transfer to a colander to drain for a few minutes. Coarsely chop the broccoli rabe. Set aside

2. Heat 6 tablespoons of the oil in a deep sauté pan or Dutch oven. Add the garlic and cook, stirring constantly, until the garlic is a light golden brown, about 2 minutes. Add the dried chile and the chopped broccoli rabe. Continue to cook until the broccoli rabe is very hot and tender, about 3 minutes. Remove and discard the chile.

3. Mix the ricotta with the remaining ¼ cup oil and season with salt and pepper. Remove 6 to 8 tablespoons of the ricotta and reserve to garnish the dish.

4. Bring a large pot of salted water to a boil over high heat. Add the pappardelle and stir to separate the pasta and submerge the noodles. Cook, uncovered, until the pasta is just tender (al dente), 2 to 3 minutes. Reserve a few ladlefuls of the pasta cooking water for finishing the sauce (you will need about ½ cup).

5. Drain the pasta in a colander. Shake well to remove any water clinging to the pasta. Pour the drained pasta into a large heated serving bowl. Add the ricotta–olive oil mixture and toss together with the pasta. Add the broccoli rabe and toss to combine. Add some of the reserved pasta cooking water if necessary to make the sauce creamy. Top with dollops of the reserved ricotta and serve at once, and pass the Pecorino Romano on the side.

Maccheroni alla chitarra con salsiccia e insalatine amare

Fresh spaghetti with sausage and bitter greens

SERVES 4 TO 6

Sausage and bitter greens

6 tbsp extra-virgin olive oil

12 oz plain fresh pork sausage, crumbled

1 cup minced shallots

4 garlic cloves, smashed

1½ cups shredded radicchio

1½ cups shredded escarole

1 cup shredded arugula

1½ cups peeled, seeded, chopped ripe plum tomatoes (see page 248)

2 tbsp chopped thyme

Red pepper flakes, as needed

Kosher salt, as needed

1 lb Maccheroni alla Chitarra (page 240)

1 oz (2 tbsp) unsalted butter

¼ cup grated Parmigiano-Reggiano

Freshly ground black pepper, as needed

1. Heat ¼ cup of the oil in a large sauté pan over medium heat and add the sausage. Cook, stirring as needed, until the sausage is golden brown, about 5 minutes. Add the shallots and garlic and cook, stirring occasionally, until fragrant, about 3 minutes.

2. Increase the heat to high. Stir in the radicchio, escarole, and arugula and continue to cook until they are wilted, about 2 minutes. Add the tomatoes, thyme, and red pepper flakes. Turn the heat off, remove and discard the garlic cloves, and set aside the sausage mixture.

3. Bring a large pot of salted water to a boil over high heat. Add the maccheroni and stir a few times to separate the pasta and submerge the strands. Cook, uncovered, until the pasta is just tender (al dente), 3 to 4 minutes. Reserve a few ladlefuls of the pasta cooking water for finishing the sauce (you will need about ½ cup).

4. Drain the pasta in a colander. Shake well to remove any water clinging to the pasta. Pour the drained pasta into a large heated serving bowl. Add ¼ cup of the reserved pasta cooking water, the reserved sausage mixture, the remaining 2 tablespoons olive oil, the butter, and cheese to the pasta. Toss together until the pasta is evenly coated. The pasta should appear creamy, not oily. If necessary, add a bit more of the pasta cooking water.

5. Serve the pasta immediately with freshly ground black pepper, as needed.

Maccheroni alla chitarra con ragù d'agnello

Fresh spaghetti with lamb sauce

SERVES 6

Lamb ragù

½ cup extra-virgin olive oil

1½ lb boneless lamb shoulder, cut into large cubes (about 2 oz each)

Kosher salt and freshly ground black pepper, as needed

1¾ cups minced yellow onion

1 garlic clove, chopped

½ cup dry white wine

1 qt canned whole San Marzano tomatoes, diced

2 bay leaves

1 dried red chile (peperoncino)

1 red pepper, quartered and seeded

Meat Broth (page 251) or water, as needed

1 lb Maccheroni alla Chitarra (page 240)

½ cup grated Pecorino Romano

1. Preheat the oven to 300°F.

2. Heat ¼ cup of the oil in a 4-quart Dutch oven over medium heat. Season the lamb cubes with salt and black pepper and add them to the hot oil in a single layer. Cook, turning as necessary, until brown on all sides, about 10 minutes total cooking time.

3. Add the onion and garlic and stir to coat them with the fat. Sauté, stirring often, until the onions are slightly tender and just starting to brown, about 10 minutes. Add the wine, tomatoes, bay leaves, dried chile, and red pepper and bring to a simmer. Transfer the pot to the oven and cook until the lamb is very tender, 3 to 4 hours. Stir the ragù as it cooks to keep it evenly moistened. If the liquid cooks away while preparing the lamb, add a bit of broth or water, as needed.

4. Remove the pan from the oven and let the ragù cool. Remove and discard the bay leaves and the chile. Break the meat into shreds with your fingers or using two forks. Season with salt, as needed.

5. Bring a large pot of salted water to a boil over high heat. Add the maccheroni and stir to submerge the pasta and separate the strands. Cook, uncovered, until the pasta is just tender (al dente), 8 to 10 minutes.

6. Drain the pasta in a colander. Shake well to remove any water clinging to the pasta. Pour the drained pasta into a large heated serving bowl. Add the ragù and toss together to combine. Serve at once and pass the cheese on the side.

Pici ai porcini

Handmade spaghetti with porcini mushrooms

SERVES 6 TO 8

1 lb fresh porcini

¼ cup extra-virgin olive oil

½ cup finely minced shallot

1 garlic clove minced

½ cup minced flat-leaf parsley

¼ cup dry white wine

1 cup canned San Marzano tomatoes, crushed through a food mill or sieve

Chicken or vegetable stock, as needed

2 rosemary sprigs

1 lb Pici (page 238)

Kosher salt, as needed

1. Trim the porcini stems with a paring knife to remove from any dirt still attached on the bottom. Quickly rinse them, one by one, under running water and spread them out on paper towels to dry. Cut the porcini lengthwise into thin slices.

2. Heat the oil in a 4-quart Dutch oven medium heat. Add the shallot and garlic and cook, stirring frequently, until tender, 2 to 3 minutes. Add the parsley and the mushrooms, increase the heat to high and sauté, stirring frequently, until the mushrooms are very hot, 2 to 3 minutes. Add the wine and cook until the wine has reduced almost completely. Add the tomatoes and simmer over low heat until the mushrooms are tender, about 10 minutes. Stir the sauce often and add the stock, as needed, to keep the sauce moistened. The sauce should have a creamy consistency. Add the rosemary during the last 5 minutes of the cooking, then remove and discard it before using the sauce.

3. Bring a large pot of salted water to a boil over high heat. Add the pici all at once and stir to submerge the pasta and separate the strands. Cook, uncovered, until the pasta is just tender (al dente), 8 to 10 minutes.

4. Drain the pasta in a colander. Shake well to remove any water clinging to the pasta. Pour the drained pasta into a large heated serving bowl. Add the porcini and toss together with the pici. Serve at once.

Rotolo di pasta con zucca e castagne

Rolled pasta with pumpkin and chestnut

SERVES 8 TO 10

Pumpkin and chestnut stuffing

One 3-lb pumpkin

Kosher salt, as needed

5 oz peeled fresh or frozen chestnuts (see page 255)

1 rosemary sprig

1 garlic clove, crushed

2 tbsp grated Parmigiano-Reggiano

4 amaretti cookies, crumbled

2 egg yolks

Zest from 1 orange

Freshly ground black pepper, as needed

12 oz Chestnut Cocoa Rotolo Sheets (page 246), cooked and cooled

6 tbsp grated Parmigiano-Reggiano

1 tbsp sugar

1 tsp ground cinnamon

½ cup heavy cream

2 oz (¼ cup) unsalted butter, melted

1. Preheat the oven to 350°F.

2. Cut the pumpkin in half and scoop out the seeds. Cut the halves into wedges and place in a baking dish. Add a few tablespoons of water, cover tightly with aluminum foil, and roast in the oven until the flesh is very tender, about 1 hour. Scoop the pumpkin flesh away from the skin, mash with a fork, transfer to a colander, and let the pumpkin drain for at least 8 hours in the refrigerator. Set the colander in a bowl to catch the liquid that will drain away.

3. Bring a large pot of salted water to a boil over high heat. Add the chestnuts, rosemary, and garlic, reduce the heat, and simmer until the chestnuts are very tender. Drain them in a colander, and when they are cool enough to handle, chop them coarsely with a knife.

4. Combine the drained pumpkin with chopped chestnuts, 2 tablespoons Parmigiano, crumbled amaretti cookies, egg yolks, and orange zest. Mix well to blend evenly. Season lightly with salt and pepper. Set aside. (If this is done in advance, hold the filling in a covered container in the refrigerator for up to 2 days.)

5. Bring a large pot of salted water to a boil over high heat. Add the pasta sheets and cook, uncovered, until just tender (al dente), 3 to 4 minutes. Carefully lift the sheets from the water, drain briefly, and then store flat on a baking sheet or platters, separating the sheets with plastic wrap.

6. Preheat the oven to 350°F.

7. Lay the sheets of cooked pasta on a flat surface and spread a ¼-inch-thick layer of pumpkin filling over the entire surface. Roll the pasta sheets up on the long side to form a log. Cool the rolls of pasta for few hours in the refrigerator to let the filling firm up and then cut the logs into 1-inch-thick pieces. Place the roll slices in a buttered baking dish.

8. Mix the 6 tablespoons Parmigiano with the sugar and cinnamon. Drizzle just enough cream to cover the bottom of the dish then sprinkle the Parmigiano-sugar mixture all over the top. Pour the melted butter over the slices. Bake until the top of the pasta has a golden color, 15 to 20 minutes. Serve from the baking dish.

Cannelloni di pescatrice con salsa di cavolo nero

Monkfish cannelloni with tuscan kale sauce

SERVES 6 TO 8

Monkfish filling

1 lb monkfish tail, trimmed and diced

Kosher salt and freshly ground black pepper, as needed

1¼ cups slivered leeks (white and light green portions only)

2 bay leaves

¼ cup extra-virgin olive oil

1 small Yukon Gold potato

¼ cup chopped flat-leaf parsley

¼ cup grated Pecorino Romano

Cavolo nero sauce

1 lb cavolo nero (Tuscan kale)

6 tbsp extra-virgin olive oil

1 shallot, slivered

1 garlic clove, thinly sliced

1. Preheat the oven to 350°F.

2. Place the monkfish in a baking dish and season with salt and pepper. Scatter the leeks over the fish, top with the bay leaves, and drizzle with the olive oil. Cover the baking dish tightly with aluminum foil and bake until the fish is cooked through, 20 to 30 minutes. Remove and discard the bay leaves.

3. While the monkfish is baking, peel and quarter the potato and cook it in simmering salted water until it is easily pierced with the tip of a knife. Drain the potato in a colander, then transfer to a mixing bowl and crush with a fork. Add the monkfish-leek mixture, the parsley, and the cheese and stir together. Set aside.

4. Separate the leaves of the kale and trim the central core from the leaves. Wash the kale well. Bring a large pot of salted water to a rolling boil. Add the kale leaves all at once and stir to submerge the leaves. Cook, uncovered, until tender and a deep green color, 3 to 4 minutes. Lift the greens out of the water with a sieve or slotted spoon and drain in a colander for a few minutes.

5. While the kale is cooking, heat 2 tablespoons of the oil a medium sauté pan over medium heat. Add the shallots and garlic. Stir to coat with the oil. Cook over low heat until the shallots are tender, about 2 minutes. Add the kale and enough water to just barely cover the leaves. Cook, stirring occasionally, until about half of the water has cooked away. Transfer the kale to a blender and let it cool for a few minutes. Purée the kale, adding the remaining 4 tablespoons oil while the blender is running to produce a fine, smooth sauce. (If you will not be using the sauce right away, cool it in an ice bath to preserve the bright green color; see page 247 for details.)

Continued

1 lb Cannelloni Sheets, cooked (page 235)

Melted unsalted butter, for brushing the baking dish and the cannelloni

Kosher salt and freshly ground black pepper, as needed

6. Preheat the oven to 300°F. Brush a baking dish or casserole with melted butter.

7. Divide the filling mixture between the sheets of cooked pasta, forming a log that runs the entire length of each sheet. Roll the pasta around the filling and then cut them into cannelloni about 4 inches long. Set them into the baking dish with the seam side down to help hold them together. Once all the cannelloni are arranged in the baking dish, brush them lightly with butter. (You may bake the dish now, or cover the baking dish and keep them refrigerated for up to 2 days.)

8. Place the baking dish in the oven and bake until the cannelloni are very hot, 15 to 20 minutes (or longer if they were held in the refrigerator). Heat the kale sauce over low heat or in the microwave while the cannelloni are baking. To serve, spoon the sauce in the center of each warmed serving plate and top with the cannelloni.

Tortelli di zucca

Tortelli filled with pumpkin, amaretti cookies, and fruit mustard

SERVES 6 TO 8

Pumpkin amaretti stuffing

One 3-lb pumpkin

1 oz amaretti cookies (about 6)

6 oz Italian fruit mostarda

2 cups grated Grana Padano

2 egg yolks

Kosher salt and freshly ground
black pepper, as needed

1 lb Pasta Sheets (page 235)

Flour, as needed

Egg wash: 1 large egg blended
with 1 tbsp water

4 oz (½ cup) unsalted butter

6 sage leaves

6 tbsp grated Parmigiano-Reggiano

1. Cut the pumpkin in half and scoop out the seeds. Cut the halves into wedges and place in a baking dish. Add a few tablespoons of water, cover tightly with aluminum foil, and roast in the oven until the flesh is very tender. Scoop the pumpkin flesh away from the skin, mash the pumpkin with a fork, transfer to a colander, and let the pumpkin drain for at least 8 hours in the refrigerator. Set the colander in a bowl to catch the liquid that will drain away.

2. Chop the amaretti and the mostarda in a food processor until evenly ground. Transfer to a bowl, add the drained pumpkin, the grated cheese, and egg yolks and blend well. Season with a pinch of salt and pepper. Set aside.

3. Lay one of the pasta sheets flat on a lightly floured work surface. Using a pastry brush, lightly wet one side of the dough with egg wash. Spoon the filling in 1-teaspoon mounds onto half of the wet side of the dough. There should be about 2 inches between the mounds so that you can cut individual tortelli. Fold the sheet in half lengthwise to cover the filling. Press the pasta sheet together to seal the edges well around the filling and press out any air. Use a fluted pasta cutter to trim the excess dough from the long edge. Cut between each mound with the cutter to make individual tortelli. As you cut out the tortelli, place them on a plate or baking sheet sprinkled with a little flour to keep them from sticking.

4. Bring a large pot of salted water to a rolling boil over high heat. Add the tortelli all at once and stir a few times to separate them. Cook, uncovered, at a gentle boil until the tortelli are just tender to the bite, 8 to 10 minutes. Drain the tortelli in a colander. Shake well to remove excess water. Transfer to a heated serving bowl.

5. Melt the butter in a sauté pan over medium heat. When the foaming subsides, add the sage and cook until the leaves are crisp. Pour the butter and sage leaves over the tortelli and toss gently to coat them evenly. Serve at once, and pass the cheese on the side.

Tortelli ai funghi con battuto al prezzemolo

Mushroom tortelli with parsley sauce

SERVES 6 TO 8

Mushroom stuffing

¼ cup extra-virgin olive oil

1 garlic clove

1 shallot, minced

2 lb mixed wild mushrooms, cleaned and cut into large dice

Kosher salt and freshly ground black pepper, as needed

3 tbsp plain dry bread crumbs, or as needed

1 lb Pasta Sheets (page 235)

Flour, as needed

Egg wash: 1 large egg blended with 1 tbsp water

4 oz (½ cup) unsalted butter

2 garlic cloves, smashed

½ cup chopped flat-leaf parsley

1. Heat the oil in a large sauté pan over medium heat. Add the garlic and the shallot and cook, stirring frequently, until the shallot is tender, about 3 minutes. Add the mushrooms, season with salt, and quickly sauté until the mushrooms are tender and all the moisture has evaporated, 5 to 6 minutes. Remove and discard the garlic clove.

2. Spread the mushrooms out on a tray to cool for at least 30 minutes. Mince the mushrooms very finely with a knife or food processor. Season with salt and pepper and add enough of the bread crumbs to hold the stuffing together. Set aside.

3. Lay one pasta sheet flat on a lightly floured work surface. Using a pastry brush, lightly wet one side of the dough with some of the egg wash. Spoon the filling in 1-teaspoon mounds onto half of the wet side of the dough. There should be about 2 inches between the mounds so that you can cut individual tortelli. Fold the sheet in half lengthwise to cover the filling. Press the pasta sheet together to seal the edges well around the filling and press out any air. Using a fluted cutter, cut individual tortelli into squares. As you cut out the tortelli, place them on a plate or baking sheet sprinkled with a little flour to keep them from sticking

4. Melt the butter in a small pan over medium-low heat. Add the garlic cloves and cook slowly until the garlic is golden brown and aromatic, about 2 minutes. Remove and discard the garlic cloves and set the butter aside to cool slightly.

5. Bring a large pot of salted water to a boil over high heat. Add the tortelli all at once and stir a few times to separate the pasta and submerge the pieces. Cook, uncovered, at a gentle boil until the pasta is almost cooked, 4 to 5 minutes Reserve a few ladlefuls of the pasta cooking water for finishing the sauce (you will need about ½ cup).

6. Drain the tortelli in a colander. Shake well to remove excess water. Pour the drained tortelli into a large heated serving bowl. Add the garlic-scented butter, the parsley, and about ¼ cup of the reserved pasta cooking water. Gently roll or toss the tortelli in the butter sauce. The butter should emulsify with the water to create a creamy consistency. Add a bit more of the pasta water if it appears oily. Serve at once.

Agnolotti di vitello col sugo d'arrosto

Veal agnolotti with its own sauce

SERVES 6

Veal and pork stuffing

Kosher salt, as needed

6 oz coarsely chopped spinach or escarole (about 2½ cups)

4 oz (½ cup) unsalted butter

1 garlic clove, minced

1 lb ground veal, preferably from shoulder

8 oz ground pork

4 large sage leaves, chopped

1 tbsp rosemary, chopped

Freshly ground black pepper, as needed

1 cup grated Parmigiano-Reggiano

2 large eggs

1 lb Pasta Sheets (page 235)

Flour, as needed

Sauce, as needed

Grated Parmigiano-Reggiano, as needed for serving

Serve this with a simple topping of browned butter and sage leaves and a generous dusting of grated Parmigiano-Reggiano. Tomato sauce and mushroom sauce are also good options. Or, if you have any juices left from braising a large cut of meat, they make an excellent sauce as well.

1. Bring a large pot of salted water to a boil. Add the chopped spinach or escarole all at once, pushing it down to completely submerge. Cook just until the greens turn a deep green color, about 2 minutes. Drain in a colander or wire-mesh sieve, rinse with cool water, and drain again. Gather the greens into a ball and squeeze in your hands to remove excess moisture. Transfer to a cutting board and chop very finely with a chef's knife. Set aside. (Keep them refrigerated if you are doing this step in advance; they will keep for up to 24 hours.)

2. Heat the butter in a saucepan over medium heat. When the butter has stopped foaming, add the garlic and cook, stirring frequently, until the garlic is lightly browned, about 2 minutes. Add the ground meats, breaking them up with a wooden spoon, and cook, stirring as necessary, until the meat no longer looks raw and has taken on some good brown color. Add the sage and rosemary and continue to cook for another 3 to 4 minutes. Add the chopped greens, stir to combine, and season with salt and pepper.

3. Transfer the meat mixture to a bowl and let it cool for about 15 minutes. Add the cheese and the eggs and stir to combine thoroughly to make a smooth filling.

4. Lay one pasta sheet on a work surface and, using a spoon or a pastry bag, distribute the filling mixture, spacing the dollops about 2 inches apart. Top with the second sheet of pasta and press the dough around the dollops of filling to create agnolotti. Using a pasta cutter, knife, or circular cutter, cut the agnolotti. Set them aside on a lightly floured baking sheet or platter until you are ready to cook them.

5. Bring a large pot of salted water to a rolling boil over high heat. Add the agnolotti all at once and stir a few times to separate the pasta and submerge the pieces. Cook, uncovered, at a boil until the pasta is almost cooked, 3 to 4 minutes. Using a slotted spoon, transfer the agnolotti to a plate. Top with any sauce you like and sprinkle with the cheese. Serve at once.

Gnocchi di patate con ragù alla finanziera

Potato dumplings with offal and mushroom sauce

SERVES 12

Finanziera sauce

8 oz chicken livers, cleaned and diced

Kosher salt and freshly ground black pepper, as needed

½ cup dry Marsala

8 oz chicken hearts, cleaned and cut in half

8 oz chicken gizzards, cleaned and diced

8 oz veal sweetbreads, blanched and diced

8 oz diced boneless beef shoulder (top blade)

¼ cup extra-virgin olive oil

1 oz (2 tbsp) unsalted butter

8 oz plain fresh pork sausage, crumbled

2 cups quartered white mushrooms

2 cups diced portobello mushrooms

2 cups diced yellow onion

3 garlic cloves, smashed

½ cup dry red wine

½ cup tomato paste

6 cups chicken broth

2 bay leaves

4 cloves

3 lb Potato Gnocchi (page 243)

2 oz (¼ cup) unsalted butter

2 tbsp extra-virgin olive oil

Grated Parmigiano-Reggiano, as needed

1. Place the chicken livers in a small bowl and season with salt, pepper, and 2 tablespoons of the Marsala. Cover and set aside in the refrigerator. Combine the hearts, gizzards, sweetbreads, and beef in a bowl and season lightly with a pinch of salt and pepper.

2. Heat the ¼ cup oil and 2 tablespoons of butter in a large saucepan over high heat until very hot, but not smoking. Add the seasoned meats and the sausage and cook, stirring as necessary, until golden brown, about 10 minutes. Add all of the mushrooms and cook, stirring occasionally for 10 minutes more.

3. Add the onions and garlic; reduce the heat to medium, and continue to cook, stirring frequently, until the onions are tender and a light golden brown, about 20 minutes.

4. Add the remaining 6 tablespoons Marsala and cook until it has nearly cooked away, about 3 minutes. Add the red wine and cook until it has reduced by half, about 5 minutes.

5. Add the tomato paste, stir it into the sauce, and cook until it has a rich, sweet aroma, about 5 minutes. Add the broth, bay leaves, and cloves and bring the sauce to a simmer. Cover the pan, reduce the heat to low, and cook slowly until the meats are extremely tender, about 2 hours. Stir the sauce often as it cooks and add a little water, if necessary, to keep the sauce from drying out. The result should be a rich, thick sauce. Remove and discard the bay leaves and cloves. Taste the sauce and season with salt and pepper, as needed. (The sauce can be made in advance and stored in a covered container in the refrigerator for up to 4 days.)

6. Bring a large pot of salted water to a boil over high heat. Add the gnocchi and stir to submerge and separate them. Cook, uncovered, at a gentle boil until the gnocchi rise to the surface and are cooked through, 2 to 4 minutes depending on their size. (To be certain, taste one of the gnocchi.)

7. Using a slotted spoon, lift the cooked gnocchi out of the water and transfer them to a large bowl. Add the ¼ cup butter and 2 tablespoons olive oil and toss with the hot gnocchi to coat them well. Add some of the finanziera sauce and some of the grated cheese. Serve the gnocchi with additional sauce on top and pass additional cheese on the side, if desired.

Gnocchi di zucca e gamberi di fiume

Pumpkin dumplings with crayfish

SERVES 4 TO 6

Crayfish stock

2 lb crayfish

2 oz (¼ cup) unsalted butter

¾ cup minced yellow onion

½ cup minced carrot

½ cup minced celery

¼ cup brandy

¼ cup dry Marsala

3 tbsp tomato paste

2 bay leaves

3 thyme sprigs

6 amaretti cookies, crumbled

Pumpkin gnocchi

14 oz (1⅔ cups) drained pumpkin purée (see Recipe note)

5 oz (1 cup plus 2 tbsp) all-purpose or tipo 00 flour

2 tbsp grated Grana Padano

2 large eggs

Kosher salt, and freshly ground black pepper, as needed

Freshly grated nutmeg, as needed

These gnocchi are not shaped in the same way that you would shape potato gnocchi. They are so soft that you will need to shape them with a spoon or a pastry bag right into the boiling water.

1. Bring a large pot of water to a boil over high heat. Lower the crayfish into the water and cook for 2 minutes. Drain the crayfish, remove the heads, and reserve. Remove the shells from the tails. Add the shells to the reserved heads and set the tail meat aside. Crush all the shells with a mortar and pestle or in a food processor.

2. Heat a medium sauté pan over medium heat. Add the ¼ cup of butter and, when it has melted, add the onion, carrot, and celery and cook, stirring frequently, until the onion is tender and lightly golden. Add the crushed crayfish shells and sauté for another 5 minutes over low heat. Add the brandy and simmer until the brandy has cooked away, about 3 minutes. Add the Marsala and cook until the Marsala has cooked away, 2 to 3 minutes more. Add the tomato paste, bay leaves, and thyme; cook, stirring frequently, until the mixture has a rich, rusty color and a sweet aroma, another 5 minutes.

3. Add water to just barely cover the shells and add the amaretti cookies. Stir to combine and simmer over very low heat for 30 minutes. Strain the stock through a wire-mesh sieve twice, pressing the solids well to extract as much liquid as possible. You should have at least 2 cups; reserve any additional stock to use in other dishes.

4. Combine the pumpkin purée, flour, cheese, eggs, salt, pepper, and nutmeg in a large bowl and stir together with a spoon. Bring a large wide pot of salted water to a boil over high heat.

5. To shape the gnocchi with a spoon, dip a serving spoon in the boiling water and then scoop up a small amount of gnocchi dough and lower it (still on the spoon) into the boiling water; it should fall off the spoon. To shape the gnocchi with a pastry bag, fill a pastry bag fitted with a large round tip with the gnocchi batter and squeeze the batter onto the surface of the boiling water, in about 1-inch lengths.

Continued

2 oz (¼ cup) unsalted butter

2 tbsp minced shallot

Reserved pumpkin, cut in small dice
(see Recipe note)

½ cup slivered almonds, toasted

3 tbsp finely chopped chives

6. Cook the gnocchi in small batches to avoid overcrowding the pot. The gnocchi will take 2 to 3 minutes to cook. Using a slotted spoon to lift the cooked gnocchi out of the water and spread each batch out on a baking sheet to cool.

7. Heat a medium sauté pan over medium heat. Add the ¼ cup butter and, when it has melted, add the shallot and diced pumpkin. Season with salt and cook, stirring from time to time, until the pumpkin starts to brown. Add 2 cups of the crayfish stock and continue to cook until the stock is reduced by half and the diced pumpkin is completely tender, about 15 minutes.

8. Reheat the gnocchi in boiling water for 30 seconds and drain well. Toss the heated gnocchi with the sauce, then add the crayfish tail meat and continue to toss until the sauce coats the gnocchi. Transfer to a heated serving bowl or individual plates and sprinkle with the almonds and chives.

Recipe note *A day before you make the gnocchi cut a 4- or 5-pound pumpkin in quarters, remove the seeds, save about 1½ cups of diced raw fresh pumpkin for the dish, then place the rest a roasting pan, cover with aluminum foil, and cook it in a 350°F oven, until tender. When done, remove the pulp from the skin and purée in a food processor. Put the purée in cheesecloth and let drain overnight.*

Gnocchi di grano saraceno con ragù di radici miste

Buckwheat and potato gnocchi with mixed root vegetable ragù

SERVES 6 TO 8

Root vegetable ragù

3 oz (6 tbsp) unsalted butter

1 garlic clove, minced

2 thyme sprigs

½ cup cubed peeled sweet potato

1 small white turnip, peeled and cubed

1 parsnip, peeled and cubed

1 carrot, cubed

⅔ cup cubed rutabaga

⅔ cup cubed celeriac

Kosher salt and freshly ground black pepper, as needed

2 cups water or vegetable broth, or as needed

Buckwheat and potato gnocchi

2 lb russet or other starchy potatoes, scrubbed

6 oz (1⅓ cups) all-purpose or tipo 00 flour, plus as needed

3 oz (¾ cup) buckwheat flour

1 large egg

½ cup grated Parmigiano-Reggiano

1. Melt the butter in a deep sauté pan or Dutch oven over low heat. Add the garlic and thyme. When the garlic is aromatic, about 1 minute, add all the vegetables. Season with salt and pepper and stir to coat the vegetables evenly with the butter. Increase the heat to medium and sauté the vegetables until they are hot, but not colored, about 2 minutes.

2. Add enough of the water or broth to cover the vegetables by half. Cover the pan with a lid, reduce the heat to low, and simmer until all the vegetables are tender, 15 to 20 minutes. Check the vegetables as they cook and, if needed, add more water or broth. When the sauce is done the vegetables should be very tender and the liquid should be almost all evaporated and blended with the butter.

3. Put the potatoes in a large pot and add enough cold water to cover them by about 2 inches. Salt the water and bring it to a boil over medium-high heat. Cook until the potatoes are easily pierced with a wooden skewer or fork (the time will depend on the size of the potatoes). Drain the potatoes and dry them in the pot over low heat, about 3 minutes. Remove the skin and pass the potatoes through a food mill.

4. Spread the milled potatoes on a clean surface area to cool. When the potatoes are cool enough to handle, add the all-purpose and buckwheat flours, egg, and with a pinch of salt. Knead the dough until all the ingredients are well combined.

5. Divide the dough into three pieces and roll each piece to form a rope about ¾ inch in diameter. (Flour your work surface as needed while you roll and cut the gnocchi.) Cut each rope on a bias to form small gnocchi. Once shaped, the gnocchi can be reserved on a floured baking sheet, loosely covered, in the refrigerator for up to 8 hours.

6. Bring a large pot of salted water to a boil over high heat. Add the gnocchi and stir a few times to separate them. Cook, uncovered, at a gentle boil until the gnocchi rise to the surface and are cooked through, 2 to 4 minutes depending on their size. (To be certain, taste one of the gnocchi.) Using a slotted spoon, lift the cooked gnocchi out of the water and transfer to a heated serving bowl.

7. Add the root vegetable ragù to the gnocchi and toss them together until they are evenly coated and the sauce is creamy. Add the cheese, toss to combine, and serve at once.

Panissa ligure

Chickpea polenta

SERVES 4 TO 6

1 lb (3½ cups) chickpea flour

6 cups boiling water, or more as needed

Kosher salt and freshly ground black pepper, as needed

Fresh lemon juice, as needed

Extra-virgin olive oil, preferably from Liguria, as needed

You may wish to add some sautéed red onion and chopped parsley to this very simple dish.

1. Put the flour in a large pot. Add the water, mixing well to prevent any lumps from forming. The mixture should be smooth and about the consistency of heavy cream. Place the pot over low heat and cook, stirring constantly, until it is very thick and creamy, about 1 hour. Add more water, if necessary, while you are cooking the panissa to keep it moist.

2. Season the panissa, as needed, with salt, pepper, and a few drops of lemon juice. Transfer to a heated serving bowl or plates and top with the oil, or pass the oil separately to add at the table.

Recipe notes *Any leftover panissa may be transferred to a pan and cooled. You can simply reheat it or cut it into slices and sauté (it will harden like polenta). Serve with some olive oil and good balsamic vinegar.*

You could also cut the panissa in "fingers" about the size of steak fries and then deep-fry them. These are called panelle, *a typical street food popular in Sicily.*

Polenta con funghi, salsiccia e fontina

Polenta with mushrooms, sausage, and fontina

SERVES 6

Mushroom ragù and sausages

½ cup extra-virgin olive oil

½ cup diced yellow onion

3 garlic cloves, chopped

1 lb fresh mushrooms, preferably porcini, trimmed and sliced

¾ cup flat-leaf parsley

½ cup dry white wine

1½ lb fresh Italian link sausage

Polenta

2 qt water

2 tbsp kosher salt

¼ cup extra-virgin olive oil

8 oz (1¾ cups) cornmeal

12 oz Fontina, diced

1. Heat the ½ cup oil in a saucepan over medium-high heat. Add the onion and cook, stirring frequently, until it is tender and translucent, about 3 minutes. Add the garlic and cook until aromatic, about 1 minute. Add the mushrooms and parsley and stir well. Add the wine, cover the pan, and continue to cook until the mushrooms are tender, about 10 minutes, depending on mushrooms you are using. Set aside.

2. Pierce the sausage links or cut them in half lengthwise. Heat a sauté pan over medium heat and sauté the sausage until it is cooked through, about 10 minutes.

3. Remove sausage from the pan, add a little bit of water, and simmer for 2 or 3 minutes to make a pan sauce with the drippings and the fat left in the pan. Set aside.

4. Bring the water to a simmer in a large saucepan over medium heat. Add the salt and the ¼ cup oil, and then slowly add the cornmeal, whisking continuously. Let simmer gently until the polenta is done, stirring frequently with a wooden spoon to make sure the polenta does not stick, 30 to 40 minutes. (The cooking time may vary depending upon the coarseness of your cornmeal.) Remove the polenta from the heat and adjust the seasoning with salt, as needed.

5. Spoon the hot polenta into heated pasta bowls or plates. Top with the cheese and the mushroom sauce. Finish with the sausage on top and then drizzle with some of the sausage pan juices. Serve at once.

Recipe notes *You may also mix the Fontina into the polenta and then serve it topped with the mushrooms and sausage.*

Different types of cornmeal and varying degrees of coarseness will give you different cooking times and consistency, so adjust the recipe based on the type of cornmeal you are using.

Polenta con sopressata all'aceto

Polenta with sopressata and vinegar sauce

SERVES 6

Polenta

2 qt water

2 tbsp kosher salt

¼ cup extra-virgin olive oil

8 oz (1¾ cups) cornmeal

6 thick slices sopressata, sliced ¼ inch thick, about 12 oz (see Recipe note)

½ cup dry white wine vinegar

The secret in this dish is a good sopressata. If you can get your hands on a real Venetian-style sopressata, that would be the best, but if not, try to find a very fresh coarse-grind salami or sopressata that is a little soft and not dry. You may want to add some freshly ground black pepper to the pan sauce to more closely approximate the taste of a Venetian-style sopressata.

1. Bring the water to a simmer in a large saucepan over medium heat. Add the salt and oil, and then slowly add the cornmeal, whisking continuously. Let simmer gently until the polenta is done, stirring frequently with a wooden spoon to make sure the polenta does not stick, 30 to 40 minutes. (The cooking time may vary depending upon the coarseness of your cornmeal.) Remove the polenta from the heat, adjust the seasoning with salt, and keep warm.

2. Heat a sauté pan over medium-high heat (you will not need any fat in the pan since the sopressata is quite fatty on its own). Add the sopressata to the pan, working in batches to cook it in a single layer. When the fat begins to melt and the sopressata is browned on both sides, remove it from the pan. Drain on paper towels.

3. Add the vinegar to the fat in the pan and simmer very briefly over medium heat, just long enough to make a thick sauce, about 1 minute. If the sauce appears too greasy, add a few teaspoons of water and mix well to thicken the sauce.

4. Spoon the hot polenta onto heated plates and top each serving with a slice of the fried sopressata. Pour the pan sauce over the sopressata and polenta and serve at once.

Recipe note *Sopressata is usually much larger in diameter than a regular salami, so one slice per person is usually enough, but if you are using any other type of good-quality soft salami, you may have to increase the number of slices for each serving.*

Farrotto con pollo e finferli

Farro with chicken and chanterelle ragù

SERVES 6 TO 8

Chicken and chanterelle ragù

½ cup extra-virgin olive oil

4 small chicken legs (8 to 10 oz each)

Kosher salt and freshly ground black pepper, as needed

1 small yellow onion, chopped

1 small carrot, chopped

1 celery stalk, chopped

½ tsp chopped rosemary

2 tsp chopped thyme

½ cup dry white wine

½ cup canned whole San Marzano tomatoes, crushed through a food mill or sieve

8 oz chanterelles

Chicken broth, as needed

1 lb (3 cups) farro, rinsed and soaked in cold water overnight

2 qt chicken broth

Chopped flat-leaf parsley, as needed

1. Preheat the oven to 350°F.

2. Heat ¼ cup of the oil in a 4-quart Dutch over medium heat. Season the chicken legs with salt and pepper and add them to the hot oil in a single layer. Cook, turning as necessary, until golden brown on all sides, about 8 minutes total cooking time.

3. Add the onion, carrot, celery, rosemary, and thyme and stir to coat them with the fat. Sauté, stirring often, until the vegetables are slightly tender and just starting to brown, about 10 minutes. Add the wine, stirring well to dissolve any juices that have reduced in the pot, and continue to cook until the wine has nearly cooked away. Add the tomatoes and the chanterelles. Transfer the pot to the oven and cook until the chicken is very tender, about 30 minutes. Turn the chicken as it cooks to keep it evenly moistened. If the liquid cooks away while preparing the chicken, add a bit of broth.

4. As soon as the legs are done, remove the pot from the oven and lift the chicken legs from the sauce. When they are cool enough to handle, pull the meat from the bones and remove and discard the skin and any tendons. Cut the meat into large dice and return it to the sauce in the pan.

5. Drain the farro and blot dry with a clean towel. Bring the broth to a boil in a large saucepan and season with salt, if needed. Heat the remaining ¼ cup oil in a casserole over medium heat. Add the farro and sauté, stirring constantly, until the grains are evenly coated with the oil, about 1 minute.

6. Add about 1 cup of the boiling broth to the farro and stir until it has been almost completely absorbed. Continue adding the broth to the farro in the same manner until all of the broth has been added and the farro is moist but not soupy, and tender but with a discernible bite, about 30 minutes. Add the chicken ragù to the farro during the last 5 minutes of cooking. Transfer to a heated serving bowl or soup plates and top with the parsley.

Paniscia

Risotto with vegetables, beans, salame, and red wine

SERVES 4 TO 6

1 qt chicken or vegetable broth

2 oz lard or pancetta, cut into small dice

1 medium yellow onion, minced

3 oz salamino or salami, diced

10 oz (1½ cups) Carnaroli or Vialone Nano rice

½ cup dry white wine

1½ cups cooked fresh or dried borlotti beans (page 254)

¼ cup canned crushed San Marzano tomatoes

2 oz (¼ cup) unsalted butter

½ cup chopped flat-leaf parsley

¾ cup grated Parmigiano-Reggiano (optional)

Kosher salt and freshly ground black pepper, as needed

According to old-time tradition, this risotto doesn't get the typical grated Parmigiano-Reggiano or Grana Padano cheese, as there is already enough fat in dish from the salamino and the lard, but we leave it up to your taste.

1. Heat the broth over low heat; keep warm.

2. Heat the lard, onion, and salamino in a large pot over low heat to make a sofrito. Cook, stirring frequently, until the onion is tender and translucent, about 4 minutes. Add the rice and cook, stirring frequently, until the rice is well coated with the oil, about 2 minutes.

3. Add the wine and cook until almost dry. Add the beans and the tomatoes and enough of the broth to come ½ inch above the rice. Cook, stirring frequently to be sure the rice doesn't stick to the bottom. As the rice absorbs the liquid, keep adding more broth, ½ cup at a time.

4. Once the rice has absorbed almost all the broth and the grains are just tender (al dente), about 15 minutes total cooking time, remove the pot from the heat. Add the butter, parsley, and cheese, if using, and stir vigorously until the rice looks very creamy. Season the risotto with salt and pepper as needed and serve immediately.

Risotto al gorgonzola, radicchio e pera

Risotto with gorgonzola, radicchio, and pear

SERVES 6

6 cups Meat Broth (page 251), or as needed

2 tbsp extra-virgin olive oil

3 oz (6 tbsp) unsalted butter

¾ cup minced yellow onion

½ head radicchio, cut into thin strips

1 lb (2⅓ cups) Carnaroli rice

½ cup dry white wine

¾ cup crumbled Gorgonzola

½ cup chopped flat-leaf parsley (optional)

Freshly ground black pepper, as needed

¾ cup peeled, diced pear

If your pear is not completely ripe, you may add it during the final 5 minutes of the cooking time for the risotto so it will cook in the risotto and become tender.

1. Heat the broth over low heat; keep warm.

2. Heat the oil and 2 tablespoons of the butter in a large pot over low heat. Add the onion and radicchio and cook, stirring frequently, until the onions are tender and translucent and the radicchio is wilted, about 4 minutes. Add the rice and toast lightly, stirring frequently, about 2 minutes.

3. Add the wine and cook until almost dry. Add enough broth to come ½ inch above the rice, and cook, stirring frequently to be sure the rice doesn't stick to the bottom. As the rice absorbs the broth, keep adding more, ½ cup at a time.

4. Once the rice has absorbed almost all the broth, and the grains are just tender (al dente), about 18 minutes total cooking time, remove the pot from the heat. Add the remaining 4 tablespoons butter and stir vigorously until the risotto is creamy.

5. Add the cheese and parsley, if using. Season with pepper, and serve immediately on flat plates topped with the pear.

Risotto con le verze

Risotto with cabbage

SERVES 6

6 cups Meat Broth (page 251), or as needed

3 tbsp extra-virgin olive oil

3 oz (6 tbsp) unsalted butter

1 cup diced yellow onion

7 cups shredded savoy cabbage

9 oz (1⅓ cups) Carnaroli, Vialone Nano, or Arborio rice

3 garlic cloves, smashed

1 cup grated Parmigiano-Reggiano

Kosher salt and freshly ground black pepper, as needed

1. Heat the broth over low heat; keep warm.

2. Heat the oil and 2 tablespoons of the butter in a large pot over low heat. Add the onion and cook, stirring frequently, until tender and translucent, about 4 minutes. Add the cabbage, cover the pan, and cook, stirring occasionally, until the cabbage is wilted and has released some of its juices, about 3 minutes. Add the rice and cook, stirring frequently, about 2 minutes.

3. Add the garlic and enough of the broth to come ½ inch above the rice, and cook, stirring frequently to be sure the rice doesn't stick to the bottom. As the rice absorbs the broth, keep adding more, ½ cup at a time.

4. Once the rice has absorbed almost all the broth, and the grains are just tender (al dente), about 18 minutes total cooking time, remove the pot from the heat.

5. Remove and discard the garlic, and add the remaining butter and the cheese and stir vigorously until the risotto is creamy. Season with salt and pepper if needed and serve immediately on flat plates.

Recipe note *Vegetable broth can be used if preferred.*

Risotto ai porcini e mirtilli

Risotto with porcini and blueberries

SERVES 6

¼ cup extra-virgin olive oil

3 garlic cloves

12 oz fresh porcini mushrooms, cleaned, trimmed, thinly sliced

10 cups Meat Broth (page 251), or as needed

5 oz (10 tbsp) unsalted butter

¾ cup minced yellow onion

1 lb (2⅓ cups) Carnaroli rice

½ cup dry red wine

½ cup fresh blueberries

1 cup grated Grana Padano

½ cup chopped flat-leaf parsley

Kosher salt and freshly ground black pepper, as needed

1. Heat the oil in a sauté pan over medium-high heat. Add the garlic cloves and cook, stirring frequently, until the garlic is aromatic and a light golden color, about 2 minutes. Add the porcini and continue to cook until light golden, 5 or 6 minutes more. Remove and discard the garlic cloves. Set the porcini aside.

2. Heat the broth over low heat; keep warm.

3. Heat 6 tablespoons of the butter in a large pot over low heat. Add the onion and cook, stirring frequently, until tender and translucent, about 4 minutes. Add the rice and toast lightly, stirring frequently, about 2 minutes.

4. Add the wine and cook until almost dry. Add the sautéed porcini and enough of the broth to come ½ inch above the rice, and cook, stirring frequently to be sure the rice doesn't stick to the bottom. As the rice absorbs the broth, keep adding more, ½ cup at a time.

5. Once the rice has absorbed almost all the broth, and the grains are just tender (al dente), about 18 minutes total cooking time, remove the pot from the heat. Add the remaining 4 tablespoons butter and the blueberries and stir vigorously until the risotto is creamy. Stir in the cheese and parsley.

6. Season with salt and pepper, if needed, and serve immediately on flat plates.

Risotto con mele, noci, porcini e fontina

Risotto with apple, walnuts, porcini mushrooms, and Fontina

SERVES 6

10 cups Meat Broth (page 251), or as needed

Kosher salt, as needed

6 oz (¾ cup) unsalted butter

¾ cup minced yellow onion

1 lb (2⅓ cups) Carnaroli rice

¼ cup extra-virgin olive oil

3 garlic cloves

18 oz fresh porcini mushrooms, cleaned, trimmed, and thinly sliced

2 small apples, peeled, cored, and thinly sliced

½ cup dry Marsala

1 cup grated Grana Padano

Kosher salt and freshly ground black pepper, as needed

4 oz Fontina, thinly sliced

1 tbsp coarsely chopped walnuts

1. Heat the broth over low heat and season with salt; keep warm.

2. Heat 7 tablespoons of the butter in a large pot over low heat. Add the onion and cook, stirring frequently, until tender, about 5 minutes. Add the rice and cook over medium heat, stirring frequently, until the grains are hot, about 2 minutes.

3. Add enough of the broth to come ½ inch above the rice, and cook, stirring frequently to be sure the rice doesn't stick to the bottom. As the rice absorbs the broth, keep adding more, ½ cup at a time.

4. In a separate sauté pan, heat the oil over medium heat. Add the garlic cloves and cook, stirring frequently, until they are a light golden color. Add the porcini and apples. Season with a pinch of salt and pepper and cook, stirring frequently, until the mushrooms are very hot and nearly tender, about 8 minutes. Add the Marsala and cook until the wine has reduced by about half, 4 to 5 minutes. Remove and discard the garlic cloves and keep the mushroom-apple mixture warm.

5. Add half of the mushroom-apple mixture to the risotto after it has cooked for about 10 minutes. Once the rice has absorbed almost all the broth, and the grains are just tender (al dente), about 18 minutes total cooking time, remove the pot from the heat.

6. Add the remaining 5 tablespoons butter and the Grana Padano and stir vigorously until the risotto is creamy. Season with salt and pepper, if needed, and serve immediately on flat plates topped with the sliced Fontina and the remaining mushroom-apple mixture and sprinkle with the walnuts.

Risotto con quaglie e erbe fresche

Herbed risotto with roasted quail

SERVES 6

Herbed quail

6 quail (4 to 5 oz each)

Kosher salt and freshly ground black pepper, as needed

2 tbsp extra-virgin olive oil

2 oz (¼ cup) unsalted butter, melted

3 garlic cloves

10 cups Meat Broth (page 251), or as needed

4 oz (½ cup) unsalted butter, cubed

¾ cup minced yellow onions

1 lb (2⅓ cups) Carnaroli rice

½ cup dry white wine

1 cup grated Grana Padano

½ cup finely minced mixed herbs, such as tarragon, chervil, parsley, marjoram, or chives

Add any bones and wingtips from the quail to the meat broth in this dish for an even richer flavor. Simmer the bones in the broth for about 45 minutes and then strain it before using to prepare the risotto.

1. Preheat the oven to 350°F.

2. With a small boning knife separate the breast and the legs from the quail. Set aside.

3. Season the quail pieces with salt and pepper. In a sauté pan, heat the oil, and quickly sauté the quail breasts and legs on both sides. Transfer the quail to a baking dish. Top with the ¼ cup butter and the garlic. Place the baking dish in the oven and roast until the meat is cooked through, about 15 minutes. Baste with the butter during cooking.

4. Heat the broth over low heat; keep warm.

5. Heat ¼ cup of the butter in a large pot over low heat. Add the onion and cook, stirring frequently, until tender and translucent, about 4 minutes. Add the rice and toast lightly, stirring frequently, about 2 minutes.

6. Add the wine and cook until almost dry. Add enough of the broth to come ½ inch above the rice, and cook, stirring frequently to be sure the rice doesn't stick to the bottom. As the rice absorbs the broth, keep adding more, ½ cup at a time.

7. Once the rice has absorbed almost all the broth, and the grains are just tender (al dente), about 18 minutes total cooking time, remove the pot from the heat. Add the remaining ¼ cup of the butter and the cheese and stir vigorously until the risotto is creamy. Add the minced herbs, season with salt and pepper, if needed, and serve immediately on flat plates topped with the quail.

Risotto con zucca e parmigiano

Risotto with pumpkin and parmigiano-reggiano

SERVES 4 TO 6

One 3-lb pumpkin

1 qt chicken or vegetable broth

½ cup extra-virgin olive oil

1 medium yellow onion, minced

10 oz (1½ cups) Carnaroli or Vialone Nano rice

4 oz (½ cup) unsalted butter, cubed

¾ cup grated Parmigiano-Reggiano

Kosher salt and coarsely ground black pepper, as needed

Top the risotto with a few leaves of sage fried in butter and a sprinkling of crumbled amaretti cookies.

1. Cut the pumpkin in half and scoop out the seeds. Peel the pumpkin and dice the flesh. Set aside.

2. Heat the broth over low heat; keep warm.

3. Heat the oil in a large pot over low heat. Add the onion and cook, stirring frequently, until tender and translucent, about 4 minutes. Add the diced pumpkin and continue to cook, stirring to coat the pumpkin with the oil, until it is hot, about 2 minutes. Add the rice and toast lightly, stirring frequently, about 2 minutes.

4. Add enough of the broth to come ½ inch above the rice, and cook, stirring frequently to be sure the rice doesn't stick to the bottom. As the rice absorbs the broth, keep adding more, ½ cup at a time.

5. Once the rice has absorbed almost all the broth, and the grains are just tender (al dente), about 20 minutes total cooking time, remove the pot from the heat. Add the butter and cheese and stir vigorously until the risotto is creamy. (The pumpkin will start to fall apart; this is what should happen and gives the risotto a brilliant orange color and additional creaminess.) Season with salt and pepper if necessary and serve immediately on flat plates. Top the risotto with a few leaves of sage fried in butter and a sprinkling of crumbled amaretti cookies.

Recipe note *Any type of winter squash or pumpkin will work in this recipe, including butternut, cheese, acorn, or Hubbard squash. The yellow color of this risotto will depend on the type of winter squash you use.*

Winter

Pennette all'arrabbiata

Pennette with spicy garlic-tomato sauce

SERVES 6

Arrabbiata Sauce

6 tbsp extra-virgin olive oil

4 small dried red chiles (peperoncini), crushed

3 garlic cloves, minced or thinly sliced

1 can (28 oz) whole San Marzano tomatoes

Kosher salt, as needed

1 lb dried pennette lisce (not rigate)

This pasta sauce is supposed to be quite spicy, so feel free to adjust the quantity of chiles to suit your taste.

1. Heat the oil in a 4-quart Dutch oven over medium heat. Add the dried chiles and garlic and stir to coat them with the oil. Sauté over low heat, stirring often, until the garlic is just starting to turn color, about 3 minutes. Add the tomatoes with their juices and simmer the sauce, uncovered, until it is very flavorful and the tomatoes are "sweet," 25 to 30 minutes. Use a wooden spoon or a potato masher to break up the tomatoes while the sauce simmers.

2. Bring a large pot of salted water to a boil over high heat. Add the pennette and stir to submerge and separate the pasta. Cook, uncovered, until just tender (al dente), 8 to 9 minutes (check the cooking time for your pasta).

3. Drain the pasta in a colander. Shake well to remove any water clinging to the pasta. Add the drained pasta to the arrabbiata sauce and toss them together until the pasta is evenly coated. Serve at once in warmed pasta plates.

Sedanini ai quattro formaggi

Tube-shaped pasta tossed with four cheeses

SERVES 6

1 lb dried sendanini, or other tube-shaped pasta

2 cups heavy cream

3 oz sweet Gorgonzola, crumbled or cubed

3 oz Gruyère, cubed

3 oz Fontina Valdostana, cubed

¾ cup grated Pecorino Romano

Kosher salt and freshly ground black pepper, as needed

1. Bring a large pot of salted water to a boil over high heat. Add the pasta and stir a few times to submerge and separate the pasta. Cook, uncovered, until just tender (al dente), 8 to 9 minutes (check the cooking time for your pasta).

2. While the pasta is cooking, heat the cream in a large saucepan over medium heat. Add all the cheeses and stir them into the cream over low heat until they have melted into a thick, smooth sauce, about 4 minutes.

3. Drain the pasta in a colander. Shake well to remove any water clinging to the pasta. Add the drained pasta to the cheese sauce and toss together until the pasta is evenly coated. Season with pepper, as needed, and serve at once in a heated serving bowl or pasta plates.

Spaghetti cacio e pepe

Spaghetti with black pepper and pecorino

SERVES 6

1 lb dried spaghetti

Kosher salt, as needed

1 cup grated Pecorino Romano, plus as needed for serving

½ cup extra-virgin olive oil

4 tsp freshly ground black pepper, or as needed

The quality of your cheese is crucial to the success of this dish. Make sure you taste your pecorino before you start, as different pecorinos can vary greatly in how salty they are. Adjust the seasoning in this sauce to adapt to the salt level in your pecorino.

1. Bring a large pot of salted water to a boil over high heat. Add the spaghetti and stir to submerge and separate the strands. Cook uncovered until the pasta is just tender (al dente), 10 to 12 minutes (check the cooking time for your pasta). Reserve a few ladlefuls of the pasta cooking water for finishing the sauce (you will need about ½ cup.)

2. Drain the spaghetti in a colander. Pour the drained spaghetti into a heated serving bowl. Add the cheese, oil, and pepper. Stir the pasta until the cheese and pepper are evenly distributed. Add about ¼ cup of the reserved pasta cooking water to the spaghetti to moisten it slightly. It should appear creamy, not oily. If necessary, add a bit more of the pasta water.

3. Serve at once, passing additional cheese on the side.

Spaghetti aglio, olio e peperoncino

Spaghetti with garlic, oil, and hot pepper

SERVES 4 TO 6

Kosher salt, as needed

1 lb dried spaghetti

1 cup extra-virgin olive oil, or as needed

1 tsp red pepper flakes

3 garlic cloves

½ cup chopped flat-leaf parsley

1. Bring a large pot of salted water to a boil over high heat. Add the spaghetti and stir to submerge and separate the strands. Cook, uncovered, until just tender (al dente), 8 to 9 minutes (check the cooking time for your pasta).

2. While the pasta is cooking, heat the oil in a large sauté pan. Add the chiles to the oil. Press the garlic through a garlic press directly into the hot oil and reduce the heat to low. Let the garlic infuse the oil and gently fry until translucent, about 1 minute. Add the parsley and remove the pan from the heat.

3. Drain the pasta in a colander. Shake well to remove any water clinging to the pasta. Add the drained pasta to the garlic oil. Toss to coat and season with salt as needed. Serve at once in a heated serving bowl or in pasta plates.

Spaghetti con acciughe, finocchietto e mollica

Spaghetti with anchovies, wild fennel, and toasted bread crumbs

SERVES 6

Kosher salt, as needed

1 lb dried spaghetti

6 salt-cured anchovy fillets

¼ cup extra-virgin olive oil

4 garlic cloves, thinly sliced

¼ tsp red pepper flakes

¼ cup chopped fennel fronds (wild fennel, if available)

Toasted Bread Crumbs (page 247)

1. Bring a large pot of salted water to a boil over high heat. Add the spaghetti and stir to submerge and separate the strands. Cook, uncovered, until the pasta is just tender (al dente), 10 to 12 minutes (check the cooking time for your pasta). Reserve a few ladlefuls of the pasta cooking water for finishing the sauce (you will need about ½ cup).

2. While the pasta is cooking, use a small knife to cut the anchovy fillets away from the bone. Scrape the salt away. Heat the oil in a large sauté pan over medium heat. Add the garlic and red pepper flakes and cook, stirring frequently, until the garlic is lightly browned, about 2 minutes. Add the anchovies and cook, mashing them into the sauce with the back of a wooden spoon, until they melt into the oil, about 2 minutes. Add ¼ cup of the reserved pasta cooking water and the fennel fronds, and simmer slowly over low heat for 5 minutes.

3. Drain the spaghetti in a colander. Shake well to remove any water clinging to the pasta. Pour the drained pasta into the pan with the garlic-fennel sauce and toss together over low heat until the pasta is evenly coated, about 1 minute. Add half the bread crumbs and quickly toss the pasta until they are evenly distributed. Serve at once on heated plates topped with the remaining bread crumbs.

Orecchiette con cime di rapa

Orecchiette with broccoli rabe

SERVES 4 TO 6

1 lb broccoli rabe

Kosher salt, as needed

1½ lb dried orecchiette

½ cup extra-virgin olive oil

4 garlic cloves, thinly sliced

Red pepper flakes, as needed (optional)

¾ cup grated Pecorino Romano

You may add some toasted thinly sliced almonds, walnuts, or even hazelnuts for some texture and flavor in this dish.

1. Trim all the leaves away from the broccoli rabe, and remove the central core from each leaf. Remove the bottom 3 inches of the stem and peel the rest up to the flower buds. Rinse well under cold running water.

2. Bring a large pot of salted water to a boil. Add the broccoli and stir to submerge. Cook, uncovered, until tender and a deep green color, 3 to 4 minutes. Lift the greens out of the water with a sieve or slotted spoon and rinse under cold running water. Drain in a colander for a few minutes. Coarsely chop the broccoli rabe and set aside

3. Bring another large pot of salted water to a boil over high heat. Add the orecchiette and stir to submerge and separate the pieces. Cook, uncovered, until the pasta is just tender (al dente), 8 to 10 minutes (check the cooking time for your pasta).

4. While the pasta is cooking, heat the oil in a large sauté pan over medium heat. Add the garlic and cook, stirring frequently, until the garlic is a light golden color, about 1 minute. Add the red pepper flakes, if using, the cooked broccoli rabe, and about ¼ cup of the reserved pasta cooking water. Simmer until the broccoli rabe is hot and tender (the time will vary depending upon how well-cooked you like your broccoli rabe). Turn off the heat and set aside.

5. Drain the orecchiette in a colander, shaking well to remove excess water. Add the drained pasta to the pan with the broccoli rabe and toss together over low heat until combined, about 1 minute.

6. Serve at once on heated plates at once, and pass the cheese on the side.

Garganelli con cipolle rosse, pancetta, olive, pecorino e panna

Garganelli with red onion, pancetta, olives, pecorino, and cream

SERVES 4 TO 6

Kosher salt, as needed

1 lb dried garganelli

¼ cup extra-virgin olive oil

4 to 6 oz pancetta, cut into small dice

1 large red onion, cut into small dice

12 large green olives, pitted, and coarsely chopped

1 cup heavy cream

½ cup grated Pecorino Romano, plus more as needed for serving

Freshly ground black pepper, as needed

1. Bring a large pot of salted water to a boil over high heat. Add the garganelli and stir to submerge and separate the pieces. Cook, uncovered, until the pasta is just tender (al dente), 8 to 10 minutes (check the cooking time for your pasta).

2. While the pasta is cooking, heat the oil and the pancetta in a large sauté pan over medium heat. Cook, stirring frequently, until the pancetta is crisp and golden, about 3 minutes.

3. Add the onion and olives and cook, stirring frequently, until the onion is very tender, about 6 minutes. Add the cream and simmer the sauce over low heat until it is thickened and flavorful, about 4 minutes. Set aside.

4. Drain the garganelli in a colander, shaking well to remove the excess water. Add the pasta to the pan with the red onion and pancetta mixture. Add the cheese and pepper and toss the pasta and the sauce together over low heat until evenly blended, about 2 minutes.

5. Serve the garganelli at once on heated plates, and pass cheese on the side.

Bucatini alla carbonara

Bucatini with eggs, cheese, and guanciale

SERVES 4 TO 6

Kosher salt, as needed

1 lb dried bucatini

1 tbsp extra-virgin olive oil

5 oz diced guanciale (cured pork jowl) or pancetta

2 large eggs

2 egg yolks

½ cup grated Pecorino Romano

1 tsp freshly ground black pepper

1. Bring a large pot of salted water to a boil over high heat. Add the bucatini and stir to submerge and separate the strands. Cook, uncovered, until the pasta is just tender (al dente), 10 to 12 minutes (check the cooking time for your pasta).

2. While the bucatini is cooking, heat a large sauté pan over medium heat. Add the oil and the guanciale. Cook, stirring to cook the guanciale evenly, until it is just starting to crisp, about 2 minutes. There should be about 2 tablespoons of rendered fat and oil in the pan. Set aside.

3. Blend together the whole eggs, egg yolks, cheese, and pepper in a medium bowl with a whisk or fork until well combined.

4. Drain the bucatini in a colander. Shake well to remove any water clinging to the pasta. Pour the drained pasta into the pan with the guanciale.

5. Add the egg mixture and stir the bucatini together with the egg mixture and the bacon. The heat from the pasta should be enough to cook the eggs, but if necessary, you can cook the sauce very gently over low heat. Stop as soon as the sauce clings well; if you cook it any longer, the eggs will scramble.

Recipe note *Make sure you taste your pecorino before you start making this dish, as different pecorinos vary in their saltiness and you may need to adjust the seasoning of the dish accordingly. Choose the best-quality cheese you can find, as it is crucial to the success of this dish.*

Strozzapreti con brodetto di pesce

Strozzapreti with fish stew

SERVES 4 TO 6

Fish stew

3 tbsp extra-virgin olive oil

1 garlic clove, smashed

1 medium sweet white onion, chopped

½ cup dry white wine

One 6-oz can tomato paste

1 qt water

Kosher salt and freshly ground black pepper, as needed

1 bay leaf

1 dried red chile (peperoncini) (optional)

1½ lb mixed seafood, such as squid, rockfish, red mullet, langoustine or prawns, cleaned or filleted, as needed

2 tbsp red wine vinegar

2 tbsp chopped flat-leaf parsley

1½ lb dried strozzapreti

4 tbsp extra-virgin olive oil

1 garlic clove, smashed

1 dried red chile, cracked

2 tbsp chopped flat-leaf parsley

1. Heat the 3 tablespoons of the oil in a Dutch oven or casserole over medium heat. Add 1 of the smashed garlic cloves and stir until the garlic begins to color, about 1 minute. Add the onion and cook, stirring frequently, until a rich golden brown, 10 to 12 minutes. Add the wine and simmer until it has cooked almost completely away, about 3 minutes. Add the tomato paste and cook, stirring frequently, until there is a rich, sweet aroma, 1 to 2 minutes. Add the water, salt and pepper as needed, bay leaf, and the whole dried chile, if using, and bring to a simmer. Simmer over low heat until the sauce has a rich flavor and is thickened, about 45 minutes. Remove and discard the bay leaf.

2. Cut the seafood into bite-size pieces, if needed. Transfer to a bowl, season with salt and pepper, and add the vinegar. Toss to coat the seafood evenly with the seasonings. Add the seafood to the stew, cover the pan, and simmer over low heat until the seafood is just cooked through, about 5 minutes. Remove the pan from the heat and gently fold in 2 tablespoons of the parsley (try to avoid breaking the seafood apart).

3. Bring a large pot of salted water to a boil over high heat. Add the strozzapreti and stir to submerge and separate the pieces. Cook, uncovered, until the pasta is just al dente, 10 to 12 minutes (check the cooking time for your pasta).

4. While the strozzapreti is cooking, heat the 4 tablespoons of the oil in a large sauté pan over medium heat. Add the remaining clove of garlic and the cracked dried chile and cook, stirring frequently, until the garlic begins to color and is aromatic, about 1 minute.

5. Drain the strozzapreti in a colander. Shake well to remove any water clinging to the pasta. Pour the drained pasta into the pan with the garlic-chile oil, add the 2 tablespoons parsley, and toss to coat the pasta evenly with the oil.

6. Transfer the strozzapreti to a warmed serving bowl or pasta plates and top with the fish stew. Serve at once.

Rigatoni con ragù di salsiccia e panna

Rigatoni with sausage and a touch of cream

SERVES 4 TO 6

Kosher salt, as needed

1 lb dried rigatoni

2 oz (¼ cup) extra-virgin olive oil or unsalted butter

½ large yellow onion, diced

1 lb plain pork sausage, casings removed and crumbled

Red pepper flakes, as needed

1 cup heavy cream

⅓ cup chopped flat-leaf parsley

½ cup grated Parmigiano-Reggiano, plus more as needed for serving

Freshly ground black pepper, as needed

1. Bring a large pot of salted water to a boil over high heat. Add the riga-toni and stir to submerge and separate the pieces. Cook, uncovered, until the pasta is almost tender (al dente), 6 to 8 minutes (check the cooking time for your pasta and cook for 1 or 2 minutes less than the recommended time). Reserve a few ladlefuls of the pasta cooking water for finishing the sauce (you will need about ½ cup.)

2. While the pasta is cooking, heat the oil or butter in a large sauté pan over medium heat. Add the onion and cook, stirring frequently, until it is a light golden color, about 1 minute. Add the sausage and a pinch of the red pepper flakes and cook, stirring as needed to break up the sau-sage, until it is cooked through and lightly browned, 4 to 5 minutes. Add the cream and simmer until the sauce is flavorful and lightly thickened, about 3 minutes. Keep the sauce warm.

3. Drain the rigatoni in a colander, shaking well to remove the excess water. Add the drained pasta to the pan with the sausage and cream sauce and toss the rigatoni and sauce together over low heat until evenly blended, about 2 minutes. If the pasta appears dry or oily, add a bit of the pasta cooking water until it looks creamy and moist.

4. Add the parsley, cheese, and black pepper and toss until combined. Serve at once in a heated serving bowl or plates. Pass additional cheese on the side.

Recipe notes *Make sure you buy a good-quality sausage.*

You can also add up to ½ cup of tomato sauce to the sausage sauce to give it a pink color.

Peas work nicely in this dish as well. Add peas while simmering the sausage with the cream, but avoid overcooking them.

Fettuccine al vino rosso con selvaggina

Red wine fettuccine with wild game

SERVES 6 TO 8

Braised game ragù

2 oz lard

2 tbsp extra-virgin olive oil

1 lb boneless game meat (wild boar, venison, or hare), cut into 2-inch cubes

Kosher salt and freshly ground black pepper, as needed

2 tbsp flour

1 large onion, diced

1 leek, white portion only, thinly sliced

1 oz dried porcini mushrooms, rehydrated in warm water and drained

3 bay leaves

1 thyme sprig

1 cup dry red wine

1 cup canned whole tomatoes, crushed through a food mill or sieve

3 cups Meat Broth (page 251) or water, plus as needed

Kosher salt, as needed

1¼ lb Red Wine Fettuccine (page 238)

½ cup chopped flat-leaf parsley

1. Heat the minced lard and oil in a 4-quart pot over medium heat until the fat melts. Season the cubed game meat with salt and pepper, and dust them lightly with the flour, and add them to the hot oil in a single layer. (Work in batches, if necessary, to avoid overcrowding the pan.) Cook, turning as necessary, until brown on all sides, about 10 minutes total cooking time. Transfer the meat to a plate and reserve.

2. Add the onion and leek to the pot and stir to coat them with the fat. Sauté, stirring often, until the onions are slightly tender and just starting to brown, about 10 minutes. Return the meat (and any juices in the plate) to the pot, add the porcini, bay leaves, thyme, and wine. Simmer until the wine is nearly reduced, about 30 minutes. Add the tomatoes and broth and bring to a simmer. Cover the pot and simmer over low heat until the game is very tender and starting to fall apart, 45 minutes more. Stir the ragù as it cooks to keep it evenly moistened. If the liquid cooks away while preparing the game, add a bit of broth or water.

3. Using a slotted spoon, lift the meat out of the ragù and transfer to a plate. Remove and discard the bay leaves and thyme sprig. Simmer the remaining sauce and adjust the consistency, either by reducing the sauce or adding a bit of water. Taste and season with salt and pepper, if necessary.

4. Break the game into shreds with your fingers or using 2 forks and return it to the sauce. (If making the sauce in advance, cool the sauce and store it in the refrigerator for up to 3 days.)

5. Bring a large pot of salted water to a boil over high heat. Add the fettuccine and stir to submerge and separate the strands. Cook, uncovered, until just tender (al dente), 3 minutes.

6. Return the ragù to a simmer over low heat. Add the parsley. Keep the ragù warm while cooking the fettuccine.

7. Drain the pasta in a colander. Shake well to remove any water clinging to the pasta. Transfer the drained fettuccine to a large heated bowl, add the ragù, and serve at once.

Pappardelle al cacao con ragù di cinghiale

Cocoa pappardelle with wild boar sauce

SERVES 4 TO 6

Boar ragù

3 oz pancetta

1 garlic clove, coarsely chopped

2 small yellow onions, chopped

2 tbsp rosemary

5 juniper berries

¼ cup extra-virgin olive oil

2 lb coarsely ground boar meat

2 tbsp tomato paste

1 cup dry red wine

1 bay leaf

Kosher salt and freshly ground
black pepper, as needed

Meat Broth (page 251) or water,
as needed

1¼ lb Cocoa Pappardelle
(page 240)

Grated Pecorino Toscano,
as needed for serving

1. Combine the pancetta, garlic, onion, rosemary, and juniper berries in the bowl of a food processor. Process to a coarse paste.

2. Heat the oil in a 4-quart Dutch oven over medium heat. Add the pancetta mixture and stir to coat with the fat. Sauté, stirring often, until just starting to brown, about 10 minutes.

3. Add the boar and cook, stirring to break up the meat and allow it color evenly, about 8 minutes. Add the tomato paste, the wine, and the bay leaf. Stir well to combine. Season with a pinch of salt and pepper. Cover the pot and simmer the sauce over very low heat until it is thick and flavorful, about 4 hours. Stir the sauce occasionally as it simmers; if it is becoming too dry, add some broth or water.

4. Bring a large pot of salted water to a boil over high heat. Add the pappardelle and stir to submerge and separate the noodles. Cook, uncovered, until just tender (al dente), 4 to 5 minutes.

5. Drain the pasta in a colander. Shake well to remove any water clinging to the pasta. Transfer the drained pappardelle to a large heated bowl, add the boar ragù, and toss together until the pasta is evenly coated.

6. Serve the pappardelle at once and pass the cheese on the side.

Pizzoccheri alla valtellinese

Buckwheat pasta with bitto, potato, and cabbage

SERVES 4 TO 6

Kosher salt, as needed

1½ cups small-dice potato

2 cups coarsely chopped savoy cabbage

1¼ lb Pizzoccheri (page 239)

1 cup grated Bitto or Fontina

¾ cup grated Parmigiano-Reggiano

4 oz (½ cup) unsalted butter

2 garlic cloves

6 sage leaves

1. Preheat the oven to 350°F.

2. Bring a large pot of salted water to a boil over high heat. Add the potatoes and cabbage and cook until they are nearly tender, about 5 minutes. Add the pasta and stir to submerge and separate the noodles. Continue to cook until the pasta and vegetables are fully cooked, about 5 minutes more.

3. Drain the pasta and vegetables in a colander. Shake well to remove any water clinging to the pasta. Layer about one-third of the pasta and vegetables in a casserole or baking dish, and top with one-third of the Bitto and one-third of the Parmigiano-Reggiano. Continue to make two more layers with remaining pasta and vegetables and cheese, ending with the Parmigiano-Reggiano.

4. Heat the butter with the garlic and sage in a small sauté pan over medium heat until the butter has a nutty aroma and a light brown color. Remove and discard the garlic and pour the melted butter and sage leaves over the casserole. Bake until the cheese is melted, 4 to 5 minutes. Serve at once directly from the casserole.

Fazzoletti con fagioli e frutti di mare

Handkerchief pasta with beans and seafood

SERVES 6

Seafood sauce with beans and tomatoes

¼ cup extra-virgin olive oil

½ cup minced shallot

3 garlic cloves, thinly sliced

1 jalapeño, minced or red pepper flakes, as needed

6 oz sea scallops, muscle tabs removed

6 large shrimp, peeled and deveined

1 lb mussels, scrubbed and debearded

1 lb littleneck clams, scrubbed

9 oz monkfish fillet, cleaned and cut into strips

¼ cup freshly torn basil

½ cup coarsely chopped flat-leaf parsley

¾ cup dry white wine

1 cup cooked white beans in their cooking water (see page 254)

1 cup halved or quartered ripe cherry tomatoes

Kosher salt and freshly ground black pepper, as needed

1¼ lb Fazzoletti (page 237)

1. Heat 2 tablespoons of the oil in a large sauté pan over medium-high heat. Add the shallot and cook, stirring frequently, until tender and translucent without any browning, 2 to 3 minutes. Add the garlic and jalapeño or red pepper flakes and cook, stirring constantly, until the garlic is aromatic and translucent, about 1 minute.

2. Add the scallops, shrimp, mussels, clams, fish, half of the basil, and half of the parsley. Toss to coat evenly with the oil, and then add the wine. When the wine comes to a simmer, add the beans and the tomatoes. Cover the pan and cook until the clams and mussels are completely opened and all the seafood is cooked through, about 8 minutes. Discard any clams and mussels that do not open.

3. Transfer the seafood to a heated serving bowl with a slotted spoon. Add the remaining herbs to the pan juices and season with salt, black pepper, or red pepper flakes, as needed. If necessary, reduce the sauce slightly over medium heat.

4. Bring a large pot of salted water to a boil over high heat. Add the pasta and stir to submerge and separate the pieces. Cook, uncovered, until the pasta is just tender (al dente), 2 to 3 minutes.

5. Drain the pasta in a colander. Shake well to remove any water clinging to the pasta. Pour the drained pasta into the serving bowl with the seafood. Add the pan juices from the seafood and mix together until the pasta is evenly coated. Drizzle with the remaining oil and serve at once.

Maccheroni con carbonara e carciofi fritti

Homemade macaroni with egg, guanciale, and fried artichokes

SERVES 6

Fried artichokes

3 large globe artichokes, cleaned, trimmed, and choke removed

Juice of 1 lemon

Olive oil for deep-frying

Kosher salt and freshly ground black pepper, as needed

Onion purée

3 tbsp extra-virgin olive oil

2 medium sweet white onions, thinly sliced

1 garlic clove, smashed

¼ cup dry white wine

Meat Broth (page 251) or water, as needed

8 oz guanciale, cut into large squares

1¼ lb Maccheroni alla Chitarra (page 240) or 1 lb dried maccheroni alla chitarra

2 oz (¼ cup) unsalted butter

2 tbsp extra-virgin olive oil

3 tbsp grated Parmigiano-Reggiano, plus more as needed for serving

3 tbsp grated Pecorino Romano, plus more as needed for serving

6 egg yolks

1. Cut the artichokes in half lengthwise if not done already and slice thinly. Place the sliced artichokes in a bowl, add the lemon juice, and toss to coat evenly.

2. Add about 3 inches of olive oil to a deep pot and heat to 325°F over medium heat. Add the sliced artichokes (work in batches so you don't overcrowd the pan) and deep-fry until crispy, about 3 minutes. Drain the artichokes on paper towels and season with salt. Set aside.

3. Heat the 3 tablespoons of the extra-virgin olive oil in a 4-quart Dutch over medium heat. Add the onions and garlic and stir to coat with the oil. Sauté, stirring often, until the onions are slightly tender and just starting to brown, about 10 minutes.

4. Add the wine and stir well to deglaze the pan. Purée the onion mixture in a food processor, adding a bit of water or broth to make a smooth sauce. Season with a pinch of salt and pepper, if needed. Keep warm.

5. Heat a medium sauté pan over low heat. Add the guanciale and cook slowly, turning as necessary to cook evenly, until crispy, about 5 minutes. Blot on paper towels and set aside.

6. Bring a large pot of salted water to a boil over high heat. Add the maccheroni and stir to submerge and separate the strands. Cook, uncovered, until just tender (al dente), about 4 minutes for fresh maccheroni or 8 to 10 minutes for dried (check the cooking time for your pasta).

7. Drain the pasta in a colander. Shake well to remove any water clinging to the pasta. Pour the drained pasta into a large serving bowl. Add the butter, the 2 tablespoons extra-virgin olive oil, the Parmigiano-Reggiano, and Pecorino Romano and toss to coat evenly.

8. To serve the pasta, spread some of the onion purée on individual plates, top with a nest of maccheroni, and place an egg yolk on the top in the center of the pasta. Garnish with the crispy guanciale and fried artichokes across the pasta. Sprinkle with additional cheese, if desired.

Ravioli di fagioli, maggiorana e sugo di cozze

Bean ravioli with marjoram and mussels

SERVES 6 TO 8

Bean ravioli

1 lb dried cranberry beans

3 sage leaves

2 garlic cloves

Kosher salt, as needed

2 tbsp chopped marjoram leaves

2 tbsp grated Pecorino Romano

Freshly ground black pepper, as needed

1 lb Pasta Sheets (page 235)

Egg wash: 1 large egg blended with 1 tbsp water

Flour, as needed

Mussels with marjoram

2 tbsp extra-virgin olive oil

1 garlic clove, peeled and left whole

½ lb mussels, scrubbed and debearded

2 tbsp chopped marjoram

¼ cup white wine

½ cup water

4 oz (½ cup) unsalted butter

4 ripe plum tomatoes, peeled, seeded, and cut into medium dice (see page 248)

2 tbsp chopped marjoram

Recipe note *If you prefer to cook the beans in advance, store them in the refrigerator, covered with some of their cooking liquid. You may use some of this liquid to adjust the consistency of the bean purée.*

1. Soak the beans in water overnight. Drain the beans; place them in a large pot and add enough cold water to cover by at least 2 inches. Add the sage and the 2 whole garlic cloves. Bring to a simmer over low heat. Continue to simmer until the beans are very tender, about 1½ hours. Season the beans with salt and remove from the cooking liquid; reserve the beans and the cooking liquid separately.

2. Process the beans to a fine purée in a food processor; add a little of the cooking liquid, if necessary, but do not let the purée become too liquid. Or push the bean purée through a fine wire-mesh sieve for a very smooth texture, if desired.

3. Transfer the bean purée to a bowl and stir in the 2 tablespoons of marjoram and the cheese. Season with salt and pepper as needed. Set aside.

4. Lay one pasta sheet flat on a lightly floured work surface. Using a pastry brush, lightly coat the dough with some of the egg wash. Spoon the bean filling in 2-teaspoon mounds onto the dough. There should be about ½ inch between the mounds so that you can cut individual ravioli. Top with a second pasta sheet. Press the pasta sheets together to seal the edges well around the filling. Using a pastry cutter or a knife, cut individual ravioli. As you cut out the ravioli, place them on lightly floured baking sheet.

5. Heat the oil in a Dutch oven or casserole over medium heat. Add the garlic and cook, stirring frequently, until it starts to get a little color, about 1 minute. Add the mussels, the 2 tablespoons chopped marjoram, wine, and ½ cup of water. Cover with a lid and let the mussels cook until they are completely open and transfer them to a bowl. Discard any unopened mussels.

6. When they are cool enough to handle remove the mussels from the shells and place them in a second bowl. Strain the cooking liquid from the pot as well as any juices that collected in the bowl and add it to the mussels.

7. Bring a large pot of salted water to a boil. Add the ravioli and stir to submerge and separate them. Cook, uncovered, until the pasta is just tender (al dente), 5 to 6 minutes.

8. Using a slotted spoon or spider, transfer the cooked ravioli and the mussels to a large sauté pan. Add the butter and shake the pan to swirl the butter into the cooking liquid; it should thicken and coat the ravioli. Add the mussels, tomatoes, and the 2 tablespoons chopped marjoram. Season with salt and pepper, as needed. Serve at once.

Ravioli con ricotta e uvetta al profumo di limone

Ravioli with cheese, raisins, and lemon zest

SERVES 6

Cheese filling

3 oz raisins (about ½ cup)

¼ cup dry Marsala or water

6 oz sheep or cow's milk ricotta
(about ¾ cup)

6 oz Taleggio, cut into small cubes

4 oz Gorgonzola, crumbled

⅔ cup grated Parmigiano-Reggiano

Zest of ½ lemon, finely grated

½ cup plain dry bread crumbs,
or as needed

Kosher salt and freshly ground
black pepper, as needed

1 lb Pasta Sheets (page 235)

Egg wash: 1 large egg blended
with 1 tbsp water

6 oz (¾ cup) unsalted butter

Flour, as needed

Zest of ½ lemon, cut into long
strips

Grated Parmigiano-Reggiano,
as needed for serving

1. Combine the raisins with the Marsala or water and let soak until soft, about 30 minutes. Drain and set aside, reserving a few tablespoons of the soaked raisins to garnish the finished ravioli.

2. Stir together the ricotta, Taleggio, and Gorgonzola, mixing well with a wooden spoon until very smooth with no lumps. Stir in the ⅔ cup Parmigiano-Reggiano cheese and the grated lemon zest. Add just enough of the bread crumbs to help the filling hold together. Season with salt and pepper and let the mixture firm in the refrigerator for at least 1 hour before filling the ravioli.

3. Lay one of the pasta sheets flat on a lightly floured work surface. Using a pastry brush, lightly wet one side of the dough with some of the egg wash. Spoon the filling in 2-teaspoon mounds onto half of the wet side of the dough. There should be about ½ inch between the mounds so that you can cut individual ravioli. Fold the sheet in half lengthwise to cover the filling. Press the pasta sheet together to seal the edges around the filling. Using a pastry cutter or a knife, cut out individual ravioli. As you cut out the ravioli, place them on a plate or baking sheet sprinkled with a little flour to keep them from sticking.

4. Bring a large pot of salted water to a boil over high heat. Add the ravioli and stir to submerge and separate them. Cook, uncovered, until the pasta is just tender (al dente), 8 to 10 minutes.

5. Using a slotted spoon or a spider, transfer the ravioli to a colander and let drain. Transfer to a large heated serving bowl, add the butter, and turn the ravioli in the butter until evenly coated.

6. Serve at once, garnished with the reserved raisins and strips of lemon zest, and pass additional Parmigiano-Reggiano on the side.

Casoncelli bergamaschi

Sausage-filled ravioli with brown butter and pancetta

SERVES 10 TO 12

Sausage stuffing

2 oz white bread, crust removed and thinly sliced (about 2 slices)

¼ cup whole milk, warm

2 oz mortadella

½ lb plain pork sausage

4 oz ground beef

⅔ cup grated Grana Padano

1 large egg

¼ cup chopped flat-leaf parsley

Kosher salt and freshly ground black pepper, as needed

Freshly grated nutmeg, as needed

1 lb Pasta Sheets (page 235)

Flour, as needed

4 oz (½ cup) unsalted butter

6 oz pancetta slices (about 6)

6 to 8 sage leaves

⅔ cup grated Grana Padano

1. Combine the bread with the milk and let soak just long enough to soften.

2. Finely chop the mortadella in a food processor, then add the soaked bread and process for 20 seconds more. Transfer to a mixing bowl and add the sausage, beef, the ⅔ cup of cheese, egg, parsley, salt, pepper, and nutmeg, as needed. Stir together with a wooden spoon, working the mixture well to thoroughly combine.

3. Lay one of the pasta sheets flat on a lightly floured work surface. Using a pastry brush, lightly wet one side of the dough with water. Spoon the filling in 2-teaspoon mounds onto half of the wet side of the dough. There should be about ½ inch between the mounds so that you can cut individual ravioli. Fold the sheet in half lengthwise to cover the filling. Press the pasta sheet together to seal the edges well around the filling. Using a pastry cutter or a knife, cut individual ravioli. As you cut out the ravioli, place them on a lightly floured baking sheet until you are ready to cook them.

4. Bring a large pot of salted water to a boil over high heat. Add the ravioli and stir to submerge and separate the ravioli. Cook, uncovered, until just tender (al dente), about 5 minutes.

5. While the ravioli are cooking, melt the butter in a sauté pan over medium high heat. When the foaming subsides, add the pancetta and the sage and cook until the leaves and pancetta are crisp.

6. Drain the ravioli in a colander, shaking gently to remove excess water. Transfer the drained ravioli to a large heated bowl, sprinkle with the ⅔ cup cheese, then add the browned butter with the sage leaves and pancetta. Gently toss together until the ravioli are evenly coated. Serve at once.

Tortelli all'uovo con tartufo bianco

Egg-filled tortelli with white truffle

SERVES 6

Ricotta-spinach filling

½ cup blanched chopped spinach

1 cup fresh ricotta (sheep's ricotta, if available)

½ cup grated Parmigiano-Reggiano

Kosher salt, as needed

Pinch of ground white pepper

Small pinch of freshly grated nutmeg

1 lb Pasta Sheets (page 235)

6 egg yolks

Egg wash: 1 large egg blended with 1 tbsp water

4 to 6 oz (½ to ¾ cup) unsalted butter

Grated Parmigiano-Reggiano, as needed for serving

2 oz white truffle, shaved (optional)

1. Stir together the spinach, ricotta, Parmigiano-Reggiano, salt, pepper, and nutmeg in a medium bowl. After the filling is well combined, transfer to a pastry bag fitted with a ½-inch round plain tip; set aside.

2. Using a 2-inch round cutter, gently press marks for the tortelli, spacing them 5 inches apart. Pipe the ricotta-spinach filling to cover the marked circle, then pipe a border making a 1-inch-high edge, leaving space in the center of each "little tower."

3. Place 1 egg yolk with a tiny bit of white in the center of each circle, making sure the yolk remains unbroken. Season each yolk with a pinch of salt and white pepper.

4. Brush a little egg wash on the border of the pasta where the filling is and gently place a second sheet of pasta over the filling, pressing the edges together to seal them and eliminate any air between the two layers.

5. Using a 4-inch wide cutter (fluted, if available), cut out each tortello. At this point you may store them in refrigerator for up to 1 hour (see Recipe notes).

6. Bring a large pot of salted water to a simmer over medium-high heat. Using a slotted spoon or a spider, lower the tortelli all at once to the boiling water and cook, uncovered, at a boil until just tender to the bite, 2 to 3 minutes.

7. Lift the tortelli from the water with a slotted spoon or spider. Divide among 6 warmed plates.

8. Heat the butter in a small pan over medium-high heat until browned and nutty, about 2 minutes. Sprinkle some of the Parmigiano-Reggiano over each tortello, pour over the brown butter, and garnish with the shaved truffle, if desired. Top the tortelli with a few leaves of sage fried in butter.

Recipe notes *These tortelli are quite fragile, and should be cooked as soon as they are assembled, although you can hold the filled tortelli for up to 1 hour in the refrigerator, if necessary.*

If white truffles are not available or too expensive for your budget, you can use a little bit of truffle oil in the filling and then add a bit more to the butter when you melt it to dress the tortelli in step 8.

Casoncelli all'ampezzana

Ravioli filled with beets, butter, and poppy seeds

SERVES 6

You can add bacon or prosciutto to the stuffing for a more complex flavor.

Beet filling

2 oz (¼ cup) unsalted butter

1 medium yellow onion, diced

4 sage leaves, finely chopped

1½ lb beets, peeled and diced

½ cup water

¾ cup grated Parmigiano-Reggiano

½ cup fresh ricotta

2 egg yolks

½ tsp finely grated orange zest

Kosher salt and freshly ground black pepper, as needed

Plain dry bread crumbs, as needed

1 lb Pasta Sheets (page 235)

Flour, as needed

4 oz (½ cup) unsalted butter

12 sage leaves

¾ cup grated Parmigiano-Reggiano

Poppy seeds, as needed

1. Heat a large sauté pan over medium heat. Add the ¼ cup of butter and let melt (it should foam but not darken in color). Add the onion and chopped sage and cook, stirring frequently, until the onion is tender, about 4 minutes. Add the beets and water. Cover, bring the liquid to a simmer, and cook, adjusting the heat as necessary, until the beets are tender enough to mash easily with a fork, about 25 minutes.

2. Remove from the heat and let the beets cool before chopping them finely with a knife or in a food processor. They should be fairly smooth. (If they are too wet, drain them in a colander or a sieve lined with a clean cloth.) Transfer to a large bowl.

3. Add the ¾ cup of the Parmigiano-Reggiano, the ricotta, egg yolks, orange zest, salt, and pepper, as needed, and stir with a wooden spoon until blended. The filling should be firm enough to mound when dropped from a spoon. If it is soft enough to run off the spoon, add some bread crumbs to help it hold together. Reserve in the refrigerator while you prepare the pasta dough.

4. Lay 1 of the pasta sheets flat on a lightly floured work surface. Using a pastry brush, lightly wet one side of the dough with water. Spoon the filling onto the wet side of the dough, mounding about 2 tablespoons of the filling for each raviolo. There should be about 2 inches between the mounds so that you can cut individual ravioli. Place a second pasta sheet on top of the first one. Press the dough together to seal the sheets together along the edges and around the filling, creating little pockets of filling. Using a fluted or plain biscuit cutter, cut out round ravioli. As you cut out the ravioli, place them on a plate or baking sheet sprinkled with flour to keep them from sticking.

5. Bring a large pot of salted water to a boil over high heat. Add the ravioli and stir to submerge and separate them. Cook, uncovered, until the pasta is just tender to the bite, 5 to 6 minutes. While the pasta is cooking, melt the ½ cup butter with the whole sage leaves in a small sauté pan over medium heat until the butter begins to brown.

6. Drain the ravioli in a colander. Shake gently to remove excess water. Transfer the drained pasta to a large heated serving bowl and top with the butter-sage sauce. Serve at once, sprinkled with the ¾ cup Parmigiano-Reggiano and the poppy seeds.

Agnolotti ripieni di brasato e spinaci al burro nocciola

Agnolotti filled with braised meat, spinach, and brown butter

SERVES 6

Braised meat and spinach filling

4 oz (½ cup) unsalted butter

2 tbsp extra-virgin olive oil

1 lb boneless beef (top blade, shank, or chuck), trimmed

Kosher salt and freshly ground black pepper, as needed

1 medium yellow onion, diced

1 celery stalk, diced

1 garlic clove, smashed

1 oz dried porcini, rehydrated in warm water and drained

3 tbsp tomato paste

1 tbsp rosemary

4 large sage leaves

½ cup roughly chopped flat-leaf parsley

2 tbsp all-purpose flour

2 cups Meat Broth (page 251) or water, plus more as needed

6 oz spinach, blanched and squeezed dry

2 egg yolks

1 cup grated Parmigiano-Reggiano

Zest of ½ lemon

Pinch of freshly grated nutmeg

1¼ lb Pasta Sheets (page 235)

Flour, as needed

3 oz (6 tbsp) unsalted butter

Grated Parmigiano-Reggiano, as needed for serving

1. Preheat the oven to 300°F.

2. Heat the ½ cup of butter and the oil in a 4-quart Dutch oven over medium heat. Season the beef with salt and pepper and add to the hot fat. Cook, turning as necessary, until brown on all sides, about 10 minutes total cooking time. Transfer to a plate and set aside.

3. Add the onion, celery, and garlic to the pot and stir to coat with the fat. Sauté, stirring often, until the onions are slightly tender and just starting to brown, about 10 minutes. Add the porcini, tomato paste, rosemary, sage, and parsley. Scatter the flour over the vegetables and stir to incorporate. Place the beef on top of the vegetables and add enough of the broth or water to cover the meat by about one-third. Cover and cook in the oven until the beef is very tender, 1½ to 2 hours, adding a bit more broth or water if necessary to keep the dish moist.

4. Remove the beef from the pot and transfer to a platter to cool. Using a slotted spoon, lift the vegetables out of the cooking liquid and transfer them to the platter as well. Reserve the pan juices.

5. Chop the cooked meat, vegetables, and the spinach together by hand or in a food processor to a fine consistency. Transfer to a large bowl and add the egg yolks and the 1 cup of cheese. Add the lemon zest, and season with salt, pepper, and the nutmeg and mix thoroughly; if the filling mixture is too dry, add a bit of the reserved pan juices.

6. Lay one of the pasta sheets flat on a lightly floured work surface. Using a pastry brush, lightly wet one side of the dough. Spoon the filling in 2-teaspoon mounds about ½ inch apart onto half of the wet side of the dough. Fold the sheet in half lengthwise to cover the filling. Press the pasta sheet together to seal the edges well around the filling. Using a pastry cutter or a knife, cut individual agnolotti. As you cut out the agnolotti, place them on a lightly floured baking sheet until ready to cook them.

7. Bring a large pot of salted water to a boil over high heat. Add the agnolotti and stir to submerge and separate them. Cook, uncovered, until just tender (al dente), 5 to 6 minutes. Drain the agnolotti and transfer to a heated serving bowl. Pour some of the reserved pan juices over the agnolotti.

8. Heat the 6 tablespoons of butter in a skillet over medium-high heat until it is golden brown and has a nutty aroma. Pour the butter over the ravioli. Serve at once, and pass the cheese on the side.

Cannelloni di patate con sugo di pomodoro

Potato and pecorino cannelloni with tomato sauce

SERVES 6

Potato and pecorino filling

¼ cup extra-virgin olive oil

1 small yellow onion, cut into julienne

2 lb Yukon gold potatoes

Kosher salt, as needed

1¼ cups grated aged Pecorino Toscano

4 oz fresh sheep's milk cheese, cut into small cubes

¼ cup chopped flat-leaf parsley

Melted unsalted butter, as needed for brushing

1 lb Cannelloni Sheets (page 235), cooked and cooled

1½ cups Tomato Sauce (page 248)

1. Heat the oil in a sauté pan over medium heat. Add the onions and cook, stirring frequently, until the onions are very tender and translucent, 10 to 12 minutes. Transfer to a mixing bowl.

2. Peel and quarter the potatoes and cook them in simmering salted water until they are easily pierced with the tip of a knife. Drain the potatoes in a colander, then transfer to the mixing bowl and crush with a fork. Add the cheeses and the parsley and stir together. Set aside.

3. Preheat the oven to 350°F. Brush a baking dish or casserole with melted butter.

4. Divide the filling mixture between the sheets of cooked pasta, forming a log that runs the entire length of each sheet. Roll the pasta around the filling and then cut them into cannelloni about 4 inches long. Set them into the baking dish seam side facing down to help hold them together. Once all of the cannelloni are arranged in the baking dish, brush them lightly with butter. (You may bake the dish now, or cover the dish and keep them refrigerated for up to 2 days.)

5. Place the baking dish in the oven and bake until the cannelloni are very hot, 15 to 20 minutes (or longer if they were held in the refrigerator). Heat the tomato sauce over low heat or in the microwave while the cannelloni are baking. To serve, spoon the tomato sauce in the center of each warmed plate and top with the cannelloni.

Crespelle di ceci con bruscandoli

Chickpea crespelle with bitter greens

SERVES 4 TO 6

Melted unsalted butter or olive oil, as needed for the baking dish

Bitter greens filling

2 tbsp extra-virgin olive oil

½ medium yellow onion, minced

1 lb dandelion greens, trimmed and coarsely chopped

½ lb fresh sheep's or cow's milk ricotta

½ cup grated Parmigiano-Reggiano

Kosher salt and freshly ground black pepper, as needed

8 Chickpea Crespelle (page 242)

1 cup heavy cream

½ cup grated Parmigiano-Reggiano

If you are making the crespelle ahead of time, or if you make more crespelle than you need for this recipe, they can be wrapped and kept in the refrigerator for up to 2 days.

1. Preheat the oven to 350°F. Brush a baking dish or casserole with melted butter or oil.

2. Heat the 2 tablespoons oil in a medium sauté pan over medium heat. Add the onion and cook over low heat, stirring frequently, until very translucent, about 3 minutes. Add the dandelion greens, stir, and cook, covered, over low heat, stirring occasionally, until the greens are very tender, about 12 minutes. Transfer the greens to a bowl and let them cool.

3. Squeeze any excess moisture from the greens mixture and combine them with the ricotta and the ½ cup of the cheese. Season with salt and pepper. Set aside.

4. To fill the crespelle, cut each one in half and spoon or pipe about ¼ cup of the filling mixture into the center of each piece. Fold the crespelle in thirds around the filling and set them in the prepared baking dish.

5. Once all the crespelle are arranged in the baking dish, pour the cream over the tops of the crespelle and sprinkle with the ½ cup cheese. (You may bake the dish now, or cover the pan and keep them refrigerated for up to 2 days.)

6. Bake until the crespelle are very hot and the cheese has formed a golden crust, about 20 minutes. Serve at once.

Malloreddus con ragù di salsiccia e finocchietto

Semolina gnocchi with sausage and wild fennel ragù

SERVES 6

Sausage and wild fennel ragù

½ small yellow onion, minced

3 oz extra-virgin olive oil

¼ cup wild fennel fronds

Kosher salt, as needed

1 lb plain pork sausage

¼ cup white wine

2 cups crushed canned San Marzano tomatoes

1 tsp saffron threads

1 tsp fennel seed

Freshly ground black pepper, as needed

Beef or chicken broth, as needed

1 lb Semolina Gnocchi (page 153)

⅔ cup grated Pecorino Romano

1. Heat the oil in a skillet over medium heat. Sweat the onions in the oil until they are translucent and soft, about 5 minutes. Meanwhile, in a separate pot, blanch the fennel fronds in salted water for 7 to 8 minutes. Strain the leaves, squeeze dry, coarsely chop, and set aside.

2. Add the sausage to the onions, stirring well to break it up into small pieces. Add the chopped fennel fronds and the wine.

3. Let the wine evaporate, about 2 minutes, and then add the tomatoes, stir, and season the sauce with the saffron, fennel seed, and salt and pepper. Bring the sauce to a boil, and then the simmer for 45 minutes. Add broth if the sauce starts to dry out. The sauce can be prepared in advance, and cooled and stored in a covered container in the refrigerator for up to 3 days.

4. Bring a large pot of salted water to a boil over high heat. Add the gnocchi and stir to submerge and separate them. Cook uncovered at a gentle boil until the gnocchi rise to the surface and are cooked through, 2 to 4 minutes depending on their size. (To be certain, taste one of the gnocchi.)

5. Use a slotted spoon to lift the cooked gnocchi out of the water and transfer them to a large serving bowl. Add some of the sauce and some of the pecorino. Serve the gnocchi with additional sauce on top and pass additional pecorino on the side.

Gnocchi di susine al profumo di cannella e speck

Potato and prune gnocchi with cinnamon and smoked prosciutto

SERVES 6 TO 8

Potato and prune gnocchi

½ cup finely chopped prunes

2 lb russet potatoes (about 3 or 4 medium potatoes)

Kosher salt, as needed

10 oz (2¼ cups) all-purpose or tipo 00 flour

Pinch of freshly grated nutmeg

1 large egg

1 tbsp ground cinnamon

1 tbsp sugar

4 oz (½ cup) unsalted butter

6 to 8 sage leaves

4 oz smoked prosciutto (speck), cut into thin strips

⅔ cup grated Grana Padano

1. Soak the prunes in a bowl of warm water to soften, about 30 minutes. Drain and set aside.

2. Peel and quarter the potatoes. Put them in a pot and add enough cold water to cover them by about 2 inches. Salt the water and bring it to a boil over medium-high heat. Cook until the potatoes are easily pierced with the tip of a knife, about 15 minutes. Drain the potatoes and dry them in the pot over low heat, about 3 minutes. Purée through a food mill or potato ricer onto a lightly floured work surface. Let the potatoes cool to room temperature.

3. Gather the potatoes into a mound and make a well in the center. Surround the well with half of the flour, and sprinkle with the nutmeg. Add the egg to the well.

4. Mix the ingredients by hand to form a soft dough. If necessary, add more of the flour, a little at a time, until the dough has the correct consistency.

5. Roll the dough to a thickness of ¼ inch and, using a 3-inch round cookie cutter, cut out gnocchi. Place a prune half in the center of each circle and wrap the dough around it to form a ball. Continue in the same way with the rest of the dough.

6. Mix the cinnamon with the sugar and set aside.

7. Bring a large pot of salted water to a boil. Add the gnocchi and stir to submerge and separate the gnocchi. Cook, uncovered, at a gentle boil until the gnocchi rise to the surface and are cooked through, 2 to 4 minutes depending upon their size. (To be certain, taste one of the gnocchi.) Using a slotted spoon, lift the cooked gnocchi out of the water and immediately transfer to a heated serving bowl or plates.

8. While the gnocchi are cooking, heat the butter with the sage and speck in a sauté pan. Cook until the sage leaves and speck are crisp and the butter is brown with a rich, nutty aroma, about 2 minutes.

9. Sprinkle the gnocchi with a generous amount of Grana Padano and pour the butter mixture over the gnocchi. Finish with a pinch of the cinnamon-sugar mixture on top and serve at once.

Gnocchi alla romana

Roman-style semolina gnocchi

SERVES 6 TO 8

1 qt whole milk

4 oz (½ cup) unsalted butter, plus more as needed for baking dish

1 tsp kosher salt

Pinch of freshly grated nutmeg

9 oz (1½ cups) semolina flour

2 egg yolks

⅔ cup grated Parmigiano-Reggiano, plus more as needed for topping the gnocchi

1. Heat the milk, half the butter, the salt, and a pinch of nutmeg in a heavy saucepot over medium heat. Slowly add the semolina, whisking continuously. Let simmer gently until the semolina is very thick, stirring with a wooden spoon, 3 to 5 minutes. Remove the pot from the heat and stir in the egg yolks and the ⅔ cup of cheese.

2. Pour the semolina mixture into a jelly roll pan or directly onto an oiled work surface. Using a rolling pin, press it into a layer about ½ inch thick. Let the semolina cool slightly, about 30 minutes, and then cut into circles with a 2½-inch round cookie cutter.

3. Preheat the oven to 375°F and generously butter a baking dish.

4. Arrange the semolina gnocchi in the baking dish, overlapping them slightly. Melt the remaining butter and pour over the gnocchi. Top with additional grated cheese. Bake until the gnocchi are very hot and the cheese has browned, about 15 minutes.

Gnocchi con carciofi e calamari

Potato gnocchi with artichokes and squid

SERVES 6

Artichoke and squid sauce

1 lb baby artichokes

Juice of 1 lemon

1 lb squid, cleaned

2 tbsp extra-virgin olive oil

2 garlic cloves, minced or thinly sliced

1 tsp red pepper flakes

2 tbsp chopped flat-leaf parsley

½ tsp marjoram leaves, torn in small pieces

¼ cup dry white wine

½ pt ripe cherry tomatoes, quartered

Kosher salt, as needed

1½ lb Potato Gnocchi (page 245)

1 tbsp extra-virgin olive oil

1. Clean the artichokes by removing the tougher outer leaves and cut into small wedges, about 8 pieces each. Place the wedges in a bowl, add the lemon juice, and toss to coat evenly.

2. Cut the squid into small strips or leave them whole if they are very small.

3. In a large sauté pan, heat the 2 tablespoons of oil over medium heat. Add the garlic and red pepper flakes and cook, stirring constantly, until aromatic, about 1 minute.

4. Add the parsley, marjoram, artichokes, and squid. Sauté for 1 minute over medium heat. Add the wine and let it cook away, about 2 minutes. Add the tomatoes and let cook to release their juices, 1 minute.

5. Bring a large pot of salted water to a boil over high heat. Add the gnocchi and stir to submerge and separate them. Cook, uncovered, at a gentle boil until the gnocchi rise to the surface and are cooked through, about 4 minutes, depending on their size. (To be certain, taste one of the gnocchi.) Using a slotted spoon, lift the cooked gnocchi out of the water and transfer to a heated serving bowl.

6. Toss the gnocchi with the sauce and serve them immediately, drizzled with the remaining 1 tablespoon oil.

Gnocchi di polenta con fonduta tartufata

Polenta dumplings with truffled cheese fondue

SERVES 6

Polenta gnocchi

1 qt water

4 tsp kosher salt

¼ cup extra-virgin olive oil

8 oz (1¼ cups) cornmeal

1 scant cup all-purpose flour

1 large egg

⅔ cup grated Parmigiano-Reggiano

Fonduta sauce

9 oz Fontina

10 tbsp whole milk

1 oz (2 tbsp) unsalted butter

1 tbsp all-purpose flour

3 egg yolks

2 tbsp truffle paste

Kosher salt, as needed

2 oz fresh truffle (optional)

2 tbsp thinly sliced chives (optional)

1. Cut the Fontina into thin strips, place it in a bowl and pour the milk over, and macerate the cheese in the milk in the refrigerator for 2 to 3 hours.

2. Bring the water for the polenta to a simmer in a large saucepan over medium heat. Add salt and the oil, and then slowly add the cornmeal, whisking continuously. Let simmer gently until the polenta is done, stirring frequently with a wooden spoon to make sure the polenta does not stick, 30 to 40 minutes. (The cooking time will vary depending on the coarseness of your cornmeal.) Remove the polenta from the heat, pour the polenta into a shallow dish, and let it cool. (This can be done ahead of time; the polenta can be covered and stored in the refrigerator for up to 3 days.)

3. Spread the 1 cup of flour on a flat work surface, then push the polenta through a fine sieve directly onto the flour and gather it into a mound. Make a well in the center of the sieved polenta and add the egg and Parmigiano-Reggiano to the well. Knead gently just until the dough is well combined and smooth.

4. Divide the dough into 4 pieces and roll it into small log about ¾ inch in diameter. Cut into ¾-inch-long gnocchi. (You may roll each dumpling over the back of a fork, if desired.)

5. Melt the 2 tablespoons of butter in a saucepan over low heat, add the flour, and stir to combine. Add the macerated cheese and milk and stir until the cheese melts, but do not allow the mixture to boil.

6. When the cheese is melted, add the egg yolks and truffle paste and stir to combine. At this point the fondue will look runny. Cook over very low heat, stirring constantly, until the mixture starts to thicken and has a creamy consistency. Do not allow the temperature go over 185°F or the eggs will scramble.

7. Bring a large pot of salted water to a boil over medium-high heat. Add the gnocchi in batches and cook, uncovered, at a gentle boil until the gnocchi rise to the surface and are cooked through, 2 to 4 minutes depending on their size. (They will float to the surface about 1 minute before they are fully cooked. To be certain, taste one of the gnocchi.) Using a slotted spoon, transfer them to a colander to drain.

8. When all the gnocchi are cooked, reheat them in boiling water for 30 seconds. Drain and combine them in a heated serving dish with the fonduta sauce, or put them on individual plates and pour the fonduta on top. Garnish with finely shaved truffle and chives, if desired.

Gnocchi soffiati al tartufo

Oven-puffed gnocchi with truffle

SERVES 6

1 cup whole milk

3 oz (6 tbsp) unsalted butter

1 tsp kosher salt, plus as needed

Pinch of freshly grated nutmeg

¾ cup all-purpose flour

⅔ cup grated Parmigiano-Reggiano, plus as needed

1 tbsp truffle paste

3 large eggs

½ cup heavy cream, or as needed

2 oz fresh black or white truffle (optional)

1. Heat the milk, 4 tablespoons of the butter, the salt, and a pinch of nutmeg in a heavy sauce pot over medium heat. Slowly add the flour, whisking continuously. Let simmer gently, stirring with a wooden spoon, until the mixture is very thick and pulls away from the sides of the pot, 3 to 5 minutes. Transfer to a bowl and stir in the cheese and truffle paste. Add the eggs, one at a time, stirring to incorporate each one before adding the next.

2. Bring a large pot of salted water to a boil over high heat. Fill a bowl with ice water and place it near the stove to cool the gnocchi as they finish poaching.

3. Transfer the dough into a pastry bag fitted with a ½-inch plain tip. Pipe the gnocchi directly over the pot of boiling water, cutting the dough into ¾-inch-long pieces while piping. As soon as the gnocchi rise to the top, lift them from the pot with a slotted spoon and transfer them to the bowl of ice water. Once they are thoroughly chilled, transfer them to paper towels to drain and blot dry.

4. Preheat the oven to 375°F and generously butter a baking dish with the remaining 2 tablespoons butter.

5. Add the gnocchi to the buttered baking dish in a single layer. Pour enough cream into the dish to cover the bottom of the dish and sprinkle the gnocchi with additional cheese. Bake until the gnocchi have doubled in size, the cheese is browned, and the cream has reduced into a thick sauce, about 15 minutes. Serve at once, topped with shaved fresh truffle, if desired.

Pisarei e fagioli

Bread gnocchi with beans

SERVES 4 TO 6

Tomato and pancetta sauce with borlotti beans

½ cup extra-virgin olive oil

2 oz pancetta, minced

1 rosemary sprig, chopped

4 large sage leaves, chopped

½ cup chopped flat-leaf parsley

2 garlic cloves, minced

1 bay leaf

1 medium onion, minced

1 tbsp tomato paste

3¾ cups canned whole San Marzano tomatoes, crushed through a food mill or sieve

2 cups drained cooked borlotti beans (page 254), cooking liquid reserved

Bread gnocchi

2½ cups plain dry bread crumbs, finely ground

1½ cups boiling water

18 oz (4 cups) all-purpose or tipo 00 flour

2 large eggs

Kosher salt, as needed

½ cup grated Parmigiano-Reggiano

1. Heat the oil in a Dutch oven over medium heat. Add the pancetta along with the herbs and garlic and cook, stirring frequently, until aromatic, about 2 minutes. Add the bay leaf and onion and cook until the onion is translucent and soft, about 5 minutes. Add the tomato paste and cook until the paste turns a deep red and smells very sweet and savory, about 5 minutes. Add the crushed tomatoes with their juices and cook for 10 minutes.

2. Add the beans with their liquid to the sauce. Simmer the sauce until it is slightly reduced, about 10 minutes. Keep the sauce warm or let it cool and store in a covered container in the refrigerator for up to 3 days.

3. Place the bread crumbs in a large bowl and pour the boiling water over them. Let rest for 5 minutes.

4. Mound the flour on a clean surface. Create a well in the center and place the eggs and the soaked bread crumbs in the well. Using a fork, start dragging the flour into the egg–bread crumb mixture. Once the flour is evenly moistened, knead well by hand on a floured surface until all of the ingredients are well combined and the dough seems smooth and elastic, 10 minutes. Wrap the dough in plastic wrap or place it in a covered bowl and let it rest for at least 10 minutes

5. Divide the dough in 2 or 3 pieces and roll it into small logs, about ½ inch in diameter. Cut the dough into pieces about the size of a bean. Using the tip of your thumb, press each piece of dough. Pull your thumb back and up in a quick motion, releasing the gnocchi. Once shaped, the gnocchi can be reserved on a floured baking sheet, loosely covered, in the refrigerator for up to 8 hours.

6. Bring a large pot of salted water to a boil over high heat. Add the gnocchi all at once and stir to submerge and separate them. Cook, uncovered, at a gentle boil until the gnocchi rise to the surface and are cooked through, 5 to 6 minutes depending on their size. (To be certain, taste one of the gnocchi.)

7. Using a slotted spoon, lift the cooked gnocchi out of the water and transfer them to a large heated bowl. Add some of the tomato and pancetta sauce and toss the gnocchi to coat well. Serve the gnocchi with additional sauce on top and pass the cheese on the side.

Recipe notes *If your bread crumbs are not dry enough, you can toast them in a little olive oil before incorporating into the eggs and flour in step 3.*

If the sauce is too dry, add some of the bean cooking liquid. The sauce is supposed to be quite dense.

Gnocchi di semolina e radicchio

Semolina gnocchi with radicchio

SERVES 6 TO 8

Radicchio and speck

1 tbsp unsalted butter

½ cup diced yellow onion

2 oz speck (smoked prosciutto), cut into thin strips

1 head radicchio, leaves cut into thin strips

Kosher salt, as needed

¼ cup dry red wine

2 oz (¼ cup) unsalted butter, plus as needed for the baking dish

1 qt whole milk

1 tsp Kosher salt

Pinch of freshly grated nutmeg (optional)

9 oz (1½ cups) semolina flour

2 egg yolks

⅔ cup grated Parmigiano-Reggiano, plus as needed for topping the gnocchi

¼ cup chopped flat-leaf parsley

½ cup heavy cream, or as needed

1. Heat the 1 tablespoon of butter in a sauté pan over medium heat. Add the onion and speck and cook, stirring frequently, until tender and the onions are translucent, about 3 minutes.

2. Add the radicchio, season with a pinch of salt, and cook until the radicchio is wilted, about 2 minutes. Add the wine and continue to cook, stirring, until the wine has cooked away, another 3 minutes. Set aside.

3. Preheat the oven to 375°F. Generously butter a baking dish and set aside.

4. Heat the milk, ¼ cup butter, salt, and a pinch of nutmeg, if using, in a heavy saucepot over medium heat. Slowly add the semolina, whisking continuously. Let simmer gently until semolina is very thick, stirring with a wooden spoon, 3 to 5 minutes.

5. Remove the pot from the heat and stir in the egg yolks and ⅔ cup of cheese. Add the radicchio and speck mixture and the parsley and stir to combine.

6. While the mixture is still hot, shape the semolina mixture with two spoons (or an ice cream scoop) and place the gnocchi into the prepared baking dish. Pour enough cream into the dish to cover the bottom and sprinkle the gnocchi with additional cheese. Bake until the cheese is browned and the cream has reduced into a thick sauce, about 15 minutes. Serve at once.

Polenta con sugo di stoccafisso

Polenta with salt cod

SERVES 6

Salt cod sauce

1 lb salt cod, soaked and rinsed (page 258)

1 cup extra-virgin olive oil

1 medium yellow onion, diced

3 garlic cloves, chopped

¾ cup chopped flat-leaf parsley

1½ tsp chopped oil-packed anchovies

Freshly ground black pepper, as needed

3 tbsp all-purpose flour

½ cup grated Parmigiano-Reggiano

½ cup chicken broth or water, or as needed

½ cup whole milk

1 qt water

4 tsp kosher salt

¼ cup extra-virgin olive oil

8 oz (1¼ cups) cornmeal

1. Remove the skin and any bones from the cod, and cut into 1-inch pieces.

2. Preheat the oven to 300°F.

3. Heat the 1 cup of oil in a sauté pan over medium-low heat. Add the onion and cook, stirring frequently, until translucent and very soft, about 10 minutes. Add the garlic, parsley, and anchovies and sauté until aromatic, about 2 minutes. Season with pepper, as needed.

4. Place the salt cod in a casserole dish, season with pepper and sprinkle the flour over the top. Add the onion mixture in a layer, top with the cheese, and pour the broth or water over the entire dish.

5. Cover the casserole and bake for 20 minutes. Check that the fish is not sticking to the bottom of the casserole as it bakes and, if necessary, add a bit more broth. Add the milk and continue baking until the fish is tender, 10 minutes more.

6. Bring the water for the polenta to a simmer in a large saucepan over medium heat. Add the salt and the ¼ cup of oil, and then slowly add the cornmeal, whisking continuously. Let simmer gently until the polenta is done, stirring frequently with a wooden spoon to make sure the polenta does not stick 30 to 40 minutes. (The cooking time will depend on the coarseness of your cornmeal.) Remove the polenta from the heat and cover the pot to keep it hot.

7. When ready to serve, gently transfer the fish to a plate. Pour the sauce from the casserole into a saucepan, bring it to a simmer over medium heat, and let it reduce slightly, about 4 minutes. Season with pepper, if needed.

8. Spoon the polenta onto heated plates, top with the baked salt cod, and spoon the sauce over the fish. Serve at once.

Recipe note *The thickness of the cod can vary so you may need to adjust your soaking and cooking time accordingly.*

Margottini bergamaschi

Polenta, cheese, and truffle timbales

SERVES 6

5 cups water or Meat Broth
(page 251)

1 tbsp kosher salt

10 oz (1¾ cups) cornmeal, plus
more as needed for coating
timbales

⅔ cup grated Grana Padano

1 tsp freshly ground black pepper

Melted butter, as needed

Shaved fresh black truffle (optional)

4 oz Northern Italian mountain
cheese, such as Fontina or similar,
thinly sliced

6 egg yolks

1. Bring the water or broth to a simmer in a large, deep pot over medium-high heat. Add the salt and then add the cornmeal gradually, whisking continuously to prevent the cornmeal from clumping. Once all the cornmeal has been added, reduce the heat to medium or low and let the polenta simmer gently, stirring frequently to make sure it does not stick, until the polenta is fully cooked and creamy, about 45 minutes. Remove the polenta from the heat and stir in the Grana Padano and black pepper.

2. Preheat the oven to 350°F. Brush six 4-ounce timbale molds or soufflé cups generously with butter. Add a pinch of cornmeal to each mold and turn to coat the sides and bottom with the cornmeal. Shake out any excess cornmeal. Set aside.

3. Fill each mold about half full with the hot polenta. Use the back of a teaspoon to push the polenta up the sides of the molds. Add a few truffle shavings, if using, and a slice of the mountain cheese. Top with an egg yolk, and then add another slice of cheese, followed by a shaving or two of truffle, if using. Spoon more polenta on top of the mold to seal in the cheese and yolk, spreading it into an even layer and sealing the cheese and yolk inside the polenta.

4. Bake the margottini until the yolk is warm, about 10 minutes; it should still be runny. To check the doneness of the yolk, use an instant-read thermometer; it should read 145°F.

5. Run a paring knife around the sides of the mold and then carefully tip the margottini out onto a warm plate. Serve at once, letting each diner break open the case to see the golden yolk-and-cheese center flow out to become the sauce for the polenta.

Recipe note *The perfect margottini have a rich polenta crust that completely surrounds a center of melted cheese with a warm runny yolk. The polenta needs to be quite warm when you assemble the timbales, so while the polenta simmers on the stove, prepare the molds, slice the cheese, and separate the yolks.*

Polenta taragna

Buckwheat polenta

SERVES 6 TO 8

12 oz (2½ cups) cornmeal

1 cup buckwheat flour

10 cups water

2 tbsp salt

6 oz (¾ cup) unsalted butter, cubed

8 oz Bitto or Fontina, cubed

6 sage leaves

1. Mix the cornmeal and buckwheat flour together in a medium bowl and set aside.

2. Bring the water for the polenta to a simmer in a large saucepan over medium heat. Add the salt, and then slowly add the cornmeal-buckwheat mixture, whisking continuously. Let simmer gently until polenta is nearly done, stirring frequently with a wooden spoon to make sure the polenta does not stick, 40 to 50 minutes. (The cooking time may vary depending on the coarseness of your cornmeal.)

3. Add ½ cup of the butter and the cheese. Continue to cook over low heat, stirring until the butter and the cheese are evenly blended into the polenta. Remove the polenta from the heat, adjust the seasoning, and keep hot.

4. Heat the remaining ¼ cup butter in a small saucepan over medium heat until it is melted and very hot. Add the sage leaves and continue to cook, swirling the pan frequently, until the butter is browned and the sage leaves are crisp, about 2 minutes.

5. Spoon the polenta into heated dishes, top with the browned butter and sage, and serve at once.

Recipe note *Bitto is the traditional cheese used for this preparation. When it is difficult to find, you can substitute Fontina.*

Riso, patate, cozze e origano

Rice, potato, mussels, and oregano

SERVES 6 TO 8

7 tbsp extra-virgin olive oil

5 garlic cloves, 2 left whole,
3 finely chopped

1 lb mussels, scrubbed and
debearded

1 cup dry white wine

1 cup water

3 medium russet potatoes, peeled
and sliced ⅛ inch thick

Kosher salt and freshly ground
black pepper, as needed

¼ cup chopped flat-leaf parsley

1 tbsp dried oregano

1 lb ripe cherry tomatoes,
quartered

⅔ cup grated Pecorino-Romano

10 oz (1½ cups) medium-grain rice,
rinsed in cold water and drained

1. Preheat the oven to 375°F.

2. Heat 2 tablespoons of the oil in a Dutch oven or casserole over medium heat. Add the whole garlic cloves and stir until the garlic starts to get a little color, about 1 minute. Add the mussels, wine, and water, cover, and let the mussels cook until they are all completely open. Transfer them to a bowl. Discard any unopened mussels. When they are cool enough to handle, remove and discard the top shell. Strain the cooking liquid and reserve separately.

3. Oil the bottom of a baking dish with 1 tablespoon of the oil and layer half of the potatoes in the pan; season with salt and pepper. Sprinkle half of the chopped garlic, half of the parsley, and half of the oregano over the potatoes. Sprinkle over half of the tomatoes and all of the cheese. Add the rice in an even layer, and arrange the cooked mussels over the rice. Add the remaining potatoes in a layer and top with the remaining garlic, parsley, oregano, and tomatoes. Pour the remaining 4 tablespoons oil over the dish.

4. Bring the reserved cooking liquid from the mussels to a boil and pour over the dish; it should barely cover the last layer (add some hot water if there is not enough cooking liquid). Cover the baking dish with aluminum foil and bake for 15 minutes, then remove the foil. Continue to bake, uncovered, until the rice and potatoes are tender and the liquid has been completely absorbed, 25 to 30 minutes more. Serve at once.

Risotto al radicchio e montasio

Risotto with radicchio and montasio

SERVES 6

10 cups Meat Broth (page 251) or chicken broth

Kosher salt, as needed

6 oz (¾ cup) unsalted butter

4 oz pancetta, minced

¾ cup minced yellow onion

1 head radicchio, cut into thin strips

1 lb (2⅔ cups) Carnaroli rice

½ cup dry red wine

1 cup grated aged Montasio

Freshly ground black pepper, as needed

1. Heat the broth in a saucepan over low heat and season with salt.

2. In a large saucepan, melt 6 tablespoons of the butter over low heat. Add the pancetta and cook until the pancetta is golden, about 2 minutes. Add the onions and cook, stirring frequently, until the onions are tender and translucent, about 3 minutes. Then add the radicchio and cook until it starts to wilt, about 2 minutes, and then add the rice. Cook the rice, stirring frequently, until it is coated with the fat and lightly toasted, about 2 minutes.

3. Add the wine and cook until almost dry, 2 or 3 minutes. Add enough of the broth to cover the rice by ½ inch, and cook, stirring frequently to be sure the rice doesn't stick to the bottom. As the rice absorbs the broth, keep adding more, ½ cup at a time.

4. Once the rice has absorbed almost all the broth, and the grains are just tender (al dente), about 18 minutes total cooking time, remove the pot from the heat. Add the remaining 6 tablespoons butter and stir vigorously until the risotto is creamy. Stir in the cheese, season the risotto with salt and pepper as needed, and serve immediately on heated plates.

Risotto con vino rosso e salamino

Red wine risotto with salami

SERVES 6

2½ qt Meat Broth (page 251), or as needed

6 oz (¾ cup) unsalted butter

¾ cup minced yellow onion

1 lb (2¼ cups) Carnaroli rice

½ cup dry red wine

1 cup grated Parmigiano-Reggiano

5 oz salami, casing removed, diced

Kosher salt and freshly ground black pepper, as needed

1. Heat the broth over low heat; keep warm.

2. Heat ½ cup of the butter in a large pot over low heat. Add the onion and cook, stirring frequently, until tender and translucent, about 4 minutes. Add the rice and toast lightly, stirring frequently, about 2 minutes.

3. Add the wine and cook until almost dry. Add enough of the broth to cover the rice by ½ inch, and cook, stirring frequently to be sure the rice doesn't stick to the bottom. As the rice absorbs the broth, keep adding more, ½ cup at a time.

4. Once the rice has absorbed almost all the broth, and the grains are just tender (al dente), about 20 minutes total cooking time, remove the pot from the heat. Add the remaining ¼ cup butter and stir vigorously until the risotto is very creamy. Stir in cheese and the salami until blended. Season with salt and pepper, if needed, and serve immediately on flat plates.

Spring

Insalata di farro con pesto

Farro salad with pesto

SERVES 4 TO 6

2 tbsp extra-virgin olive oil

1 small carrot, halved

1 small yellow onion, quartered

1 celery stalk, halved

2 bay leaves

10 oz (about 1½ cups) farro

2 qt water

1 teaspoon kosher salt, plus as needed

½ cup shelled fresh garden peas, cooked

¼ cup chopped flat-leaf parsley

1 small seedless cucumber, peeled, halved lengthwise, and thinly sliced

5 radishes, halved and thinly sliced

4 baby carrots, peeled and thinly sliced (see Recipe Note)

½ small red onion, thinly sliced

2 tsp finely minced mint

1 pt ripe grape tomatoes, halved or quartered

3 tbsp thinly sliced garlic scapes (optional)

1 cup Pesto (page 247), or as needed

Freshly ground black pepper

2 tbsp lemon or lime juice or red wine vinegar

1. Heat the oil in a large saucepan over medium heat. Add the halved carrot, onion, celery, and bay leaves. Cover and cook on low heat, until barely softened, about 5 minutes. Add the farro and stir to coat with the oil. Add the water and bring to a boil over high heat.

2. Lower the heat, cover the pot, and simmer for about 10 minutes. Add 1 teaspoon salt and simmer until the farro is al dente, 15 to 20 minutes more.

3. Drain the farro and discard the onion, carrot, celery and bay leaves. Spread in a thin layer on a platter or baking dish and let cool completely.

4. In large bowl combine the cooled farro with the peas, parsley, cucumber, radishes, sliced carrots, onion, mint, tomatoes, and garlic scapes. Toss the salad with the pesto and season with salt and pepper, if needed. Just before serving add the lemon juice or vinegar. Serve at room temperature or chilled.

Cooking farro *If you need the farro to cook faster you may soak the farro for at least 6 hours before you begin cooking; wash it well after soaking. Cooking time will change.*

Usually when farro has been soaked it will take about 25 to 30 minutes to cook. If starting from dry stage about 40 to 45 minutes.

Spelt, wheat berries, barley, or any other grains may be substituted for the farro. You may also use brown or white rice for this recipe.

Linguine con vongole e pancetta

Linguine with clams and pancetta

SERVES 4 TO 6

Kosher salt, as needed

1 lb dried linguine

½ cup extra-virgin olive oil

3 oz pancetta, cut into small dice

3 garlic cloves, thinly sliced

1 dried chile (peperoncino) (optional)

32 to 40 Manila clams, or other small clams, well scrubbed

¾ cup dry white wine

¾ cup chopped flat-leaf parsley

½ cup Tomato Sauce (page 248) (optional)

Freshly ground black pepper, as needed

1. Bring a large pot of salted water to a boil over high heat.

2. Add the linguine all at once to the boiling water and stir a few times to separate the pasta. Cook, uncovered, until just slightly undercooked, 6 to 7 minutes (check the cooking time for your pasta and cook 1 to 2 minutes less).

3. While the linguine is cooking, heat 2 tablespoons of the oil and the pancetta in a 4-quart Dutch oven over medium heat. Add the garlic and the dried chile and stir to coat them with the oil. Sauté over low heat, stirring often, until the garlic is just starting to turn color, about 1 minute. Add the clams, the wine, half of the parsley, and the tomato sauce, if using. Simmer, covered, until the clams are completely open, 3 to 4 minutes. Discard any unopened clams.

4. Drain the linguine in a colander. Shake well to remove any water clinging to the pasta. Add the linguine to the clams and toss them together until the pasta is evenly coated. Simmer to finish cooking the pasta, 2 minutes more. Add enough of the remaining oil to make a rich, slightly thickened sauce. Season with salt and pepper, as needed.

5. Arrange the clams around the outside of a serving platter or individual plates, arrange the linguine in the center. Sprinkle with the remaining parsley, and serve at once.

Recipe notes *Ideally you want to toss the pasta with whole clams, and the smaller they are the better. As an alternative, you may use littleneck clams or whatever is available. In this case, if they are too big you might want to make the sauce first, remove the mollusk, and discard the shells. The amount of clams is up to you, and usually the more the better.*

If you would like to add some tomato sauce, add it while the clams are opening.

Maccheroncini al pesce spada, capperi, olive e pignoli

Maccheroncini with swordfish, capers, olives, and pine nuts

SERVES 6 TO 8

½ cup extra-virgin olive oil

10 oz swordfish, trimmed and diced

3 garlic cloves, peeled and minced

1 fresh chile (jalapeño or serrano), minced

Kosher salt, as needed

1 lb dried maccheroncini

½ cup chopped mint

3 tbsp salted capers, rinsed with cold water

3 tbsp toasted pine nuts

¼ cup chopped pitted black olives

Freshly ground black pepper, as needed

1. Heat the oil in a sauté pan over medium-low heat. Add the swordfish and cook, stirring from time to time, until it no longer appears raw, about 2 minutes. Add the garlic and chile and sauté until the garlic is aromatic, 1 minute more. Set aside while you prepare the pasta.

2. Bring a large pot of salted water to a boil over high heat. Add the maccheroncini and stir to and separate the pieces. Cook, uncovered, until the pasta is just tender to the bite (al dente), 8 to 10 minutes. Reserve a few ladlefuls of pasta cooking water for finishing the sauce (you will need about ½ cup).

3. Drain the pasta in a colander. Shake well to remove any water clinging to the pasta. Add the drained pasta to the pan with the swordfish, tossing over medium heat until the pasta is evenly coated with oil. Add the mint, capers, pine nuts, olives, salt and pepper as needed, and a little of the reserved pasta cooking water. Continue to toss over medium heat until the dish is combined and very hot. Add more pasta water, if necessary, to keep the dish from becoming too dry. Serve at once in a heated serving bowl or pasta plates.

Orecchiette con ricotta, piselli e scorza di limone

Orecchiette with ricotta, peas, and lemon zest

SERVES 4 TO 6

½ cup extra-virgin olive oil, plus more as needed for serving

2 spring onions, white and green portions, thinly sliced (about ½ cup)

½ cup chopped flat-leaf parsley

2 lb fresh garden peas, shelled

¾ cup chicken or vegetable broth, or more as needed

Kosher salt, as needed

1 lb dried orecchiette

1½ cups fresh ricotta

½ cup grated Parmigiano-Reggiano

Zest of ½ lemon, cut into very fine strips

Freshly ground black pepper, as needed

1. Heat the oil in a large sauté pan over medium heat. Add the green onions and cook, stirring frequently, until tender, about 2 minutes. Add half the parsley and cook for 2 minutes more. Add the shelled peas and the broth and bring to a simmer, stirring well. Reduce the heat to medium-low or low and continue to cook, covered, until the peas are tender but not mushy, 4 to 5 minutes (the time may vary depending upon the size of your peas). Take the pan off the heat and set aside.

2. Bring a large pot of salted water to a boil over high heat. Add the orecchiette and stir to submerge and separate the pieces. Cook, uncovered, until just tender (al dente), 8 to 10 minutes (check the cooking time for your pasta).

3. Drain the orecchiette in a colander. Shake well to remove any water clinging to the pasta. Pour the drained pasta into the peas and return the pan to low heat. Gently stir the orecchiette into the peas until well combined. (If there is a lot of liquid, continue cooking for a few minutes to cook it off.)

4. Remove the pan from the heat, add half of the ricotta to the orecchiette and fold together. Fold in the remaining parsley, the Parmigiano-Reggiano, and lemon zest. Season with salt and pepper as needed.

5. Serve the orecchiette at once in a warmed serving bowl or in pasta plates topped with spoonfuls of the remaining ricotta and drizzled with some extra-virgin olive oil.

Recipe notes *You can add some prosciutto in with the onions in step 1 for more flavor.*

If you want a richer flavor, you can also add some butter when the pasta gets tossed with the peas in step 4.

You can substitute orange zest for the lemon zest.

Cavatelli con fave fresche, pancetta e pecorino

Cavatelli with fava beans, pancetta, and pecorino

SERVES 4

Kosher salt, as needed

1 lb dried cavatelli

4 oz pancetta (about 8 slices), cut into 1-inch-wide strips

¼ cup extra-virgin olive oil

2 garlic cloves

1 cup shelled fresh fava beans, peeled (see page 256)

Freshly ground black pepper, as needed

1 cup grated Pecorino Romano, plus more as needed

1. Bring a large pot of salted water to a boil over high heat. Add the cavatelli and stir to submerge and separate the pieces. Cook until the pasta is just tender (al dente), 8 to 10 minutes (check the cooking time for your pasta). Reserve a few ladlefuls of the pasta cooking water to finish the sauce in step 4 (you will need about ¼ cup).

2. Heat a large sauté pan over medium-high heat. Add the pancetta and cook on both sides until it is crisp and the fat has rendered into the pan. Transfer the pancetta to a plate and set aside. Add the oil to the rendered fat in the pan. Add the garlic and cook, stirring constantly, until it is just aromatic, about 45 seconds. Add the fava beans and toss to coat in the oil. Immediately take the pan off the heat and season with salt and pepper. (You do not want to cook the favas; you just want to warm them.)

3. Drain the cavatelli in a colander. Shake well to remove any water clinging to the pasta. Pour the drained cavatelli into the pan with the fava beans. Add the cheese and a little of the reserved pasta cooking water to help melt the cheese and give the pasta a creamy consistency. Season with salt, pepper, or additional cheese, as needed.

4. Add the cooked pancetta and serve at once in a heated serving bowl or in pasta plates.

Garganelli con spugnole

Garganelli with leeks and morels

SERVES 6

Leek and morel sauce

1½ lb morels

3 oz (6 tbsp) unsalted butter

2 small leeks, well washed, halved lengthwise and thinly sliced (white part only)

2 garlic cloves, minced

¼ cup dry white wine

Meat Broth (page 251) or chicken broth, as needed

Kosher salt, as needed

1 lb dried garganelli

½ cup chopped flat-leaf parsley

1. Clean the morels by soaking them in a bowl of water for 1 minute and then swirling them in the water to gently remove any dirt. Lift the morels out of the water and discard the water. Repeat this step until there is no more dirt in the water. Drain them on paper towels and when they are dry, cut the morels in halves or quarters, depending upon the size of the morels.

2. Heat the butter in a large sauté pan large over medium heat. Add the leeks and cook, covered, stirring from time to time, until they are tender and translucent, about 3 minutes. Add the garlic and cook, stirring frequently, until the garlic is aromatic, about 2 minutes.

3. Add the morels and stir well. Reduce the heat to low and cook, stirring as needed, until the mushrooms are hot and tender, about 5 minutes. Add the wine and enough broth to keep the mixture moistened (it should not be soupy, however).

4. Bring a large pot of salted water to a boil over high heat. Add the garganelli and stir to submerge and separate the pieces. Cook, uncovered, until the pasta is just tender (al dente), 8 to 10 minutes (check the cooking time for your pasta).

5. Drain the garganelli in a colander. Shake well to remove any water clinging to the pasta. Pour the drained garganelli into the pan with the leek and morel sauce. Add the parsley and toss together over medium heat until combined and the liquid in the sauce has reduced enough to coat the pasta, about 2 minutes. Season with salt, as needed.

6. Serve the garganelli at once in a heated serving bowl or in pasta plates.

Penne con zucchine, noci e provolone

Penne with zucchini, walnuts, and provolone

SERVES 4 TO 6

½ cup extra-virgin olive oil

½ medium red onion, very thinly sliced

3 garlic cloves

1 lb zucchini, trimmed, quartered lengthwise, and thinly sliced

½ cup chopped flat-leaf parsley

Kosher salt and freshly ground black pepper, as needed

1 lb dried penne rigate

½ cup grated Parmigiano-Reggiano

8 oz provolone, diced, or as needed

½ cup chopped toasted walnuts

1. Heat the oil in a sauté pan large enough to hold the cooked penne over medium heat. Add the onions and cook, stirring, until they are tender and translucent, about 3 minutes. Press the garlic through a garlic press directly into the pan and cook, stirring frequently, until the garlic is aromatic, about 1 minute.

2. Add the zucchini and stir well. Increase the heat to medium-high and cook, stirring as needed, until the zucchini is cooked through and tender but not falling apart, about 5 minutes. Add the parsley and season with a pinch of salt and pepper. Set aside.

3. Bring a large pot of salted water to a boil over high heat. Add the penne all at once and stir to submerge and separate the pieces. Cook, uncovered, until the pasta is al dente, 8 to 10 minutes (check the cooking time for your pasta).

4. Drain the penne in a colander. Shake well to remove any water clinging to the pasta. Pour the drained penne into the pan with the zucchini and toss together over medium heat. Add the Parmigiano-Reggiano and the provolone and fold together to distribute the cheeses evenly (they should not melt into the sauce, however).

5. Serve the penne at once in a heated serving bowl or pasta plates topped with the walnuts.

Recipe note *When buying zucchini, look for small, firm, and very green ones; these are good signs of freshness. The youngest zucchini are also the most flavorful. Avoid large zucchini that are soft to the touch.*

Maccheroni freschi con ragù di fave, piselli e carciofi

Fresh maccheroni with fava bean, pea, and artichoke ragù

SERVES 4 TO 6

Fava bean, pea, and artichoke ragù

3 tbsp extra-virgin olive oil

1½ cups minced yellow onion

2½ oz (3 tbsp) unsalted butter

3 garlic cloves, minced

1 thyme sprig

2 to 3 artichokes, trimmed and cut in wedges (page 255)

Kosher salt and freshly ground black pepper, as needed

½ cup dry white wine

1 cup water

1 cup shelled fresh garden peas

2 cups shelled fresh fava beans, peeled if necessary (page 256)

1¼ lb Maccheroni alla Chitarra (page 240)

¼ cup grated Parmigiano-Reggiano, plus more as needed for serving

1. Heat the oil in a sauté pan over medium heat. Add the onions and cook, stirring from time to time, until they are tender and translucent, about 3 minutes. Add the butter, garlic, thyme, and artichoke wedges. Season with salt and pepper and cook, stirring frequently, until the garlic is aromatic, about 3 minutes. Add the wine and continue to cook until the wine has nearly cooked away.

2. Add the water, cover the pan, reduce the heat to low, and cook, stirring from time to time, until the artichokes are very tender, about 20 minutes. Add the peas and cook until they are bright green, about 2 minutes. Add the fava beans and cook until they are hot, 2 minutes more. Taste and season with salt and pepper. Remove and discard the thyme sprig. Keep warm.

3. Bring a large pot of salted water to a boil over high heat. Add the maccheroni all at once and stir a few times to separate the strands. Cook, uncovered, at a boil until just tender to the bite (al dente), about 6 minutes.

4. Drain the maccheroni in a colander. Shake well to remove any water clinging to the pasta. Transfer the hot pasta to a heated serving bowl and add the fava bean and artichoke ragù and the cheese, tossing them gently together.

5. Serve at once, and pass the cheese on the side, if desired.

Trofiette con aragosta, porri, zucchine e fave

Trofiette with lobster, leeks, zucchini, and fava beans

SERVES 4 TO 6

Lobster, leek, zucchini, and fava sauce

¼ cup extra-virgin olive oil

1 leek, well washed, cut in half, and thinly sliced (white part only)

2 shallots, minced

2 garlic cloves, chopped

1½ tsp minced thyme

⅓ cup cognac

½ cup dry white wine

3 cooked lobsters (about 1½ lb each), meat diced, and coral and tomalley reserved (see Recipe note)

Kosher salt and freshly ground black pepper, as needed

Red pepper flakes or minced jalapeño, as needed

½ cup chopped flat-leaf parsley

10 oz zucchini, quartered and sliced

2 lb fresh unshelled fava beans

1 lb dried trofiette

Marjoram leaves for garnish (optional)

Any type of long pasta will also work here, such as spaghetti, linguine, or bucatini. You may omit the fava beans and the zucchini and add ¾ pint of cherry or grape tomatoes (red or yellow or a mix), halved or quartered, then proceed with the recipe as described below.

1. Heat the oil in a large sauté pan large over medium heat. Add the leek and shallots and cook, until they are tender and translucent, about 3 minutes. Add the garlic and thyme, and cook, stirring frequently, until the garlic is aromatic, about 3 minutes. Add the cognac and when the cognac is hot, light it with a match and let the alcohol burn away. Add the wine, the lobster, the reserved tomalley and coral, and any juices from the lobster. Season with salt, black pepper, red pepper flakes or jalapeño, and half of the parsley.

2. Add the zucchini and fava beans, stir well, and cover the pan. Cook, stirring as needed, until the zucchini and lobster are cooked through and tender, 5 to 6 minutes. Season with a pinch of salt and pepper. Set aside.

3. Bring a large pot of salted water to a boil over high heat. Add the trofiette and stir to submerge and separate the pasta. Cook, uncovered, until the pasta is just tender (al dente), 8 to 10 minutes (check the cooking time for your pasta).

4. Drain the trofiette in a colander. Shake well to remove any water clinging to the pasta. Pour the drained trofiette into the pan with the lobster and zucchini and toss together over medium heat. Add the rest of the parsley.

5. Serve the trofiette at once in a heated serving bowl or in pasta plates topped with the marjoram, if using.

Recipe note *To prepare the lobster for this dish, bring a large pot of water to a rolling boil. Add the lobsters, one at a time, head first, to the pot. Return the water to boil. Cook, uncovered, until the shells are a brilliant red, 2 to 3 minutes. Transfer the lobster to a cutting board and let it cool enough so that you can handle it. Use kitchen shears to cut off the claws and pull out the meat, including knuckle meat. Use a nutcracker to crack the shells open, if necessary. Cut the tails away from the body and cut through the underside of the shell; pull out the meat and cut it into dice. Reserve the claw and tail meat. Cut each lobster body in half lengthwise, and pull out the any coral (bright orange part) or tomalley (green part) and transfer with any juices into a separate bowl.*

Farfalline nere con calamari, gamberetti e fave

Squid ink farfalline with shrimp, calamari, and fava beans

SERVES 6

Shrimp, calamari, and fava bean sauce

¾ cup extra-virgin olive oil

1 shallot, minced

2 garlic cloves, peeled and minced

12 small shrimp, shelled and deveined

12 small calamari, cleaned

½ cup chopped flat-leaf parsley

¼ cup dry white wine

2 ripe plum tomatoes, peeled, seeded, and diced (see page 248)

1½ cups shelled fresh fava beans, peeled if necessary (see page 256)

Kosher salt, as needed

1¼ lb Squid Ink Farfalline (page 236)

1. Heat the oil in a wide saucepan over medium heat. Add the shallot and garlic and cook, stirring frequently, until the shallot is tender and the garlic is aromatic, about 2 minutes.

2. Add the shrimp and calamari and sauté, stirring frequently, until the seafood becomes opaque, about 5 minutes. Add the parsley and sauté for another minute.

3. Add the wine and the tomatoes and cook until the wine has nearly evaporated, 3 to 4 minutes. Add the fava beans and stir to combine. Cook just long enough to heat the fava beans. Remove from the heat and reserve.

4. Bring a large pot of salted water to a boil over high heat. Add the farfalline and stir to submerge and separate the pasta. Cook, uncovered, until the pasta is just tender (al dente) 3 to 4 minutes).

5. Drain the farfalline in a colander. Shake well to remove any water clinging to the pasta. Pour the drained farfalline into the pan with the fava beans and toss together over medium heat until all the ingredients are very hot and the pasta is evenly coated. Serve at once from a heated serving bowl or on heated pasta plates.

Paglia e fieno con piselli e prosciutto cotto

Straw-and-hay pasta with peas and ham

SERVES 6 TO 8

4 oz (½ cup) unsalted butter

1 shallot, minced

⅔ cup fresh garden peas, blanched

4 oz ham, cut into thin strips

1 cup heavy cream

10 oz White Pasta (page 237)

10 oz Green Pasta (page 237)

Kosher salt, as needed

½ cup grated Parmigiano-Reggiano, plus more as needed for serving

1. Heat the butter in a large sauté pan over medium heat. Add the shallot and cook, stirring frequently, until tender and translucent, about 2 minutes. Add the peas and ham and cook, stirring, until the peas are hot, about 2 minutes. Add the heavy cream, reduce the heat to low, and simmer until the cream is thickened and slightly reduced, about 5 minutes.

2. Bring a large pot of salted water to a boil over high heat. Add the green and white pastas and stir to submerge and separate the strands. Cook, uncovered, until just tender (al dente), about 3 minutes.

3. Drain the pasta in a colander. Shake well to remove most of the water clinging to the pasta. Transfer the hot pasta to the sauté pan with the cream, ham, and peas and toss together over low heat until the pasta is evenly coated. Add the cheese and stir until evenly blended.

4. Transfer the pasta to a heated serving bowl or pasta plates and serve at once, passing additional cheese on the side.

Tagliatelle al ragù bianco di vitello

Tagliatelle with white veal ragù

SERVES 6 TO 8

White veal ragù

3 oz (6 tbsp) unsalted butter

1 large yellow onion, minced

½ cup minced celery

½ cup minced carrot

1½ lb coarsely ground veal

½ cup dry white wine

2 bay leaves

3 cups Meat Broth (page 251) or chicken broth, or as needed

1 cup heavy cream

Kosher salt, as needed

1¼ lb Tagliatelle (page 237)

Grated Parmigiano-Reggiano, as needed for serving

Freshly ground black pepper, as needed

1. Heat the butter in a 4-quart Dutch oven over medium-low heat. Add the onions, celery, and carrot and cook, stirring frequently, until they are tender and the onions are translucent, about 15 minutes.

2. Add the veal and cook, stirring often, until the meat is no longer pink, about 8 minutes. Add the wine and cook until the wine has nearly cooked off, about 2 minutes. Add the bay leaves and about ½ cup of the broth. Reduce the heat to low, cover the pot, and simmer gently until the ragù is thick and flavorful, 3 to 4 hours. Stir the ragù occasionally as it cooks and add more broth, as needed, to keep the ragù from drying out. Add the cream and simmer until the sauce is very rich and thick, about 1 hour. Remove and discard the bay leaves. Season with salt and pepper as needed.

3. Bring a large pot of salted water to a boil over high heat. Add the tagliatelle and stir to submerge and separate the strands. Cook, uncovered, until just tender to the bite (al dente), about 3 minutes.

4. Drain the tagliatelle in a colander. Shake well to remove any water clinging to the pasta. Transfer the drained pasta to a heated serving bowl, and add the white veal ragù, and toss gently together.

5. Serve at once, and pass the cheese on the side.

Pappardelle con coniglio e carciofi

Pappardelle with rabbit and artichoke ragù

SERVES 4 TO 6

Rabbit and artichoke ragù

¾ cup extra-virgin olive oil

1 lb boneless rabbit legs, cut in small pieces

Kosher salt and freshly ground black pepper, as needed

2 medium shallots, minced

1 cup dry white wine

2 tsp torn basil

1 tsp thyme

2 qt canned whole San Marzano tomatoes, crushed or coarsely chopped

6 baby artichokes, trimmed and quartered

1¼ lb Pappardelle (page 237, see Recipe note)

½ cup grated aged Pecorino Romano, plus more as needed for serving

1½ tsp torn marjoram

1. Heat 4 tablespoons of the oil in a 4-quart pot Dutch over medium heat. Season the rabbit with salt and pepper and add to the hot oil in a single layer. Cook, turning as necessary, until brown on all sides, about 10 minutes total cooking time. Transfer the rabbit to a plate and set aside.

2. Add the shallots to the pot and cook, stirring often, until the shallots are slightly tender and translucent, about 3 minutes. Return the rabbit to the pot along with any accumulated juices, the wine, basil, and thyme. Continue to cook until the wine has nearly cooked away. Add the tomatoes and bring to a simmer. Cover the pot and cook, stirring from time to time, until the rabbit is nearly tender, about 15 minutes. Add the artichokes and continue to cook until the rabbit and artichokes are very tender, 15 to 20 minutes. Season with salt and pepper, if necessary.

3. Bring a large pot of salted water to a boil over high heat. Add the pappardelle and stir to submerge and separate the strands. Cook, uncovered, until just tender (al dente), about 4 minutes.

4. Drain the pappardelle in a colander. Shake well to remove any water clinging to the pasta. Transfer the hot pasta to a heated serving bowl and add the rabbit and artichoke ragù, tossing them gently together. Add the cheese and toss together.

5. Serve at once, topped with the marjoram, and pass additional cheese on the side, if desired.

Recipe note *You can add some very finely chopped rosemary to the dough when kneading in step 3, and then proceed as directed.*

Mezzelune agli asparagi e burro al tartufo nero

Asparagus-filled half-moon ravioli with truffle butter

SERVES 4 TO 6

Asparagus ravioli

1 lb asparagus, trimmed and peeled

¼ cup extra-virgin olive oil

1 shallot, minced

¼ cup chopped flat-leaf parsley

Kosher salt and freshly ground black pepper, as needed

1⅓ cups fresh ricotta

½ cup grated Parmigiano-Reggiano

2 egg yolks

1 lb Pasta Sheets (page 235)

Truffle sauce

4 oz (½ cup) unsalted butter, softened

2 oz black truffle, half minced and half shaved

2 garlic cloves, thinly sliced

1 bunch chives, thinly sliced just before using

Grated Parmigiano-Reggiano, as needed for serving

Recipe note If you can't find fresh black truffle, you may substitute canned black truffle or use a little bit of truffle oil mixed into the butter. It will still be delicious without the truffle!

1. Blanch the asparagus in boiling salted water for about 1 to 2 minutes, depending on their size. Immediately remove from the water and rinse under cold running water to stop the cooking and keep the bright green color. Cut away the tips and reserve 12 to 18 of them to garnish the dish. Cut the rest of the asparagus into small pieces and set aside.

2. Heat the olive oil a sauté pan over medium heat. Add the shallot and the parsley and cook, stirring, until the shallot is tender, about 2 minutes. Add the cut asparagus and cook until tender but not to soft, 1 to 2 minutes. Season with salt and pepper and set aside to cool.

3. Once the asparagus has cooled completely, place it in a clean cloth and squeeze to remove any excess moisture.

4. Stir together the asparagus, ricotta, Parmigiano-Reggiano, and egg yolks until well combined. Set aside.

5. Using a round cutter, cut the pasta sheets into 3-inch circles. Place 1 teaspoon of the asparagus-ricotta filling in the center of each circle. Fold the pasta circle in half and press the edges together, making a half-moon shape.

6. Bring a large pot of salted water to a boil over high heat. Add the mezzelune and stir to submerge and separate the pieces. Cook, uncovered, until just tender (al dente), about 5 minutes. Reserve a few ladlefuls of the pasta cooking water to finish the sauce (you will need about ¼ cup).

7. While the mezzelune are cooking, heat the butter in a sauté pan with the truffle and garlic just until the garlic is aromatic, about 1 minute. Remove and discard the garlic cloves and remove the pan with the truffle butter from the heat.

8. Drain the mezzelune in a colander. Shake well to remove excess water. Transfer the hot mezzelune to skillet with the truffle butter, tossing them gently together. Add the reserved asparagus tips and a few tablespoons of the pasta cooking water and toss the ravioli into the truffle butter over low heat until the sauce is thick and creamy.

9. Transfer to a heated serving bowl or pasta plates, topped with the chives. Pass the Parmigiano-Reggiano on the side.

Corzetti con maggiorana e pignoli

Corzetti with marjoram and pine nuts

SERVES 6

Kosher salt, as needed

1¼ lb Corzetti
(page 238)

4 oz (½ cup) unsalted butter

¼ cup pine nuts

Leaves from 4 to 6 marjoram
sprigs, chopped

¼ cup grated Parmigiano-Reggiano

The only way to make corzetti pasta is with a corzetti stamp, a traditional two-piece pasta-making tool that is carved with a design. The bottom of the stamp is used to cut out pasta circles and the top is used to press the pasta and imprint it with the carved design on the tool.

1. Bring a large pot of salted water to a boil over high heat. Add the corzetti to the boiling water and stir a few times to submerge and separate the pieces. Cook, uncovered, until just tender to the bite (al dente), about 3 minutes. Reserve a few ladlefuls of the cooking water to finish the dish (you will need about ¼ cup).

2. Drain the corzetti in a colander. Shake well to remove excess water. Transfer the drained pasta to a heated serving bowl, add the butter, and toss gently together, adding a little of the reserved pasta cooking water to thicken the butter and make it cling to the pasta.

3. Top the pasta with the pine nuts, marjoram leaves, and cheese and serve at once.

Tortelli di ricotta e asparagi con gamberi di fiume

Tortelli with ricotta, asparagus, and crayfish

SERVES 4 TO 6

Asparagus tortelli

1 lb asparagus, trimmed and peeled

¼ cup extra-virgin olive oil

1 shallot, minced

¼ cup chopped flat-leaf parsley

Kosher salt and freshly ground black pepper, as needed

1⅓ cups fresh ricotta

½ cup grated Parmigiano-Reggiano

2 egg yolks

1 lb Pasta Sheets (page 235)

Flour, as needed

Crayfish sauce

2 tbsp extra-virgin olive oil

2 garlic cloves, sliced

24 crayfish (about 2 lb)

½ cup dry white wine

2½ oz (5 tbsp) unsalted butter

¼ cup chopped flat-leaf parsley

Grated Parmigiano-Reggiano, as needed for serving

1. Blanch the asparagus in boiling salted water for 1 to 2 minutes, depending on their size. Immediately remove them from the water and rinse under cold running water to stop the cooking and keep the bright green color. Cut away the tips and reserve 12 to 18 of the tips to garnish the dish. Cut the rest of the asparagus into small pieces and set aside.

2. Heat the ¼ cup of oil in a sauté pan over medium heat. Add the shallot and the ¼ cup of parsley and cook, stirring, until the shallot is tender, about 2 minutes. Add the blanched asparagus and cook until tender but not to soft, 1 to 2 minutes. Season with salt and pepper and set aside to cool.

4. In a large bowl, stir together the asparagus, ricotta, Parmigiano-Reggiano, and egg yolks until well combined. Set aside.

5. Using a cutter, cut the pasta sheets into 3-inch circles. Place a teaspoon of asparagus filling in the center of each circle. Fold the pasta circle in half over the filling and pinch the corners together to form a tortello. As you cut out the tortelli, place them on a plate or baking sheet sprinkled with a little flour to keep them from sticking.

6. Heat the 2 tablespoons of oil in a sauté pan over medium heat. Add the garlic and cook, stirring frequently, until aromatic, about 1 minute. Add the crayfish and toss until they are coated with oil. Add the wine, cover the pan, and cook over low heat until the shells are bright red. Transfer to a plate and let the cool until they can be handled easily. Peel the crayfish and transfer the tails to a bowl. Place the shells in a sieve set over the bowl holding the crayfish tail meat. Press firmly to extract as much liquid as possible. Discard the shells and set aside the crayfish.

7. Bring a large pot of salted water to a boil over high heat. Add the tortelli and stir to submerge and separate them. Cook, uncovered, until just tender (al dente), 8 to 10 minutes. Drain the tortelli in a colander.

8. Heat 2 tablespoons of the butter in a wide pan over medium heat. Add the reserved asparagus tips and cook until very hot, about 1 minute. Season with salt and pepper. Add the ¼ cup parsley and add the drained tortelli to the asparagus. Add the crayfish with any accumulated juices and the remaining butter and toss together over medium heat until well blended.

9. Serve the tortelli in a heated serving bowl or pasta plates.

Pansotti di ricotta e cicoria

Pansotti with ricotta and bitter greens

SERVES 6 TO 8

Ricotta and bitter greens pansotti

Kosher salt, as needed

3 oz dandelion greens, trimmed

4 oz Swiss chard

1 oz (2 tbsp) unsalted butter

½ cup fresh ricotta

⅔ cup grated Pecorino Romano

1 large egg

1 lb Pasta Sheets (page 235)

Flour, as needed

Walnut sauce

2 slices white bread, crusts remove (about 2 slices)

3 oz (¾ cup) walnuts

3 tbsp walnut oil

1 small garlic clove

½ cup sour cream

Grated Grana Padano, as needed for serving

1. Bring a large pot of salted water to a boil. Add the dandelion greens and stir to submerge the leaves. Cook, uncovered, until tender and a deep green color, 3 to 4 minutes. Lift the greens out of the water with a sieve or slotted spoon and transfer to a bowl of ice water. Repeat with the chard. After the greens are chilled, drain in a colander for several minutes and then squeeze to remove as much water as you can. Finely chop the greens and set aside.

2. Heat a sauté pan over medium heat. Add the butter and, when it has melted, add the chopped greens and cook, stirring occasionally, until any moisture remaining in the greens has cooked away, about 5 minutes. Transfer the greens to a bowl and cool. Add the ricotta, Pecorino Romano, and the egg to the cooled greens and stir to blend evenly. Set aside.

3. Cut the pasta sheets into 3-inch squares. Place a teaspoon of ricotta filling in the center of each square. Fold the square over the filling to form a triangle, pressing the edges well to seal them. As you cut out the pansotti, place them on a plate or baking sheet sprinkled with a little flour to keep them from sticking.

4. Combine the bread in a bowl with enough water to moisten. Let the bread soak for about 15 minutes, then lift it from the water and squeeze out the excess water.

5. Combine the bread, walnuts, walnut oil, and garlic in a mortar and pound the ingredients together to form a thick paste. Transfer to a bowl and stir in the sour cream. Set aside.

6. Bring a large pot of salted water to a boil over high heat. Add the pansotti and stir to submerge and separate the pieces. Cook, uncovered, until just tender (al dente), 8 to 10 minutes. Drain the pansotti in a colander. Shake well to remove any excess water. Transfer to a large heated serving bowl, add the walnut sauce, and toss together until well coated. Serve at once with Grana Padano on the side.

Ravioli di branzino con salsa ai frutti di mare

Striped bass ravioli with seafood sauce

SERVES 4 TO 6

Branzino ravioli

3 slices white bread, torn into pieces

12 oz skinless branzino or striped bass fillets, pinbones removed and cut into small dice

2 egg yolks

2 tbsp grated Parmigiano-Reggiano

1 tbsp chopped flat-leaf parsley

½ tbsp chopped marjoram

Kosher salt and freshly ground black pepper, as needed

1 lb Pasta Sheets (page 235)

Egg wash: 1 large egg blended with 1 tbsp water

Flour, as needed

Seafood sauce

1½ lb langoustines or shrimp, head on if possible

6 tbsp extra-virgin olive oil

½ cup dry white wine

1½ lb baby clams, scrubbed

3 garlic cloves smashed

4 ripe plum tomatoes, peeled, seeded, and diced (see page 248)

½ cup chopped flat-leaf parsley

Extra-virgin olive oil, as needed for serving

1. Combine the bread in a bowl with enough water to moisten. Let the bread soak for about 15 minutes, then lift it from the water and squeeze dry.

2. Combine the branzino in a food processor with the egg yolks, the soaked bread, cheese, the 1 tablespoon parsley, marjoram, and a pinch of salt and pepper. Process just until it has come together to form a paste (it does not have to be totally smooth). Set aside.

3. Place one pasta sheet on a work surface and spoon mounds (about 1 tablespoon) of the branzino filling down the center of the sheet, placing them about 1½ inches apart. Brush the egg wash around the filling and then top with a second sheet of pasta. Press the pasta around the filling, eliminating any air pockets and sealing the pasta sheets together. Cut between the ravioli with a round or square cutter (or cut them with a knife). Set aside on a lightly floured baking sheet.

4. Peel and devein the langoustines or shrimp and pull off the heads. Reserve the shells and head separately from the meat.

5. Heat 3 tablespoons oil in a large pot over medium heat. Add the wine and the clams. Cover the pot and cook until the shells open, 6 to 8 minutes. Discard any unopened clams. Remove the clams from the pot and once they are cool enough to handle, pull the meat from the shells and place in a bowl. Strain the cooking liquid over the meat and set aside.

6. Heat the remaining 3 tablespoons oil in a wide saucepan over medium heat. Add the garlic and cook, stirring frequently, until the garlic is aromatic, about 1 minute.

7. Add the langoustine or shrimp shells and heads and sauté, stirring frequently, until the shells turn color and then remove and discard the shells and heads. Add the peeled langoustines or shrimp, the tomatoes, and half of the parsley and sauté until the shrimp change color and start to become opaque, about 2 minutes. Add the clams and cooking juices, bring to a simmer, and then keep warm while you cook the ravioli.

8. Bring a large pot of salted water to a boil over high heat. Add the ravioli to the boiling water and stir to submerge and separate them. Cook uncovered until just tender (al dente), 8 to 10 minutes. Drain the ravioli in a colander. Shake well to remove any excess water. Transfer to a large heated serving bowl and add the seafood sauce. Serve at once topped with a drizzle of oil and the remaining parsley.

Tortelli con stracchino e zucchine

Tortelli with stracchino cheese and zucchini

SERVES 4 TO 6

Stracchino tortelli

12 oz stracchino

½ cup fine fresh white bread crumbs

¼ cup grated Parmigiano-Reggiano, plus more as needed for serving

Kosher salt and freshly ground black pepper, as needed

1 lb Pasta Sheets (page 235)

Flour, as needed

2 tbsp extra-virgin olive oil

1 garlic clove smashed

1 lb zucchini (about 2 to 3 small), thinly sliced

¼ cup chopped flat-leaf parsley

1. Mix the stracchino with the bread crumbs in a bowl and then add the Parmigiano-Reggiano and a pinch of salt and black pepper. Cover the bowl and keep the filling refrigerated while you prepare the pasta.

2. Using a cutter, cut the pasta sheets into 3-inch circles. Place a teaspoon of cheese filling in the center of each circle. Fold the pasta circle in half over the filling and pinch the corners together to form a tortello. As you cut out the tortelli, place them on a plate or baking sheet sprinkled with a little flour to keep them from sticking.

3. Heat the oil in a wide sauté pan over medium heat. Add the garlic and cook until the garlic is light brown, about 1 minute. Add the zucchini and cook, stirring, until softened slightly, about 3 minutes. Season with salt and pepper. Add the parsley, and set aside.

4. Bring a large pot of salted water to a boil over high heat. Add the tortelli and stir to submerge and separate them. Cook, uncovered, until just tender (al dente), 8 to 10 minutes. Drain the tortelli in a colander. Shake well to remove any excess water. Transfer the drained tortelli to the pan with the zucchini and toss together over medium heat until well blended.

5. Serve the tortelli in a heated serving bowl or in pasta plates, and pass the Parmigiano-Reggiano on the side.

Recipe note *You can also dice the zucchini very small, sauté them, and mix them into the filling in step 1. Serve with tomato sauce or butter and sage sauce.*

Ravioloni con piselli e scampetti

Large ravioli with peas and langoustines

SERVES 6

Ham and fresh pea ravioloni

Kosher salt, as needed

6 oz shelled fresh garden peas

1 oz (2 tbsp) unsalted butter

2 tbsp minced shallot

2 oz ham, diced

Freshly ground black pepper, as needed

⅓ cup grated Parmigiano-Reggiano

2 tbsp chopped chervil

1 lb Pasta Sheets (page 235)

Egg wash: 1 large egg mixed with 1 tbsp water

Flour, as needed

Langoustine and tomato broth

3 ripe plum tomatoes, peeled (see page 248)

3 oz (6 tbsp) unsalted butter

6 langoustines

2 shallots, thinly sliced

2 garlic cloves, smashed

¼ cup dry white wine

1 bay leaf

2 thyme sprigs

2 cups water, or as needed

1. Bring a pot of salted water to a boil. Add the peas and cook until they are just tender, about 3 minutes (time will vary depending upon the size and freshness of the peas). Drain and rinse under cold running water; this will stop the cooking and retain the peas' bright green color. Let the peas drain thoroughly after they are cool.

2. Heat the 2 tablespoons of butter in a saucepan over medium heat. Add the shallot and cook, stirring frequently, until it is tender, about 2 minutes. Add the ham and sauté until it is hot, about 2 minutes, then add the peas. Cook until all of the ingredients are very hot, about 2 minutes. Season with a pinch of salt and pepper, and transfer the mixture to a food processor. Let it cool for about 5 minutes and then purée, pulsing the machine on and off, just until it is finely ground but not pasty.

3. Transfer the purée to a bowl and stir in the cheese and chervil. Refrigerate the filling to make it easier to fill the ravioloni.

4. Cut the tomatoes in half lengthwise and scoop out the seeds and core; reserve these tomato trimmings in a small bowl for the broth (step 5). Cut the tomato flesh into small dice and reserve in a separate bowl to finish the dish (step 9).

5. Pull the heads and shells from the langoustines. Reserve the tails to finish the ravioloni (step 7). Heat ¼ cup of the butter in a saucepan over medium heat. Add the langoustine shells and heads and sauté, stirring frequently, until they are brightly colored, about 2 minutes. Add the shallots and the garlic and continue to cook, stirring, until the shallots are golden, about 3 minutes.

6. Add the white wine and simmer until it evaporates, and then add the herbs and the tomato trimmings. Add enough water to cover the shells, reduce the heat to low, and simmer the broth until flavorful, about 20 minutes. Strain the broth into a clean pan and continue to simmer until it has reduced to about ¾ cup. Set aside.

Continued

7. Brush one sheet of the pasta with some of the egg wash. Spoon the filling in 6 mounds (about 2 ounces each) down the center of the dough. Place a langoustine tail on top of each mound. Cover with the second pasta sheet and press the dough together around the filling to seal the sheets together and to remove any air pockets. Using a 4-inch round cutter, cut out the ravioloni. Transfer to a lightly floured baking sheet as the ravioloni are completed.

8. Heat the remaining butter in a saucepan over medium heat. Add the reserved diced tomatoes and the langoustine-tomato broth and simmer just until the tomatoes are hot, about 2 minutes. Set aside.

9. Bring a large pot of salted water to a boil over high heat. Add the ravioloni and cook, uncovered, at a gentle boil until just tender (al dente), 4 to 5 minutes. Using a skimmer or slotted spoon, lift the ravioloni from the pan and transfer to the pan with the langoustine-tomato broth. Swirl the pan over low heat until the ravioloni are coated and the sauce has thickened, about 2 minutes.

10. Serve the ravioloni on heated pasta plates.

Fagottini di crespelle con caprino fresco, miele e maggiorana

Crespelle bundles filled with fresh goat cheese, honey, and marjoram

SERVES 6

Goat cheese filling

12 oz fresh goat cheese

2 tbsp chopped marjoram

Kosher salt and freshly ground
black pepper, as needed

2 tbsp heavy cream, use only
if needed

1 tbsp unsalted butter, plus more
as needed for the baking dish

6 Crespelle (page 242)

6 long pieces of chives to tie up
the crespelle

¼ cup minced yellow onion

½ cup almonds

¼ cup raisins

½ cup heavy cream

3 tbsp honey, gently warmed,
as needed for serving

Slivered almonds, toasted,
as needed for garnish

Chopped marjoram leaves, as
needed for garnish

1. Mix the goat cheese with the marjoram and a pinch of salt and pepper until evenly blended. If the filling seems too dry and crumbly, you may add some of the cream, but keep in mind that the goat cheese will get soft once it bakes.

2. Preheat the oven to 350°F. Lightly brush a baking dish with butter.

3. Fill the crespelle with about 2 ounces of filling. Fold the crespelle over and tie the crespelle around the top with a piece of chive. Place the fagottini in the prepared baking dish.

4. Bake the fagottini until the goat cheese is hot and the crespelle have a golden color, 10 to 15 minutes.

5. While the fagottini are baking, heat the 1 tablespoon of butter in a sauté pan over medium-low heat. Add the onion and cook, stirring, until tender, about 2 minutes. Add the almonds and raisins and cook until the almonds turn brown and have a good aroma, about 1 minute. Add the cream and simmer long enough to blend the flavors and thicken the sauce slightly, about 5 minutes, then blend to a smooth sauce.

6. To serve the fagottini, spoon some of the cream and almond sauce on a warmed plate and place the fagottini on top. Drizzle with the warmed honey and sprinkle with toasted almond slivers and marjoram leaves.

Crespelle al vapore con verdurine primaverili

Gratin of crespelle stuffed with spring vegetables

SERVES 6

Herb emulsion

¼ cup shredded basil

¼ cup minced flat-leaf parsley

¼ cup minced tarragon

½ cup extra-virgin olive oil, or as needed

Kosher salt and freshly ground black pepper, as needed

Spring vegetable filling

1 cup diced leek or spring onion (white and light green parts)

1 cup sliced baby zucchini

1½ cups diced white mushrooms

1 cup diced carrot

1 cup trimmed peeled asparagus pieces

3 tbsp extra-virgin olive oil

1½ oz (3 tbsp) unsalted butter

3 garlic cloves

1 cup shelled fresh garden peas

3 tbsp grated Parmigiano-Reggiano

6 Crespelle (page 242)

Wrapping the crespelle in a zucchini blossom gives this dish a special look. This is a little more advanced in technique than other dishes.

1. Combine the basil, parsley, and tarragon with ¼ cup of the olive oil in a food processor or blender and purée until you have a very smooth sauce. Add more oil as you are puréeing the herbs, if necessary. Transfer the purée to a small bowl and season lightly with salt and pepper. Set aside. If made in advance, the purée can be stored in a covered container in the refrigerator for 2 days.

2. Bring a pot of salted water to a boil over high heat. Add the leeks or green onions; once the water returns to a boil, scoop them out of the boiling water with a slotted spoon and transfer to colander to drain and cool. Add the zucchini and mushrooms to the water and let the water return to the boil. Scoop them out of the water and transfer to the colander with the leeks or green onions.

3. Add the carrots to the boiling water and let them cook at a boil until tender, about 2 minutes; transfer to the colander with the other vegetables. Add the asparagus and cook at a boil until tender and still bright green, about 2 minutes; transfer to a bowl of ice water (this will keep the asparagus nice and green) and, once cooled, transfer to the colander with the remaining vegetables.

4. Heat 3 tablespoons of oil and the butter in a sauté pan over low heat. When the butter has melted, add the garlic and cook, gently swirling the garlic in the oil, until the garlic is aromatic, about 1 minute.

5. Add the vegetables and the peas. Season with a pinch of salt and pepper, cover the pan, and stew the vegetables gently until they are fully cooked and tender, 3 to 4 minutes.

6. Transfer the vegetables to a bowl and stir in the cheese. Taste and season with salt and pepper as needed. Remove and discard the garlic cloves. Set aside.

Continued

Spring vegetable filling

1 oz (2 tbsp) unsalted butter

6 zucchini blossoms, cleaned

Robiola and mascarpone sauce

1 cup fresh robiola or cream cheese

½ cup mascarpone

2 cups whole milk, or as needed

2 tbsp extra-virgin olive oil

2 or 3 ripe plum tomatoes, peeled, seeded, and diced (page 248)

3 tbsp pitted and thinly sliced green olives, such as Taggiasche

7. Fill each crespella with about ½ cup of the stuffing as follows: Mound the filling mixture near the center of the crespella. Fold in each side (about 1 inch) and then fold the bottom of the crespella up and over the filling. Roll the crespella up until you have the filling completely enclosed.

8. Heat the 2 tablespoons of butter in a sauté pan over low heat. Add the zucchini blossoms, one or two at a time, and cook just long enough for the blossom to wilt, 10 to 15 seconds. Transfer to a plate.

9. Wrap each filled crespella with one of the zucchini blossoms and place the finished crespelle on a steaming rack. (The crespelle can be prepared and filled ahead of time and held in the refrigerator for up to 2 days.)

10. Place the crespelle, still on the steaming rack, over simmering water. Cover tightly and steam until very hot, 6 to 8 minutes.

11. Drizzle the 2 tablespoons of oil over the diced tomatoes, season them with salt and pepper, and set aside.

12. Make the sauce by combining the robiola or cream cheese and mascarpone with the milk in a saucepan over medium-low heat until the sauce is heat through, creamy, and smooth, about 3 minutes. Season with a pinch of salt, if necessary.

13. To serve the crespelle, spoon some of the robiola sauce onto warmed plates. Drizzle a few drops of the herb emulsion around the edge of the sauce and add some of the olives and the diced tomatoes. Place a crespella on the top of the sauce, brush the top lightly with oil, and sprinkle with salt. The crespelle may be served hot or warm.

Rotolo di pasta con ricotta, spinaci e prosciutto cotto

Pasta rolled with ricotta, spinach, and ham

SERVES 6 TO 8

Ricotta, spinach, and ham filling

Kosher salt, as needed

8 oz fresh spinach

2 oz (¼ cup) unsalted butter

1 shallot, minced

4 oz ham, thinly sliced and coarsely chopped

1⅓ cups fresh ricotta

⅔ cup grated Parmigiano-Reggiano

2 egg yolks

Freshly ground black pepper, as needed

Freshly ground nutmeg, as needed

Melted butter as needed for the baking dish and to brush the rotolo

1 lb Rotolo Sheets (page 235), cooked and cooled

Grated Parmigiano-Reggiano, as needed for the topping

1. Cook the spinach in boiling salted water for 1 minute. Drain in a colander and rinse under running cold water. When cool enough to handle, squeeze dry and finely chop. Set aside.

2. In a sauté pan, melt the ¼ cup of butter and sweat the shallot over medium heat until tender, about 5 minutes. Add the ham and sauté for 3 minutes, then add the chopped spinach and cook for 2 minutes more.

3. Let the mixture cool slightly. In a mixing bowl, combine the ricotta with the Parmigiano-Reggiano, egg yolks, and the spinach-ham mixture. Mix well and season with salt, pepper, and nutmeg.

4. Preheat the oven to 375°F. Brush a baking dish or casserole with melted butter and set aside.

5. Place each pasta sheet on a flat surface and spread a ¼-inch-thick layer of filling over the entire sheet, then roll the pasta to form logs about 3 inches in diameter.

6. Cool the rolls of pasta for few hours, then cut in 1-inch-thick pieces. Place the pieces, cut side down, in the buttered baking dish, sprinkle with Parmigiano-Reggiano, and drizzle with melted butter. Bake until very hot and golden brown, 15 to 20 minutes. Serve directly from the baking dish.

Lasagna con asparagi e fontina

Lasagna with asparagus and fontina

SERVES 6 TO 8

Melted butter, as needed for baking dish

Besciamella Sauce (page 249)

1 lb Lasagna Sheets (page 325), cooked and cooled

1 lb asparagus, peeled if necessary and blanched

6 large hard-cooked eggs (see page 6), peeled and chopped (optional)

10 oz Fontina, thinly sliced or cut into small dice

½ cup chopped flat-leaf parsley

1¼ cups grated Parmigiano-Reggiano

2 tbsp thinly sliced chives

1. Preheat the oven to 350°F. Brush a baking dish with some melted butter.

2. Spread about ¾ cup of the besciamella sauce on the bottom of the baking dish, then add a layer of the lasagna sheets. Top the pasta with another ¾ cup of besciamella, a layer of the asparagus, and a layer of egg, if using. Add about one-third of the Fontina, parsley, and Parmigiano-Reggiano. Repeat this layering sequence two more times, ending with a layer of lasagna sheets, topped with besciamella, the remaining asparagus, and the remaining Parmigiano-Reggiano.

3. Bake the lasagna until it is very hot all the way through and the top is golden brown and bubbly, about 30 minutes. Let the lasagna rest for about 15 minutes before cutting and serving. Serve the lasagna topped with the chives.

Recipe notes *If you don't have time to make your own pasta, you can buy good-quality lasagna pasta at any supermarket. We recommend a parboiled lasagna, which does not need to be cooked before assembly, but make sure you leave your besciamella sauce a little looser so the pasta can absorb some liquid.*

If you have some sauce left over, you can store it refrigerated for about 3 days.

Gnocchi soffiati al salmone affumicato e aspergi

Baked smoked salmon gnocchi with asparagus

SERVES 6

1 cup whole milk

3 oz (6 tbsp) unsalted butter, plus more as needed for baking dish

Kosher salt, as needed

Pinch of freshly grated nutmeg (optional)

¾ cup all-purpose flour

8 oz smoked salmon, processed to a paste

3 large eggs

18 asparagus spears (about 1 lb), trimmed, peeled, and blanched

⅔ cup grated Parmigiano-Reggiano

1 cup heavy cream, or as needed

1. Heat the milk, ¼ cup of the butter, salt to taste, and a few grains of nutmeg in a heavy sauce pot over medium heat. Slowly add the flour, making sure you are whisking continuously. Let simmer gently, stirring with a wooden spoon, until the mixture is very thick and pulls away from the sides of the pot, 3 to 5 minutes. Transfer to a bowl and stir in the salmon paste. Add the eggs, one at a time, stirring to incorporate each one well before adding the next.

2. To shape the gnocchi: Transfer the dough into a pastry bag fitted with a ½-inch plain tip. Pipe gnocchi directly over a pot of salted boiling water, cutting the dough into ¾-inch-long pieces while piping. As soon as the gnocchi rise to the top, lift them from the pot and transfer them to a bowl of ice water. Once they are thoroughly chilled, transfer them to paper towels to drain and blot dry.

3. Preheat the oven to 375°F and generously butter a baking dish.

4. Add the asparagus to the buttered baking dish in a single layer and sprinkle with the cheese. Add the gnocchi in a single layer; do not place them too close to each other as they will double in size as they bake. Pour enough cream into the dish to cover the asparagus by half. Bake until the gnocchi have doubled in size and the cream has reduced into a thick sauce, about 15 minutes. Serve at once, directly from the baking dish on heated plates.

Gnocchi di pane, pancetta e cicoria

Bread and dandelion dumplings

SERVES 6

1½ lb bread, cut in thin slices and dried overnight

4 qt Meat Broth (page 251) or chicken broth

Kosher salt, as needed

1 lb dandelion greens, trimmed

2 oz (¼ cup) unsalted butter

2 oz pancetta, minced

1 medium yellow onion, minced

2 large eggs

½ cup all-purpose flour

1¼ cups grated Parmigiano-Reggiano

Freshly grated nutmeg, as needed

1. Place the bread in a bowl and add enough of the broth to moisten the bread without making it soggy, about 4 cups. Cover with plastic wrap and let it rest for 1 hour.

2. Bring a large pot of generously salted water to a boil. Add the dandelion greens all at once and stir to submerge the leaves. Cook, uncovered, until tender and a deep color, 3 to 4 minutes. Lift the greens out of the water with a sieve or slotted spoon and transfer to a bowl of ice water. After the greens are chilled, drain in a colander for several minutes and then squeeze them with your hands to remove as much water as you can. Use a chef's knife to finely chop the dandelion.

3. Heat the butter in a sauté pan over medium-high heat. Add the pancetta and cook, stirring as needed, until it is crisp, about 1 minute. Add the onions and continue to cook, stirring frequently, until they are tender, about 3 minutes. Add the greens and sauté just long enough to combine them with the onions and flavor them with the pancetta and butter, about 2 minutes.

4. Lift the bread out of the broth and squeeze lightly. Transfer to a second bowl, add the greens, eggs, flour, and half of the cheese. Season with salt and nutmeg and knead to make a uniform dough. Pat the dough into rough dumplings about 1 inch in diameter.

5. Bring the rest of the broth to a boil. Add the dumplings, reduce the heat, and let them simmer until cooked through to the center, about 10 minutes.

6. Serve the gnocchi in heated soup plates and ladle enough of the broth over the top to cover them by about half. Sprinkle with the rest of the cheese.

Gnocchi di patate con asparagi, coniglio e fegatini

Potato gnocchi with asparagus, rabbit, and liver

SERVES 6

Rabbit ragù

1 whole rabbit (about 2½ lb)

6 rabbit or chicken hearts, split lengthwise

Kosher salt and freshly ground pepper, as needed

¼ cup extra-virgin olive oil

1 medium yellow onion, chopped

2 or 3 cups Rabbit Broth (page 253), or as needed

Rabbit loins and livers sautéed with pancetta

Boneless rabbit loins from trimmed rabbit

2 tsp thyme

3 oz pancetta (about 4 slices)

3 rabbit or chicken livers, cut in half

2 tbsp dry Marsala

1 tbsp extra-virgin olive oil

1 tbsp unsalted butter

Continued

1. Trim the rabbit and cut as much meat as possible from the bones. Remove the rabbit loins in one piece and set aside. Cut the remaining meat into 1-inch cubes for the ragù and reserve separately. Reserve the heart and liver for the ragù separately as well. Reserve the bones to make the rabbit broth as directed on page 253.

2. Season the cubed rabbit meat and the rabbit and chicken hearts with salt and pepper.

3. Heat the ¼ cup oil in a deep pot or Dutch oven over medium-high heat. Add the rabbit meat and hearts and brown, turning as necessary to color evenly, about 6 minutes total. Add the onion and continue cooking, stirring frequently, until the onion is a rich, gold color, about 8 minutes. Add enough of the rabbit broth to barely cover the meat and bring to a simmer over low heat.

4. Cook slowly, covered, until the meat is tender, 2 to 3 hours. Stir occasionally to keep the rabbit evenly moistened. The liquid should reduce to a rich sauce that coats the meat. Taste and season with salt and pepper. If the ragù is made in advance, let cool and store it in a covered container in the refrigerator for up to 3 days. Reheat the ragù over medium-low heat before serving, if necessary.

5. While the meat is cooking, season the rabbit loins with salt and pepper and some thyme. Lay each loin on top of 2 pancetta slices and roll. Secure with butcher's twine or toothpicks. Season the livers with salt, pepper, and the Marsala. Heat the 1 tablespoon oil and 1 tablespoon butter in a sauté pan over medium heat. Add the rabbit loins and sauté, turning until they are a rich golden brown and just cooked through, about 5 minutes. Remove from heat, remove the string or toothpick and keep warm.

Continued

Pan-steamed asparagus

3 tbsp extra-virgin olive oil

1 tbsp butter

1 garlic clove, peeled and smashed

12 asparagus spears, trimmed, stem peeled, cut into 1½-inch lengths

1½ lb Potato Gnocchi (page 245)

3 oz (6 tbsp) unsalted butter

6 tbsp grated Parmigiano-Reggiano, plus as needed for serving

6. In the same pan, cook the livers and the Marsala over medium-low heat until they are just cooked but still slightly pink in the center, about 2 minutes on each side. Sprinkle the livers with thyme and keep warm.

7. In a separate sauté pan, heat the 3 tablespoons extra-virgin olive oil and 1 tablespoon of butter over medium heat. Add the garlic. As soon as the garlic starts frying, add the asparagus and sauté for a few minutes. Add about 2 tablespoons of water to help steam the asparagus, cover the pan, and cook them until just done. Season with salt and pepper and keep warm.

8. Bring a large pot of salted water to a boil over high heat. Add the gnocchi and cook just until they float to the surface, 3 to 4 minutes. Transfer the cooked gnocchi to a large bowl and add the 6 tablespoons of butter. Toss to coat in butter. Add the cheese and toss to coat.

9. Place the gnocchi on heated pasta plates. Cut the loins into 3 pieces each. Top the gnocchi with one piece of loin, one heart, and one piece of liver per serving. Serve immediately. Sprinkle with additional cheese and/or freshly cracked black pepper if desired.

Strangolapreti

Bread and swiss chard dumplings

SERVES 6 TO 8

1 loaf Italian bread (about 2 lb), thinly sliced

1 qt whole milk, warmed, or as needed

Kosher salt, as needed

1 lb Swiss chard

3 oz (6 tbsp) unsalted butter

2 oz pancetta (2 or 3 slices)

1 small yellow onion, minced

¼ cup all-purpose or tipo 00 flour

1 large egg

2 egg yolks

1¼ cups grated Parmigiano-Reggiano

Freshly grated nutmeg, as needed

6 sage leaves

1. Place the bread in a bowl and add enough of the milk to moisten the bread without making it soggy. Cover with plastic wrap and let rest for 1 hour.

2. Bring a large pot of salted water to a boil over high heat. Add the Swiss chard and stir to submerge the leaves. Cook, uncovered, until tender and a deep green color, 3 to 4 minutes. Remove the chard from the water with a sieve or slotted spoon and transfer to a bowl of ice water. After the chard is chilled, drain in a colander for several minutes and then squeeze dry. Finely chop the chard and set aside.

3. Heat 3 tablespoons of the butter in a sauté pan over medium-high heat. Add the pancetta and cook, stirring as needed, until crisp, about 1 minute. Add the onions and continue to cook, stirring frequently, until they are tender, about 3 minutes. Add the chopped chard and sauté just long enough to combine them with the onions and flavor them with the pancetta and butter, about 2 minutes.

4. Lift the bread out of the milk and squeeze lightly. Transfer to a large bowl and add the sautéed greens, whole egg, egg yolks, flour, and half of the cheese. Season with salt and nutmeg and knead to form a uniform dough. Pat the dough into rough dumplings about 1 inch in diameter.

5. Bring a large pot of salted water to a boil. Add the dumplings, reduce the heat, and let simmer until cooked through, about 3 minutes.

6. While the dumplings are cooking, heat the remaining 3 tablespoons butter in a saucepan over medium heat, swirling the pan occasionally, until is it browned, about 2 minutes. Add the sage leaves and continue to cook until they are crisp, about 1 minute.

7. Drain the dumplings in a colander. Shake well to remove any excess water. Serve the dumplings in heated soup plates sprinkled with the remaining Parmigiano-Reggiano and topped with the brown butter and crisped sage leaves.

Risotto with calamari and fresh peas

SERVES 6

2½ qt Meat Broth (page 251) or Fish Broth (page 252)

6 oz (¾ cup) unsalted butter

¾ cup minced yellow onion

1 lb (2¼ cups) Carnaroli rice

½ cup dry white wine

1 cup shelled fresh garden peas

1 lb calamari, trimmed and cut into thin strips

¼ cup minced chervil

¼ cup grated Parmigiano-Reggiano

Kosher salt, as needed

1. Heat the broth over low heat; keep warm.

2. Heat ½ cup of the butter in a large pot over low heat. Add the onion and cook, stirring frequently, until the onion is tender and translucent, about 4 minutes. Add the rice and toast lightly, stirring frequently, about 2 minutes.

3. Add the wine and cook until the wine evaporates, 2 minutes. Add enough of the broth to come ½ inch above the rice and cook, stirring frequently to be sure the rice doesn't stick to the bottom. As the rice absorbs the broth, keep adding more, ½ cup at a time.

4. Once the rice has absorbed almost all the broth, and the grains are al dente, about 12 minutes total cooking time, add the peas and continue to cook, for about 4 minutes. Add the calamari, stir into the risotto, and cook for about 1 minute. Remove the pot from the heat. Add the chervil, the remaining ¼ cup butter, and the cheese and stir vigorously until the risotto is creamy. Taste and season with salt, as needed.

5. Serve the risotto on flat plates.

Risotto di scampi con erbette fresche

Risotto with langoustines and fresh herbs

SERVES 6

6 cups Langoustine Broth (page 253)

6 oz (¾ cup) unsalted butter

¾ cup minced yellow onion

1 lb (2¼ cups) Carnaroli rice

2 tbsp extra-virgin olive oil

Tails from 18 small langoustines, peeled and deveined, cut into 1-inch pieces

½ cup minced mixed herbs, such as chervil, chives, tarragon, parsley, and marjoram

2 tbsp grated Parmigiano-Reggiano cheese

Kosher salt, as needed

1. Heat the broth over low heat; keep warm.

2. Heat ½ cup of the butter in a large pot over low heat. Add the onion and cook, stirring frequently, until the onion is tender and translucent, about 4 minutes. Add the rice and toast lightly, stirring frequently, about 2 minutes.

3. Add enough of the broth to come ½ inch above the rice and cook, stirring frequently to be sure the rice doesn't stick to the bottom. As the rice absorbs the broth, keep adding more, ½ cup at a time.

4. While the risotto is cooking, heat the oil in a sauté pan over medium heat. Add the sliced langoustine tails and sauté until they are just cooked through, about 2 minutes.

5. Once the rice has absorbed all the broth, and the grains are al dente, about 18 minutes total cooking time, remove the pot from the heat. Add the herbs, the remaining ¼ cup butter, and the cheese and stir vigorously until the risotto is creamy. Taste and season with salt, as needed.

6. Serve the risotto on flat plates topped with the sautéed langoustines.

Risotto con cozze, zafferano e fiori di zucchine

Risotto with mussels, saffron, and zucchini blossoms

SERVES 6

Pan-steamed mussels

2 tbsp extra-virgin olive oil

2 garlic cloves

1 lb mussels, scrubbed and debearded

½ cup white wine

1 bay leaf

10 to 12 baby zucchini with blossoms

2½ qt Meat Broth (page 251)

7 oz (14 tbsp) unsalted butter

¾ cup minced yellow onion

1 lb (2¼ cups) Carnaroli rice

½ cup dry white wine

¼ cup grated Parmigiano-Reggiano

Kosher salt, as needed

1. Heat the oil in a large pot over medium-high heat. Add the garlic and saute, stirring frequently, until golden and aromatic, about 2 minutes. Add the mussels, wine, and bay leaf. Cover the pot tightly and let the mussels steam until they are completely open and transfer to a bowl. Discard any mussels that do not open. When they are cool enough to hand, pull the mussels from the shells and transfer to a bowl. Strain the cooking liquid over the mussels and set aside.

2. Pull the blossoms from the zucchini. Cut the blossoms in thin strips and cut the zucchini crosswise in thin disks. Set aside.

3. Heat the broth over low heat; keep warm.

4. Heat ½ cup of the butter in a large pot over low heat. Add the onion and cook, stirring frequently, until the onion is tender and translucent, about 4 minutes. Add the rice and toast lightly, stirring frequently, about 2 minutes.

5. Add the wine and cook until the wine evaporates, about 2 minutes. Add enough of the broth to come ½ inch above the rice and cook, stirring frequently to be sure the rice doesn't stick to the bottom. As the rice absorbs the broth, keep adding more, ½ cup at a time.

6. Once the rice has absorbed almost all the broth, and the grains are just tender (al dente), about 14 minutes total cooking time, add the zucchini blossoms and zucchini and continue to cook until the rice and zucchini are cooked, another 2 minutes. Add the mussels and their cooking liquid and cook until the mussels are heated through, another 2 minutes. Remove the pot from the heat. Add the remaining 6 tablespoons butter and stir vigorously until the risotto is creamy. Taste and season with salt, as needed.

7. Serve the risotto on flat plates.

Riso e bisi

Rice and peas

SERVES 4 TO 6

8 oz (½ cup) unsalted butter

1 medium onion, minced

½ cup chopped flat-leaf parsley

2 lb fresh garden peas, shelled

1 qt chicken or vegetable broth

Kosher salt, as needed

10 oz (1½ cups) Carnaroli or Vialone nano rice

¾ cup Parmagiano-Reggiano, grated

Freshly ground black pepper, as necessary

1. Heat ¼ cup of the butter in a small saucepan over medium heat. Add half of the onion and cook, stirring frequently, until tender and translucent, about 4 minutes. Add half of the parsley, and then the peas. Stir to coat the peas with the butter. Add 1 cup of the broth and bring to a gentle simmer until the peas are cooked but still firm, 5 to 7 minutes. Set aside.

2. Heat the remaining broth over low heat; keep warm. Season with salt.

3. Heat 4 tablespoons of the butter in a large pot over low heat. Add the remaining onion and cook, stirring frequently, until the onion is tender and translucent, about 4 minutes. Add the rice and toast lightly, stirring frequently, about 2 minutes.

4. Add enough of the broth to come ½ inch above the rice the broth and cook, stirring frequently to be sure the rice doesn't stick to the bottom. As the rice absorbs the broth, keep adding more, ½ cup at a time.

5. Once the rice has absorbed almost all the broth, and is al dente, about 16 minutes total cooking time, add the peas and their cooking liquid and continue to cook until the all of the ingredients are fully cooked, 2 minutes more. Remove the pot from the heat. Add the remaining ¼ cup butter and parsley and the cheese and stir vigorously until the risotto is creamy. Season with salt and pepper as needed.

6. Serve the risotto on flat plates.

   Recipe note *This type of risotto dish is supposed to be a little soupy. Allow the rice to rest for few minutes and then serve it.*

Risotto con asparagi selvatici e spugnole

Risotto with wild asparagus and morels

SERVES 6

½ lb morels

Kosher salt, as needed

½ lb wild asparagus, trimmed

5 oz (10 tablespoons) unsalted butter, cubed

3 garlic cloves, peeled and minced

2 thyme sprigs

2½ qt Meat Broth (page 251)

1¼ cups minced yellow onion

1 lb (2¼ cups) Carnaroli rice

½ cup dry white wine

½ cup grated Parmigiano-Reggiano

Freshly ground black pepper, as needed

1. Soak the morels in a bowl of water for 1 minute and use your fingertips to gently stir them to remove any dirt. Remove the mushrooms from the bowl, and pour out the water. Repeat this step until the mushrooms are clean. Spread them on a tray lined with a paper towels to remove any excess water, then cut in half or quarters, if they are large.

2. Bring a large pot of salted water to a boil over high heat. Add the asparagus and cook, uncovered, until the asparagus is tender-crisp and a bright color, about 2 minutes. Drain and rinse under cold running water. Set aside.

3. Heat 3 tablespoons of the butter in a sauté pan over medium heat. Add the garlic cloves and the thyme. When the garlic is just starting to take on a little color, about 2 minutes, add the morels and continue to cook until the mushrooms are hot, 2 or 3 minutes more. Remove the pan from the heat and reserve.

4. Heat the broth over low heat; keep warm. Season with salt.

5. Heat 4 tablespoons of the butter in a large pot over low heat. Add the onion and sweat until tender, about 5 minutes. Add the rice and toast lightly without letting the rice or onion take on any color.

6. Add the wine and cook until almost dry, about 2 minutes. Add enough of the broth to come ½ inch above the rice, and cook, stirring frequently to be sure the rice doesn't stick to the bottom. As the rice absorbs the broth, keep adding more, ½ cup at a time. During the last 5 minutes of the cooking time (after about 14 minutes), add the reserved morels and asparagus.

7. Once the rice has absorbed almost all the broth, and is just tender (al dente), about 18 minutes total cooking time, remove from the heat. Add the remaining butter and the cheese, and stir vigorously to develop a creamy texture.

8. Taste the risotto, season with salt and pepper as needed, and serve on flat plates.

Risotto con fave, piselli e menta

Risotto with fava beans, peas, and mint

SERVES 4 TO 6

2 lb unshelled fresh fava beans

1 lb unshelled fresh garden peas

1 qt chicken or vegetable broth

Kosher salt, as needed

6 tbsp extra-virgin olive oil

1 medium onion, minced

10 oz (1½ cups) Carnaroli or Vialone nano rice

1 cup dry white wine

4 oz (½ cup) unsalted butter, cut into cubes

½ cup chopped flat-leaf parsley

¼ cup thinly sliced mint

¾ cup grated Parmigiano-Reggiano cheese

Freshly ground black pepper, as needed

When shopping for favas, look for small, smooth pods; the ones that are a little split or broken are past their prime.

1. Shell the favas and the peas and keep them separate. If necessary, remove the tough outer skin from the fava beans by pinching the outer skin between your thumb and forefinger, and discard the skins.

2. Heat the broth over low heat; keep warm. Season with salt.

3. Heat the oil in a large pot over low heat. Add the onion and sweat until tender, about 5 minutes. Add the rice and toast lightly without letting the rice or onion take on any color.

4. Add the wine and cook until almost dry, about 2 minutes. Add enough of the broth to come ½ inch above the rice, and cook, stirring frequently to be sure the rice doesn't stick to the bottom. As the rice absorbs the broth, keep adding more, ½ cup at a time. After the rice has cooked for about 6 minutes, add the fava beans and peas. Continue adding broth and cooking the risotto until the rice is cooked but still al dente.

5. Once the rice has absorbed almost all the broth, and it is still al dente, about 18 minutes total cooking time, remove from the heat. Add the butter, parsley, mint, and cheese and stir vigorously to develop a creamy texture.

6. Taste the risotto, season with salt and pepper as needed, and serve on flat plates.

Risotto con fiori di zucchine e tartufo

Risotto with zucchini blossoms and truffles

SERVES 4 TO 6

Zucchini purée

2 tbsp extra-virgin olive oil

1 medium shallot, minced

3 cups sliced baby zucchini

2 tbsp chopped flat-leaf parsley

¼ cup beef or chicken broth

Risotto

1 qt chicken or vegetable broth

Kosher salt and freshly ground black pepper, as needed

6 tbsp extra-virgin olive oil

1 medium yellow onion, minced

10 oz (1½ cups) Carnaroli or Vialone Nano rice

1 cup dry white wine

4 oz (½ cup) unsalted butter, cut into cubes

½ cup chopped flat-leaf parsley

¾ cup grated Parmigiano-Reggiano cheese

12 to 15 zucchini blossoms, pistils removed and torn

2 oz black or white truffle, shaved

1. Heat 2 tablespoons of the oil in a saucepan over medium heat. Add the shallot and zucchini and toss for 1 minute, add the 2 tablespoons parsley and the ¼ cup broth. Cover the pan and simmer gently simmer until zucchini is tender, 3 to 5 minutes. Remove from heat and let the zucchini cool for a few minutes. Transfer to a blender and purée.

2. Heat the 1 quart of broth over low heat; keep warm. Season with salt.

3. Heat the 6 tablespoons oil in a large pot over low heat. Add the onion and sweat until tender, about 5 minutes. Add the rice and toast lightly without letting the rice or onion take on any color.

4. Add the wine and cook until almost dry. Add enough of the broth to come ½ inch above the rice, and cook, stirring frequently to be sure the rice doesn't stick to the bottom. As the rice absorbs the broth, keep adding more, a ½ cup at a time. When the risotto has absorbed all the broth, add the zucchini purée and continue to cook until the rice is fully cooked but still al dente, about 18 minutes total cooking time, remove from the heat. Add the butter, cheese, zucchini blossoms, and stir vigorously to develop a creamy texture.

5. Taste the risotto, season with salt and pepper as needed, and serve on flat plates topped with the truffle shavings.

Risotto nero integrale con ragù di vedurine primaverili

Whole grain black risotto with spring vegetable ragù

SERVES 6

Ragù of spring vegetables

Kosher salt, as needed

1 cup sliced ramps

½ cup diced carrot

½ cup shelled fresh garden peas

½ cup shelled fresh fava beans, peeled if necessary (see page 256)

1 cup asparagus pieces

1½ oz (3 tbsp) unsalted butter

3 tbsp extra-virgin olive oil

3 garlic cloves

1 cup sliced baby zucchini

1 cup diced white mushrooms

Freshly ground black pepper, as needed

6 tbsp peeled, seeded, and diced tomatoes (see page 248)

Spring onion sauce

2 tbsp extra-virgin olive oil

1 cup sliced spring onions

1 dried red chile

Risotto

2 qt Meat Broth (page 251) or vegetable broth

2 tbsp extra-virgin olive oil

1 cup minced onion

9 oz (1¼ cups) black rice, preferably Venere

3 tbsp unsalted butter

1½ cups grated Parmigiano-Reggiano, or as needed

1. Bring a pot of salted water to a boil over high heat. Add the ramps, carrots, peas, fava beans, and asparagus and cook just until barely tender and brightly colored. Drain and rinse with cold running water.

2. Heat the 3 tablespoons butter and 3 tablespoons olive oil in a sauté pan over medium heat. Add the garlic cloves and cook, stirring frequently, until aromatic, about 1 minute. Add the ramps, carrots, peas, fava beans, asparagus, zucchini, and mushrooms. Season with salt and pepper and cook, stirring frequently, until all of the ingredients are very hot, about 5 minutes. Remove and discard the garlic. Set aside.

3. Heat the 2 tablespoons extra-virgin olive oil in a saucepan over medium heat. Add the spring onions and cook, stirring frequently, until tender, about 2 minutes. Add a pinch of salt, the chile, and about 2 tablespoons of water. Cover the pan and cook slowly until very tender and sweet, about 15 minutes. Add more water while the spring onions cook, if necessary. Remove from the heat and let the mixture cool slightly. Transfer to a blender and purée until smooth. Transfer to the reserved vegetable ragù and stir to combine; adjust the seasoning with salt and pepper and set aside. Reheat this ragù over medium before serving it on the risotto, if necessary.

4. Heat the broth over low heat; keep warm. Season with salt.

5. Heat the 2 tablespoons olive oil in a large pot over low heat. Add the onion and sweat until tender, about 5 minutes. Add the rice and toast lightly without letting the rice or onion take on any color.

6. Add enough of the broth to come ½ inch above the rice, and cook, stirring frequently to be sure the rice doesn't stick to the bottom. As the rice absorbs the broth, keep adding more, ½ cup at a time. When the risotto is fully cooked but still al dente, about 18 minutes total cooking time, remove from the heat. Add the butter and the cheese, and stir vigorously to develop a creamy texture.

7. Season with salt and pepper, as needed, and serve on flat plates topped with vegetable ragù.

Basics

Pasta Secca

A BOX OF PASTA IN THE PANTRY means you always have something to cook. Be sure to seek out high-quality dried pastas. Artisanal pasta has a rougher appearance, which means you'll have better texture and flavor in the finished dish. All dried pasta should be cooked until it is "al dente," meaning that the pasta has a pleasant "chew" but is not undercooked. However, keep in mind that when a recipe calls for you to finish the pasta by combining it with a sauce and cooking it further before serving or to bake the pasta dish (*al forno*), you'll want the pasta to be slightly undercooked because it absorbs more liquid and completes cooking as it cooks or bakes in a sauce. Read the cooking time on the package, and stop cooking the pasta 1 or 2 minutes earlier than it suggests.

There aren't a lot of tricks to cooking pasta beyond these: plenty of rapidly boiling water, enough salt to make the water taste salty, and a big colander for draining.

Cooking Dried Pastas

Different pasta manufacturers may produce similar shapes with the same names, but due to the differences in sizes and shapes, they all take a slightly different amount of time to cook properly. You can usually find a cooking time on the package, and that is a good general guide. But don't rely just on the package; tasting a piece is the best way to tell when the pasta is properly cooked.

1. Bring a large pot of salted water to a full boil over high heat.

   The general suggestion is 1 gallon of water for every 1 pound of pasta, which means you will want a pot that holds at least 5 quarts. Remember to cover the pot so that it comes to a boil more quickly.

2. Add enough salt to make the water taste salty: 1 tablespoon is about enough for a gallon of water, but you could use a little less or more. Don't skip the salt entirely, however; pasta cooked in unsalted water has very little flavor. The pasta absorbs the salt as it cooks.

3. Add the pasta all at once and stir until the strands or pieces are softened and submerged. Long shapes like linguine may need to be pushed down under the water with a spoon until they have softened enough to stay there. Stir all pasta a few times to make sure the pieces are separated. If you don't take the time to do it at this point, you'll end up with large clumps of stuck-together pasta.

4. Let the pasta cook until it is fully cooked with a good bite (al dente). The pasta should be cooked through, but it should not be so soft that you can't feel it resisting a little bit when you bite into it.

5. Save some of the pasta cooking water to adjust the sauce, if needed. Once the pasta is done, scoop out a cup or so of the pasta water to finish the sauce. This is the "secret ingredient" that keeps sauces from feeling oily and slipping off the pasta, and also keeps the finished dish creamy. You may only need a few tablespoons, but sometimes you may need more than ½ cup.

6. Immediately drain the pasta in a colander and let as much water as possible drain away. You can shake the colander a few times to be sure that any water trapped inside tube-shaped pasta is drained.

Fresh Pasta

FRESH PASTA IS MADE FROM FLOUR AND EGGS. Sometimes you may add a bit of oil or water for pliability, or additional ingredients to add flavor or color—spices, vegetable purées, wine, or herbs. While you can buy fresh pasta, it is not difficult to make your own. The only tools you need are a flat work surface, your hands, a fork, and a rolling pin. We also include instructions here for mixing a dough using a food processor or mixer with a dough hook.

All-purpose flour works well for making fresh pasta at home. We make our fresh pasta with a flour known as "tipo 00," which you can find in some markets or specialty stores. We also call for semolina and durum flours to make pastas that have a bit more "chew."

Eggs provide moisture, flavor, and structure in most pastas, although there are a few made with just flour and water. (Dried pasta sometimes includes eggs, but water is typically the only liquid used.)

Some fresh pasta recipes also call for a small amount of water or oil to make the dough tender and pliable. Whenever you are mixing a pasta dough, have a bit of water on hand so that you can make adjustments. The amount of moisture in your flour or in the air or the size of your eggs may vary from day to day.

If the dough seems too stiff or crumbly as you work with it, sprinkle a teaspoon or two of water over the dough. Don't add too much at once, though, or you could end up with a dough that is too wet.

You can substitute a quantity of whole wheat, semolina, cornmeal, buckwheat, rye, or chickpea flour for all-purpose flour to give the pasta a unique flavor and texture. Ingredients such as spinach or saffron also may be added for flavor and color.

Making Fresh Pasta by Hand

Small batches of pasta dough can be efficiently mixed by hand.

MIXING INGREDIENTS AND KNEADING BY HAND

Mound the flour directly on a flat work surface and make a well in the center. Place the eggs and flavoring ingredients in the well. Using a fork and working as rapidly as possible, incorporate the flour into the liquid ingredients, little by little, working from the outside toward the center, until a shaggy mass forms. As the dough is mixed, adjust the consistency with additional flour or a few drops of water to compensate for the natural variations in ingredients, humidity, and temperature or for the addition of either dry or moist flavoring ingredients.

Once the dough is mixed, knead the dough until its texture becomes smooth and elastic. Use the heels of your hands to push the dough away from you, and then reverse the motion, folding the dough over on itself toward you. Give the dough a quarter turn periodically so that it is evenly kneaded.

Kneading by hand generally takes 10 to 12 minutes. Do not rush the kneading process, or the texture of the finished pasta will suffer. Properly kneaded dough is uniform in texture and no longer tacky to the touch. Divide the dough into balls about the size of an orange, place in a bowl, and cover loosely with plastic wrap or a cotton towel. Allow the dough to rest at room temperature for at least 30 minutes. This will relax the dough and make it easier to roll out.

ROLLING AND CUTTING BY HAND

You can use a straight wooden rolling pin to roll out pasta dough as described here, or a pasta machine (see page 235). Lightly dust a work surface with just enough flour to prevent the dough from sticking. Too much flour will make the pasta dough too dry. Work with one ball of dough at a time, and keep the remaining dough covered with plastic wrap or a slightly damp cotton towel to prevent it from drying out. Flatten the dough by pressing it into a disk, and then begin rolling. Try to keep the dough's thickness even as you work. Turn the dough to keep it from sticking and lightly flour the rolling pin and the work surface as necessary.

When the dough is as thin as you want it, you can cut it into sheets to the length you wish with a knife. If you are making long, flat pasta shapes like pappardelle, linguine, or fettuccine, lay the sheets out flat and let them dry slightly, just until the surface is leathery to the touch. If you are making filled pastas like ravioli and tortellini, however, you will have better results if the dough is not allowed to dry before you fill and cut the shapes.

To cut long shapes by hand, roll a sheet of pasta dough up into a cylinder and make crosswise cuts of the desired width: very wide for pappardelle to very narrow for linguine. The sheets can also be cut into squares or circles using plain or fluted pastry wheels, knives, or round or square cutters. These can be filled and folded into tortellini or ravioli, as described on page 241.

Making Fresh Pasta by Machine

Large batches of pasta dough are easier to make with a food processor or stand mixer.

MIXING INGREDIENTS AND KNEADING THE DOUGH

To mix pasta dough in a food processor, fit the machine with the metal blade and combine all of the ingredients in the work bowl. Process just until the dough is blended into a coarse meal that forms a ball when gathered together. Do not overprocess. Remove the dough, transfer to a lightly floured work surface, and knead by hand as described above.

To use a stand mixer, fit it with the dough hook attachment to combine all the ingredients, and then mix at low speed for 3 to 4 minutes, until the dough is just moistened. Increase the speed to medium and knead the dough for 3 minutes longer, until the dough forms a smooth ball that pulls cleanly away from the sides of the bowl.

ROLLING AND CUTTING THE DOUGH IN A PASTA MACHINE

Gather the dough into a ball, cover it, and let it relax at room temperature for at least 30 minutes. Letting the dough relax allows it to be rolled into thin sheets more easily. Cut off a piece of dough and flatten it. The amount will vary according to the width of your pasta machine. Cover the remaining dough to keep it from drying out. Set the rollers to the widest opening, fold the dough in thirds, and guide the flattened dough through the machine as you turn the handle. Roll the dough to form a long, wide strip. Pass the dough through the widest setting 2 or 3 times, folding the dough in thirds each time.

Lightly flour the dough strip to prevent it from sticking. Set the rollers to the next thinnest opening and run the dough through the rollers again, this time without folding. Repeat, lightly dusting the dough with flour each time, and passing the dough through the rollers twice on each setting, until it reaches the desired thinness—the second-to-last setting for most pastas, or the thinnest setting for lasagna or stuffed pasta such as ravioli.

DRYING THE DOUGH

Cut each rolled sheet of dough into shorter lengths, about 1 foot long, for easier handling. For best results with cleaner cuts and no sticking when you are cutting pasta with your machine, let the pasta sheets dry slightly until the surface is leathery to the touch.

Once the dough for long shapes is slightly dried, you can cut it using the attachment on your machine. There are usually two options, one for wider noodles (fettuccine) and another for narrower noodles (tagliatelle). Feed the dough through the desired cutting attachment.

If you are not cooking the pasta immediately, you can dry it for storage. Spread small shapes in a single layer on a clean, dry towel or baking sheet. Gather long pasta into loose nests, arrange them on a clean baking sheet with plenty of space between each one, and let the pasta dry completely in a cool, dry place before placing in an airtight container. Store in the refrigerator for up to 2 days.

Pasta Sheets for Lasagna, Cannelloni, and Rotolo

MAKES 1 POUND DOUGH

10 oz (2¼ cups) all-purpose or tipo 00 flour

3 medium eggs

1. Combine the flour and eggs by hand or using a machine. Knead until all of the ingredients are well combined and the dough is smooth and elastic. Wrap the dough in plastic wrap or place it in a covered bowl and let it rest for at least 30 minutes.

2. Dust a work surface with flour. Cut off pieces of the dough about the size of an egg. Working with one piece of dough at a time, roll the dough with a pasta machine or with a rolling pin into sheets about ¹⁄₁₆ inch thick. Cut the sheets into pieces 10 to 12 inches long.

3. Bring a large pot of salted water to a boil over high heat. Cook the sheets until they are almost cooked through, about 3 minutes. Remove the pasta from the water, drain well, and lay them flat on a table or flat surface to cool.

Ravioli Pasta Sheets

MAKES ¾ POUND DOUGH

7 oz (1½ cups) all-purpose or tipo 00 flour

2 large eggs

1. Combine the flour and eggs by hand or using a machine. Knead until all of the ingredients are well combined and the dough is smooth and elastic. Wrap the dough in plastic wrap or place it in a covered bowl and let it rest for at least 30 minutes.

2. Dust a work surface with flour. Cut off pieces of dough about the size of an egg. Working with one piece of dough at a time, roll the dough with a pasta machine or with a rolling pin into sheets about ¹⁄₁₆ inch thick. Cut the sheets into pieces about 12 inches long.

Potato Ravioli Sheets

MAKES 1¼ POUNDS DOUGH

10 oz (about 2 medium) russet potatoes

8 oz (1¾ cups) all-purpose flour

1 large egg

1. Put the potatoes in a large pot and add enough cold water to cover them by about 2 inches. Salt the water and bring it to a boil over medium-high heat. Cook until the potatoes are easily pierced with a wooden skewer or fork (the time will depend on the size of the potatoes). Drain the potatoes and dry them in the pot over low heat, about 3 minutes. Remove the skins and purée through a food mill or potato ricer onto a lightly floured work surface.

2. Gather the potatoes into a mound and make a well in the center. Surround the well with half of the flour. Add the egg to the well. Mix the ingredients by hand to form a soft dough. If necessary, add more flour, a little at a time, until the dough has the correct consistency. It should be firm enough to roll out, but not too stiff.

3. Divide the dough in half. Working with one piece at a time, roll the dough with a pasta machine or a rolling pin into sheets about ⅛ inch thick, dusting the working surface and the dough with additional flour, as necessary, to keep if from sticking.

Squid Ink Pasta Sheets

MAKES 1 POUND DOUGH

10 oz (2¼ cups) all-purpose or tipo 00 flour

3 large eggs

1 tbsp squid ink

1. Combine the flour, eggs, and ink by hand or using a machine. Knead until all of the ingredients are well combined and the dough is smooth and elastic. Wrap the dough in plastic wrap or place it in a covered bowl and let it rest for at least 30 minutes.

2. Dust a work surface with flour. Cut off pieces of dough about the size of an egg. Working with one piece of dough at a time, roll the dough with a pasta machine or with a rolling pin into sheets about ¹⁄₁₆ inch thick.

Squid Ink Rotolini or Cannelloni Cut the sheets into pieces that are about 10 inches long. Bring a large pot of salted water to a rolling boil over high heat. Cook the pasta for 1 minute, then remove the pasta sheets from the water, drain well, and lay them flat on a table or work surface to cool.

Squid Ink Farfalline Cut the dough into disks with a 3-inch-diameter cutter. Pinch each disk together in the middle to make bow ties.

Squid Ink Tagliolini Cut the sheets into noodles about ⅛ inch wide using a knife or the cutting attachment for a pasta machine.

Casonsei

MAKES 1½ POUNDS DOUGH

1 lb (3½ cups) all-purpose or tipo 00 flour

2 large eggs

¼ cup whole milk

1. Combine the flour, eggs, and milk by hand or using a machine. Knead until all of the ingredients are well combined and the dough is smooth and elastic. Wrap the dough in plastic wrap or place it in a covered bowl and let it rest for at least 30 minutes.

2. Dust a work surface with flour. Cut off pieces of dough about the size of an egg. Working with one piece of dough at a time, roll the dough with a pasta machine or with a rolling pin into sheets about ¹⁄₁₆ inch thick.

Basic Pasta for Tagliatelle, Fettuccine, Pappardelle, Maltagliati, and Fazzoletti, and Stracci

MAKES 1¼ POUNDS DOUGH

14 oz (3 cups) all-purpose or tipo 00 flour

4 large eggs

1. Combine the flour and eggs by hand or using a machine. Knead until all of the ingredients are well combined and the dough is smooth and elastic. Wrap the dough in plastic wrap or place it in a covered bowl and let it rest for at least 30 minutes.

2. Dust a work surface with flour. Cut off pieces of dough about the size of an egg. Working with one piece of dough at a time, roll the dough with a pasta machine or with a rolling pin into sheets about ¹⁄₁₆ inch thick.

Tagliatelle Cut the sheets into pieces about 10 inches long and then into ¼-inch-wide noodles with a knife or using the cutting attachment for a pasta machine.

Fettuccine Cut the sheets into pieces about 10 inches long and then into ³⁄₈-inch-wide noodles with a knife or using the cutting attachment for a pasta machine.

Pappardelle Cut the sheets into pieces about 8 inches long and then into 1-inch-wide noodles with a knife or using the cutting attachment for a pasta machine.

Maltagliati Cut the sheets into irregular pieces with a knife, about 2 inches wide and 3 inches long,

Fazzoletti Cut the sheets into 3-inch square pieces with a knife.

Stracci Cut the sheets into pieces about 4 inches wide and then into 4-inch squares.

Straw and Hay Pasta

MAKES 1¼ POUNDS DOUGH

White Pasta

7 oz (1½ cups) all-purpose or tipo 00 flour

2 large eggs

Green Pasta

7 oz (1½ cups) all-purpose or tipo 00 flour

2 oz chopped spinach, blanched, squeezed dry, and chopped

1 large egg

1. Combine the flour and eggs for the white pasta by hand or using a machine. Knead until all of the ingredients are well combined and the dough is smooth and elastic. Wrap the dough in plastic wrap or place it in a covered bowl and let it rest for at least 30 minutes. Repeat the procedure for the green pasta, combining the flour, spinach, and egg.

2. Dust a work surface with flour. Cut off pieces of dough about the size of an egg. Working with one piece of dough at a time, roll the dough with a pasta machine or with a rolling pin into sheets about ¹⁄₁₆ inch thick. Cut into noodles about ¼ inch thick with a knife or the attachment on a pasta machine.

Red Wine Fettuccine

MAKES 1½ POUNDS DOUGH

2 cups dry red wine

12 oz (2⅔ cups) all-purpose or tipo 00 flour

8 oz (1¼ cups) durum semolina flour

4 large eggs

1. Simmer the wine in a small pot over medium heat until it is reduced by a little more than half. Let the wine cool to room temperature.

2. Combine the flour, eggs, and wine by hand or using a machine. Knead until all of the ingredients are well combined and the dough is smooth and elastic. Wrap the dough in plastic wrap or place it in a covered bowl and let it rest for at least 30 minutes.

3. Dust a work surface with flour. Cut off pieces of dough about the size of an egg. Working with one piece of dough at a time, roll the dough with a pasta machine or with a rolling pin into sheets about 1/16 inch thick. Cut into noodles about ⅜ inch wide with a knife or the attachment on a pasta machine.

Corzetti Pasta

MAKES 1¼ POUNDS DOUGH

1 lb (3½ cups) all-purpose or tipo 00 flour

3 large eggs

2 tbsp dry white wine

1 tsp oil

1. Combine the flour, eggs, wine, and oil by hand or using a machine. Knead until all of the ingredients are well combined and the dough is smooth and elastic. Wrap the dough in plastic wrap or place it in a covered bowl and let it rest for at least 30 minutes.

2. Dust a work surface with flour. Cut off pieces of dough about the size of an egg. Working with one piece of dough at a time, roll the dough with a pasta machine or with a rolling pin into sheets about ⅛ inch thick.

3. To shape the corzetti, cut the dough into disks with a 2-inch-diameter corzetti cutter. Press the disks with the wooden corzetti tool; this will give them their characteristic decoration. Transfer the corzetti to a lightly floured baking sheet.

Pici

MAKES 1¼ POUNDS DOUGH

14 oz (3 cups) all-purpose or tipo 00 flour

2 oz (⅓ cup) durum semolina flour

2 large eggs

½ cup water

1. Combine the flours, eggs, and water by hand or using a machine. Knead until all of the ingredients are well combined and the dough is smooth and elastic. Wrap the dough in plastic wrap or place it in a covered bowl and let it rest for at least 30 minutes.

2. Dust a work surface with flour. Cut off pieces of dough about the size of an egg. Working with one piece of dough at a time, roll the dough with a pasta machine or with a rolling pin into sheets about ⅜ inch thick.

3. Cut the strips into pieces about 10 inches long and then into strips about ⅜ inch wide. Roll each strand on a flat surface with the palms of your hand to shape into a thick, long spaghetti.

Pizzoccheri

MAKES 1¼ POUNDS DOUGH

12 oz (3 cups) all-purpose or tipo 00 flour 4 oz (1 cup) buckwheat flour

3 large eggs

4 to 6 tbsp whole milk

1. Combine the flour, eggs, and milk by hand or using a machine. Knead until all of the ingredients are well combined and the dough is smooth and elastic. Wrap the dough in plastic wrap or place it in a covered bowl and let it rest for at least 30 minutes.

2. Dust a work surface with flour. Cut off pieces of dough about the size of an egg. Working with one piece of dough at a time, roll the dough with a pasta machine or with a rolling pin into sheets about 1⁄16 inch thick. Cut the sheets with a knife into noodles that are ½ inch wide and 4 inches long.

Chestnut Pappardelle and Tagliatelle

MAKES 1¼ POUNDS

12 oz (2⅔ cups) all-purpose flour

5 oz (1¼ cups) chestnut flour

3 large eggs

¼ cup water

1. Combine the flours, eggs, and water by hand or using a machine. Knead until all of the ingredients are well combined and the dough is smooth and elastic. Wrap the dough in plastic wrap or place it in a covered bowl and let it rest for at least 30 minutes.

2. Dust a work surface with flour. Cut off pieces of dough about the size of an egg. Working with one piece of dough at a time, roll the dough with a pasta machine or with a rolling pin into sheets about 1⁄16 inch thick.

Chestnut Pappardelle Cut sheets into 8-inch-long pieces and then into ½-inch-wide noodles.

Chestnut Fettucine Cut sheets into 8-inch-long pieces and then into ⅜-inch-wide noodles.

Farfalline and Tajarin Pasta

MAKES 1¼ POUNDS DOUGH

1 lb (3½ cups) all-purpose of tipo 00 flour

2 large eggs

7 egg yolks

1. Combine the flour, eggs, and egg yolks by hand or using a machine. Knead until all of the ingredients are well combined and the dough is smooth and elastic. Wrap the dough in plastic wrap or place it in a covered bowl and let it rest for at least 30 minutes.

2. Dust a work surface with flour. Cut off pieces of dough about the size of an egg. Working with one piece of dough at a time, roll the dough with a pasta machine or with a rolling pin into sheets about 1⁄16 inch thick.

Farfalline Cut the dough into disks with a 3-inch-diameter cutter. Pinch each disk together in the middle to make bow ties.

Tajarin Cutting the dough with a sharp knife into ⅛-inch-wide noodles.

Scialatielli

MAKES 1¼ POUNDS DOUGH

1 lb (3¾ cups) durum flour

4 to 5 oz water

1. Combine the flour and water by hand or using a machine. Knead until all of the ingredients are well combined and the dough is smooth and elastic. Wrap the dough in plastic wrap or place it in a covered bowl and let it rest for at least 30 minutes.

2. Dust a work surface with flour. Cut off pieces of dough about the size of an egg. Working with one piece of dough at a time, roll the dough with a pasta machine or with a rolling pin into sheets about ¹⁄₁₆ inch thick.

3. Cut each sheet into ¼-inch-wide noodles using the attachment on your pasta machine or with a knife.

Maccheroni alla Chitarra and Troccoli

A chitarra is a special tool used to cut pasta. The sheet of fresh pasta is pushed against the wires in the chitarra frame to make long noodles. To make troccoli, you use a cutting tool that looks like a rolling pin with grooves.

MAKES 1¼ POUNDS DOUGH

7 oz (1 cup plus 2 tbsp) semolina flour

7 oz (1½ cups) all-purpose or tipo 00 flour

4 large eggs

1. Combine the flours and eggs by hand or using a machine. Knead until all of the ingredients are well combined and the dough is smooth and elastic. Wrap the dough in plastic wrap or place it in a covered bowl and let it rest for at least 30 minutes.

2. Dust a work surface with flour. Cut off pieces of dough about the size of an egg. Working with one piece of dough at a time, roll the dough with a pasta machine or with a rolling pin into sheets about ⅛ inch thick.

Maccheroni alla Chitarra Cut the sheets into pieces as long as your chitarra. Place the sheet on the chitarra and use a rolling pin to push it through the wire.

Troccoli Cut the sheets into pieces about 10 inches long. Cut into noodles using a troccoli tool, or cut them by hand with a knife into noodles about ¼ inch thick.

Cocoa Pappardelle

MAKES 1¼ POUNDS DOUGH

1 lb (3½ cups) all-purpose or tipo 00 flour

3 tbsp cocoa powder

5 medium eggs

1. Combine the flour, cocoa powder, and eggs by hand or using a machine. Knead until all of the ingredients are well combined and the dough is smooth and elastic. Wrap the dough in plastic wrap or place it in a covered bowl and let it rest for at least 30 minutes.

2. Dust a work surface with flour. Cut off pieces of dough about the size of an egg. Working with one piece of dough at a time, roll the dough with a pasta machine or with a rolling pin into sheets about ¹⁄₁₆ inch thick.

3. Cut each sheet into 8-inch-long pieces and then into ¾-inch-wide noodles, about 10 inches long.

Chestnut Cocoa Rotolo Sheets Replace 4 oz (1 cup) all-purpose flour with chestnut flour and add 3 tablespoons unsweetened cocoa powder. Roll into sheets as directed in step 2 for use in recipe on page 76.

MAKING STUFFED PASTA

When making stuffed pasta, you may be instructed to add a small amount of oil to the dough to help it stick together better when sealed around a filling. Roll the pasta out to the thinnest setting on a pasta machine. While rolling and filling one portion of the dough, keep the rest covered with plastic wrap to make sure it stays moist and pliable. Cut and fill the sheets as soon as possible after they are rolled. As they dry, they become more difficult to seal properly.

FORMING RAVIOLI

Lightly flour a clean dry work surface and lay down a thinly rolled pasta sheet. Use a round cookie cutter to cut out as many rounds as possible, or a sharp knife to cut squares.

Using a teaspoon or pastry bag, place or pipe a small amount of the filling in the center of each circle or square. The amount of filling will vary depending on the size of the pasta round or square. Lightly moisten the edges of the pasta round or square with a pastry brush dipped in cool water or egg wash. Top each with another pasta round or square and press firmly with your fingertips to seal. Use the tines of a fork to crimp the edges together. Refrigerate the finished ravioli while you roll out, cut, and fill the remaining pasta dough.

Or you can fill the pasta by scooping or piping the filling onto the pasta sheet then topping it with a second sheet, and then cutting out the shape. Brush the sheet with egg wash or water before topping it with filling. Press the sheets together around the filling to seal the top sheet to the bottom sheet and press out any air pockets that might surround the filling. Use a ravioli cutter, knife, or a pastry wheel to cut the ravioli into squares or rounds.

FORMING TORTELLINI

Lightly flour a clean dry work surface and lay down a thinly rolled pasta sheet. Use a round cookie cutter to cut out as many rounds as possible, or a sharp knife to cut squares. Using a teaspoon or a pastry bag, place or pipe a small amount of the filling in the center of each circle or square. The amount of filling will vary depending on the size of the pasta round or square. Lightly moisten the edges of the pasta round or square with a pastry brush dipped in cool water or egg wash, fold in half to make a half-moon or triangle, and press firmly to seal with your fingertips.

To shape the tortellini, wrap the half-moon or triangle around the tip of your forefinger, pull the 2 corners together to overlap, and pinch them firmly to seal.

COOKING FRESH PASTA

A large pot that is taller than it is wide is best for boiling most pasta. Stuffed pasta such as ravioli can be cooked in wide, shallow pans that allow for easier removal. Fill the pot with plenty of water, salt generously, and bring the water to a gentle boil. Delicate and fragile pasta might fall apart if the water is boiling rapidly.

Once the water comes to a full boil, add the pasta all at once. Stir the pasta a few times to separate and submerge the strands or shapes, then cook until al dente. Fresh pasta cooks rapidly, often taking less than 1 minute. When it is ready, pour the pasta into a colander and toss well to drain away as much water as possible.

Ravioli, tortellini, and other filled pastas are less likely to fall apart if you use a skimmer or a slotted spoon to lift them from the pot and transfer them to a colander to drain.

Saucing the Pasta

YOUR PASTA SHOULD BE FRESHLY DRAINED and very hot when you combine it with a sauce. The way you combine it depends upon the type of sauce.

Ragù-style sauces are thick and have a substantial body. To combine your pasta with a ragù-style sauce, drain the pasta as much as possible, and shake it well. Pour the pasta into a heated pasta bowl (or fill individual pasta plates), and then ladle the hot sauce over the pasta.

Other sauces, including pesto, carbonara, and raw tomato sauces are tossed together with the hot pasta. Drain the pasta and pour it into a bowl or the pan you cooked the sauce in. Add the prepared sauce and use a lifting motion to combine the pasta and sauce. Add some of the pasta water you set aside (a few spoonfuls at a time) to keep the sauce loose enough for an even, creamy coating on each strand. This can be done over medium heat to finish cooking the pasta in the sauce.

Crespelle

Crespelle are the Italian version of crêpes. They are perfect for making ahead, since they can be cooked, stacked, and stored in the refrigerator for 2 days, or well wrapped and frozen for up to 3 weeks.

Crespelle

MAKES 8 CRESPELLE

10 oz (2¼ cups) all-purpose or tipo 00 flour

2 cups whole milk

4 large eggs

Kosher salt, as needed

Freshly grated nutmeg, as needed

1. Sift the flour into a large bowl. Whisk together the milk and eggs and add to the flour, whisking until the mixture is smooth and creamy. Season with a pinch of salt and a few grains of nutmeg and then strain the batter through a fine wire-mesh sieve into a clean bowl. Let the batter rest for up to 30 minutes.

2. Heat a 10-inch nonstick sauté pan or crêpe pan. With one hand, grasp the handle of the pan so that you can lift the pan up and tilt it as you pour the batter over the surface with the other hand. Add about ¼ cup of the batter for each crespella.

3. Return the pan to the heat and let the crespella cook undisturbed for about 40 seconds. Check the underside; it should be set but not browned. Turn the crespella with a long spatula and let it cook on the second side until just cooked, 10 to 20 seconds longer. Transfer the finished crespella to a plate. Continue until all of the batter is used; you should have at least 8 crespelle.

Chickpea Crespelle

MAKES 8 CRESPELLE

1 cup chickpea flour

⅓ cup all-purpose flour

¾ tsp kosher salt

1½ cups whole milk

1 large egg

1. Sift the flours and salt into a large bowl. Add the milk and egg and mix until evenly blended and smooth, but do not overmix. Strain the batter through a wire-mesh sieve into a clean bowl and let it rest for up to 30 minutes.

2. Heat a 10-inch nonstick sauté pan or crêpe pan. With one hand, grasp the handle of the pan so that you can lift the pan up and tilt it as you pour the batter over the surface with the other hand. Add about ¼ cup of the batter for each crespella.

3. Return the pan to the heat and let the crespella cook, undisturbed, for about 40 seconds. Check the underside; it should be set but not browned. Turn the crespella with a long metal spatula and let it cook on the second side until just cooked, 10 to 20 seconds more. Transfer the finished crespella to a plate. Continue making crespelle until all of the batter is used; you should have at least 8 crespelle.

Gnocchi

Gnocchi may have a longer history than pasta in Italy. A cookbook from the fourteenth century includes a recipe for gnocchi made by mashing together cheese and egg and mixing them with flour to make a dumpling. Today, you can find gnocchi made from potatoes, semolina, polenta, squash, ricotta, and bread. There are savory gnocchi for *primi piatti*, gnocchi served as an accompaniment to the main course, and even sweet gnocchi for dessert. There are gnocchi made as you would a ravioli filling, except that there is no pasta involved; these are known as *gnudi* ("naked"). Gnocchi, like pasta, can be enhanced by a number of different sauces, and there are stuffed and filled gnocchi as well.

Potato Gnocchi

It seems that you can find thousands of recipes for potato gnocchi. That doesn't mean that gnocchi are difficult to make, however. In fact, it shows just how adaptable a simple gnocchi recipe can be when it travels from one cook to another. Some cooks may want to use whole eggs, some yolks only, and others no eggs at all.

What is true about gnocchi is that it is one of those recipes that you have to make a couple of times to get the feel for it. There is a famous story from one of Italy's most renowned cookbook authors, Pellegrino Artusi (*La scienza in cucina e l'arte di mangiar bene* or *The Science of Cooking and the Art of Eating Well*). Apparently, a woman trying to prepare the little dumplings for the first time failed to use enough flour. When she stirred the pot, the gnocchi disappeared.

"'Where'd they go?" asked another lady, to whom I had told the story, wondering if a fairy had spirited them away. "Don't raise your eyebrows, madam," replied I. "Though unexpected, it's perfectly normal. The gnocchi were made with too little flour, and dissolved upon coming into contact with the boiling water."

Cooking and drying your potatoes properly, and mixing in just the right amount of flour, is the key to success. While you are just learning to make these dumplings, we strongly suggest that you prepare a couple of test gnocchi first so that yours won't disappear as they cook.

Some potatoes are starchy (russet), while others have a waxy texture (red, new, and Yukon Gold). If you use starchy potatoes, you will get the best result; if you use waxy potatoes, you may need a bit more flour. Some recipes call for eggs or egg yolks to help hold the dumplings together. It is a little more difficult to keep the gnocchi from falling apart as they cook if you don't use eggs.

MAKING POTATO GNOCCHI

1. Put the potatoes into a pot with enough salted water to cover, and simmer long enough for the potatoes to become tender. Test them by piercing them with a wooden skewer or fork.

2. Drain the potatoes in a colander. There will still be some moisture left in the potatoes; you can let it cook away by returning the potatoes to the pot and letting them dry over very low heat for a few minutes. Another option is baking the potatoes in their skins, which is a good way to ensure that they don't become waterlogged, but baking potatoes takes longer than boiling them.

3. Peel and purée the potatoes while they are hot for light, tasty gnocchi. Use a kitchen towel to protect your hands as you peel off the skin. Use a potato ricer or a food mill to purée the potatoes. These tools give the potatoes a lighter texture, but if you don't have one of these tools you can use a handheld potato masher instead. We purée the potatoes directly onto a floured work surface, mounding them and making a well in the center.

4. Combine the potatoes with the other ingredients. The potatoes should still be warm as you mix the gnocchi, but you should let them cool enough so that you can work the dough without burning your hands. Pour about half of the flour called for in the recipe around the outside of the potato mound. Add the eggs to the well and use the fingertips of one hand to mix in the egg. Use your other hand to hold up the potato wall and to pull in the flour until you've got a light dough. You may need to add more of the flour if the dough seems very wet or soft; the amount you need to add depends on the way you cooked the potatoes and the amount of water they absorbed during cooking. Before going on to shape the gnocchi, test a few pieces to be sure they have the right taste and texture.

Testing Gnocchi

Since you want add enough flour to bind the gnocchi but not so much that they become heavy or dense, you need to test them to see if they are holding together.

Put a small pot of salted water over medium-high heat and bring it to a gentle simmer, not a rolling boil. Pull off a couple of pieces of the dough that are about the size you want your finished gnocchi to be. Add them to the water and simmer over medium heat until the gnocchi rise to the surface and float there for 2 or 3 minutes.

If the gnocchi fall apart as they cook or when you try to lift them from the water, add a bit more flour to the dough and test again. Repeat, if necessary, until the test gnocchi hold together. Pay attention to the way the dough feels when the gnocchi hold together so that you can reproduce the texture next time. You should add more seasoning now, as well, if the gnocchi didn't have as much flavor as you wanted.

Shaping Gnocchi

Cut the dough into pieces about the size of an egg and roll each piece out on a floured surface into a long coil or rope about ½ to 1 inch thick. Cut the ropes into pieces about the same length as the rope is thick. You can simply cook them shaped that way, if you like, or you can roll them over the tines of a fork or a grooved surface (there are specific tools for shaping gnocchi available). Once they are shaped, you can keep the gnocchi on a lightly floured tray or baking sheet for a little while, but if you plan to serve them later, it is best to cook them right away and then, when ready to serve, reheat them in salted water.

Very soft gnocchi (like those made with vegetable purées or ricotta) are easier to shape by scooping them using spoons and dropping them into the water, or using a piping bag with a wide plain opening to squeeze the dough out, cutting it into ½- to 1-inch-long pieces as it drops from the bag into the water.

Cooking Gnocchi

For most gnocchi, you need a generous amount of boiling salted water. Use the same pot that you would use to cook your pasta—tall and deep. The water should be at a gentle boil, with just a few lazy bubbles rising to the surface.

When you add the gnocchi to the water, they'll drop to the bottom of the pot. As they cook, they will rise to the surface and float. After they have risen, let them cook for 2 or 3 minutes longer. Use a slotted spoon or a skimmer to lift the cooked gnocchi from the water; pouring them through a colander might smash them.

Souffléd Gnocchi

Very light, puffed ("soufflé") dumplings are also called *alla parigina* (Parisienne). The method for making them is a little more complex than for other gnocchi. They are poached, not boiled, and they are cooled by putting them into a bowl of ice-cold water. As soon as they are cool, lift them from the water and put them on a baking sheet or tray. When ready to serve, you will combine them with a sauce and bake them until very hot. They puff up as they bake, nearly doubling in size. You need to serve them right away, though, or they will fall flat, just like a soufflé that falls once you take it from the oven.

Serving Gnocchi

Gnocchi are delicious served very simply with just a bit of butter or some grated Parmigiano-Reggiano. We like the flavor of brown butter and fried sage leaves for something a little more interesting. There are other sauces that are perfect for gnocchi as well. A simple tomato sauce works well, as does a more elaborate ragù made with rabbit. Cream sauces are also a tasty accompaniment. A classic sauce is *fonduto*, a cheese sauce made with Fontina, eggs, and milk. You might also serve them with sautéed mushrooms or other vegetables.

Potato Gnocchi

MAKES 1½ POUNDS DOUGH

1½ lb russet or other starchy potatoes

7 oz (1½ cups) all-purpose or tipo 00 flour, or as needed

2 large eggs

½ cup grated Parmigiano-Reggiano

1 tsp kosher salt

Pinch of freshly grated nutmeg

1. Put the potatoes in a pot and add enough cold water to cover them by about 2 inches. Salt the water and bring it to a boil over medium-high heat. Cook until the potatoes are easily pierced with a wooden skewer or fork (the time will depend on the size of the potatoes). Drain the potatoes and dry them in the pot over low heat, about 3 minutes. Remove the skins and purée through a food mill or potato ricer onto a lightly floured work surface.

2. Gather the potatoes into a mound and make a well in the center. Surround the well with half the flour. Add the eggs, egg yolks, Parmigiano-Reggiano, 1 teaspoon salt, and nutmeg to the well.

3. Mix the ingredients by hand to form a soft dough. If necessary, add more flour, a little at a time, until the dough has the correct consistency. Make a few test gnocchi and adjust the dough, if necessary, with additional flour or seasoning.

4. Roll the dough into 1-inch-thick ropes, and cut them into 1-inch-long pieces. (Flour your work surface as needed while you roll and cut the gnocchi.) Roll the gnocchi over a fork to shape them, if desired. Once shaped, the gnocchi can be reserved on a floured baking sheet, loosely covered, in the refrigerator for up to 8 hours.

Risotto

Italy's most famous rice dish is likely risotto. There are differences in the cooking qualities of different types of rice, and the results you get from a recipe will vary depending upon the rice you use. Once you find a good-quality brand of rice that you like, stick with it for the most consistent results.

Types of Italian Rice

All varieties of rice can be divided into short-, medium-, and long-grain varieties. Italian rice varieties are strains of a thick, short-grained rice called japonica (*Oryza sativa japonica*). They may not taste different from one another, but they do behave differently when cooked. There are four grades of rice:

COMUNE or **ORIGINARIO:** The cheapest, most basic rice, typically short and round, used for soups and desserts but never risotto.

SEMIFINO: This medium-length grade maintains some firmness when cooked. Risotto can be made with a *semifino* grade, although *semifino* is better employed in soups.

FINO: The grains are relatively long and large and taper at the tips. *Fino*-grade rice remains firm when cooked. Several varieties are commonly graded *fino,* including Ribe, Rizzotto, and San Andrea.

SUPERFINO: This grade represents the fattest, largest grains. They take the longest to cook, and they can absorb more liquid than any of the others while still remaining firm. *Superfino* rices include Baldo, Arborio, Roma, and Carnaroli.

In Italy they say *è' un peccato mortale* (it's a mortal sin) to use the wrong pot to cook risotto. You need a deep saucepan (choose a 2-quart size for about 1½ cups of rice, which makes about 4 cups of risotto, including the garnish). Absolutely avoid using a sauté pan or skillet—you will find that the liquid evaporates too quickly before the rice has a chance to absorb it.

1. Most risottos include aromatic vegetables cooked in a bit of butter or oil, just long enough to become tender and release their flavors.

2. Add the rice all at once to the butter or oil and the aromatics and stir the rice as it cooks. It will change color slightly and give off a nice, toasty aroma, but it should never cook long enough to scorch.

3. Add the wine to the rice and let it evaporate completely, and then add the broth in stages. A good broth is one of the keys to a successful risotto, and for the best results, it should be boiling hot when you add it to the rice in the pan. You can combine the wine with the broth, if your recipe calls for wine. There are many myths about stirring the risotto as it cooks. Our opinion is that you don't need to stir the rice constantly, especially during the first 10 minutes. Just make sure to keep the rice uniformly wet at all times during the first stage of cooking, and gently stir it every few minutes during the simmering stage to make sure that the rice doesn't stick to the bottom of the pan. Use a good saucepan and a wooden spoon to cook and stir the risotto. Make sure you keep the rice quite dry toward the end; you can always adjust the consistency by adding more broth. Some additional ingredients, like vegetables or seafood, can be added during the last 5 to 7 minutes of cooking time so that they will finish cooking at the same time as the rice.

4. Add butter and any other finishing ingredients to the risotto off the heat. The last step in preparing a good risotto is to vigorously stir butter into the rice to develop the characteristic creaminess. This last step is called *mantecatura,* and it is crucial to a good risotto. You may also add grated cheese or other garnishes at this point. The risotto is supposed to be *all'onda* (wavelike) when it is finished and ready to serve; it should "pour" in a thick wave off the spoon and spread on the plate slightly.

Serving Risotto

There is also strong sentiment regarding the proper way to serve (and eat) risotto. Serving risotto in a bowl instead of on a flat plate is another *peccato mortale.* You are supposed to eat your risotto from the outside edge of the plate inward, so that the rice has time to cool slightly as you eat it, enabling you to really enjoy the flavor.

Basil

Basil comes in many different varieties: Thai, Genovese, holy, opal, purple, and more. No matter what specific type of basil you are using, be sure to smell it first. The basil should have a pungent, aromatic smell that almost "tickles" the inside of your nose. Basil can be simply cleaned and torn into pieces to add to a sauce, cut into shreds to finish a salad or garnish a dish, or made into pesto, a classic sauce made from basil, olive oil, garlic, nuts, and cheese (see page 247).

Handling Basil

The traditional basil variety for pesto is Genovese. This variety has much smaller leaves than the Italian basil you most commonly find in the market. The leaves have a strong aroma, too.

Fresh basil is fragile. The leaves will start to turn limp and even darken to black within a very short time. Chilling this herb too much actually speeds this process and robs the herb of its flavor, although you can store it for a day or two loosely wrapped in a lightly dampened towel inside a plastic bag (but don't close the bag tightly).

CLEANING FRESH BASIL

1. Pull the leaves away from the stems; this is known as "picking" the leaves. Put the leaves in a bowl or sink filled with cold water and gently swish them around. A lot of dirt can hide on the back of the leaves, so check a few to make sure they are all clean.

2. Lift the leaves out of the water and check the bottom of the bowl or sink by running your fingertips over the bottom; you should not feel any bits of grit. If you do, refill the bowl, add the leaves to rinse again, and check the water again.

3. Keep repeating this process until the leaves (and the water) are clean.

4. Transfer the leaves to a salad spinner and spin them dry.

Making Pesto

A really great pesto has a good balance of flavors. This isn't always easy when you are dealing with seasonal produce, like basil. We strongly recommend that you weigh out the ingredients when you prepare basil pesto, especially if you are making a large batch. Use a digital scale for accuracy.

Keeping Basil Bright

Basil can lose its fresh, vibrant green color when you make it into pesto, although you can improve the color by blanching the leaves in boiling water.

Be sure to remove them after just a few seconds to retain the most flavor. Put the blanched leaves into a bowl of ice water immediately to stop them from overcooking.

Garlic is an important ingredient in pesto. However, its flavor intensifies in the pesto over time, so if you are making a large batch of pesto that you plan to store for a few days, you may wish to blanch the garlic first to remove any harsh or bitter flavors. If you are going to be using the pesto right way, you can skip this step.

Nuts are another important part of a pesto. The traditional pesto from Genoa incorporates pine nuts (pignoli). Almonds and walnuts are also commonly used to make pesto.

PREPARING PESTO

1. Pick and clean the basil leaves (as well as any other greens, like arugula or spinach), slice the garlic very thinly (and blanch if desired), and grate the cheeses.

2. Transfer the basil (and any other herbs or greens you want to add), pine nuts (or other nuts), and garlic to a food processor or a blender. (See below for the mortar and pestle method.) Chop them on low speed until they are of a relatively even size. With the machine running, add the olive oil in a stream. The pesto should be a bright green, lighter in color than the leaves were.

3. Open the lid and add the cheese. Pulse the machine on and off just enough to blend in the cheese. If you run the machine at high speed or for too long, the sauce will start to change color.

4. The pesto is ready to use right now, or you can transfer it to a storage container. Even out the top of the pesto to make a smooth layer, and pour a bit of olive oil on top; this will keep the pesto from turning a dark color (oxidizing). Do this before storing the pesto in the refrigerator and after each use.

Pesto

MAKES ABOUT 3 CUPS

1 oz (3 tbsp) pine nuts

1 small garlic clove

Kosher salt as needed

¾ cup extra-virgin olive oil, plus as needed

8 oz basil leaves (about 4 cups loosely packed leaves)

2 oz (½ cup) grated Pecorino Romano

2 oz (½ cup) grated Parmigiano-Reggiano

In a large mortar, using the pestle, crush the pine nuts, garlic and a generous pinch of salt with about 2 tablespoons of oil. Add the basil leaves and continue mashing the mixture and gradually adding the remaining oil until a semi-liquid paste forms. Add both cheeses at the end and mix to combine. (To prepare in a food processor, add all the ingredients to the bowl of the processor and purée just until a paste forms.) Store in a jar, covered, with extra-virgin olive oil, for up to 3 days.

Toasted Bread Crumbs

MAKES 1¼ CUPS

1 cup plain dry bread crumbs

¼ cup grated Pecorino Romano

2 tbsp extra-virgin olive oil

1 tbsp red pepper flakes

Heat a sauté pan over medium heat, add the bread crumbs and toss until they are golden brown and toasted, about 2 minutes. Pour them into a bowl and let cool. Add the cheese, oil, and the pepper flakes. Mix well to distribute the oil evenly throughout the bread crumbs. These bread crumbs will last up to 1 week at room temperature in airtight containers.

Tomatoes

Tomatoes are one of the signature ingredients of Italian cooking. When tomatoes are in season, we like to enjoy them either fresh or cooked quickly in a simple sauce. You'll find plenty of debate about what goes into an authentic tomato sauce. We recommend that you taste your tomatoes, whether they are fresh or canned, before you cook with them. That way, you have the chance to evaluate how sweet, savory, or tart they are and make adjustments that result in the perfect sauce for any dish.

Fresh Tomatoes

Our recipes call for a number of different types of tomatoes, from large beefsteak tomatoes to golden grape tomatoes. For most cooked dishes, you want to remove the peel and seeds. You can save the seeds and juices and add them to other dishes like broths or soups.

PEELING AND SEEDING FRESH TOMATOES

To be successful at peeling and seeding tomatoes, take the time to set up your work area. Fill a large pot with water and let it come to a boil. Fill a large bowl with ice water. Have a slotted spoon or a skimmer ready to lift the tomatoes from the pot. They usually only need a few seconds in the hot water, so you want to be ready to transfer them to the ice bath before they overcook.

1. Use a paring knife to cut out the stem end of the tomato. If you wish, you can also make a small X-shaped cut on the blossom end of the tomato to make peeling easier, but don't cut too deeply.

2. Lower the tomatoes into a pot of boiling water. Use a slotted spoon or a skimmer to do this, and only add a few tomatoes at once, otherwise the water temperature will drop too much.

3. After a few seconds (10 or 15 if the tomatoes are very ripe, and up to 25 seconds if they are somewhat underripe), lift the tomatoes out of the boiling water and immediately put them into the ice bath.

4. Use your fingers to pull away the skin. If the skin is sticking in a few spots, use a paring knife to help remove it.

5. Cut the tomatoes in half across the widest part. Squeeze the seeds and juices from the tomatoes into a bowl. Use your fingertips to scoop out any seeds that don't come out when you squeeze. The tomatoes are ready to cut as called for in your recipe.

Canned Tomatoes

There are many different varieties of tomatoes on the market. They can be found as whole peeled tomatoes, crushed tomatoes, tomato purée, diced tomatoes, and tomato paste. We prefer the flavor and texture of whole peeled San Marzano tomatoes for most cooked sauces because they are less watery and have a richer flavor, but regardless of the type you choose, remember to taste the tomatoes before using them.

CRUSHING AND SIEVING CANNED TOMATOES

Whole peeled tomatoes still contain seeds, so you will need to cut them in half and squeeze out the seeds. Catch the seeds and juices in a bowl and use them in other dishes. To crush tomatoes, you can simply chop them up with a potato masher as they cook in the sauce or you can crush them in your hands by squeezing them before you add them to a sauce.

If you want the texture a little finer than you would get from simply crushing the tomatoes, you may wish to crush them through a sieve. Set a wire mesh sieve over a bowl, add the drained and seeded tomatoes, and push them through the sieve with your hands or a wooden spoon.

Tomato Sauce

MAKES 4 CUPS

¼ cup extra-virgin olive oil

½ cup chopped yellow onion

2 garlic cloves, minced

2 qt canned whole San Marzano tomatoes with their juices

Kosher salt, as needed

Heat the oil in a large saucepan over low heat. Add the onions and garlic and cook, stirring frequently, until tender and translucent, and then add the tomatoes. Season the sauce lightly with salt and simmer the sauce until it is thickened and flavorful, 20 to 30 minutes. When the sauce is cooked, pass it through a food mill. The sauce is ready to use now, or it can be stored in covered containers in the refrigerator for up to 4 days.

Fresh Tomato Sauce

MAKES 4 CUPS

¼ cup extra-virgin olive oil

½ cup minced yellow onion

2½ lb ripe plum tomatoes, peeled, seeded, and coarsely chopped (see page 248)

Kosher salt, as needed

Heat the oil in a large saucepan over low heat. Add the onions and cook, stirring frequently, until tender and translucent, then add tomatoes. Season the sauce lightly with salt and simmer the sauce until it is thickened and flavorful, 20 to 30 minutes. When the sauce is cooked, pass it through a food mill. The sauce is ready to use now or it can be cooled and stored in covered containers in the refrigerator for up to 4 days.

Herbed Fresh Tomato Sauce
Replace the onions with 2 smashed garlic cloves and cook until golden. Then add 1 dried red chile and 1 teaspoon dried Sicilian oregano and stir well. Add 6 to 8 large basil leaves along with the tomatoes. Cook as directed above. Remove and discard the garlic, chile, and basil leaves before putting through a food mill.

Besciamella Sauce

This is a classic white sauce that we feature in a number of dishes. It is simple to make and holds well for a few days.

Besciamella

MAKES 4 CUPS

6 oz (¾ cup) unsalted butter

⅓ cup minced yellow onion

1 cup all-purpose flour

1 qt whole milk

1 bay leaf

Kosher salt and freshly ground black pepper, as needed

Freshly grated nutmeg, as needed

1. Heat the butter in a saucepan over low heat. Add the onion and cook, stirring frequently, until the onion is tender and translucent, about 5 minutes. Add the flour and cook, stirring frequently, until the mixture reaches a golden color, about 6 minutes.

2. Add the milk and the bay leaf and stir well with a whisk to break up any lumps and smooth the sauce. Stir the sauce constantly with a wooden spoon as it returns to a simmer.

3. Once it is simmering, lower the heat slightly and continue to cook the sauce until it is thickened and creamy, 10 to 15 minutes. Season the sauce with salt, pepper, and nutmeg as needed. Strain through a fine-mesh sieve and reserve. You may make the sauce up to 3 days in advance. After straining it, let it cool completely, then store in a covered container in the refrigerator. Warm the sauce over very low heat or in a microwave when you are ready to assemble your dish.

Eggplant

According to traditional Italian recipes, eggplant is seasoned with salt, garlic, and hot pepper and then left to dry in the sun for a day. After that, it is fried and made into a sauce with fresh tomato, garlic, and basil. Without the warm Mediterranean sun to help prepare eggplant for cooking, this salting and draining technique changes the texture of the flesh a bit, giving it more substance and reducing any bitterness in the flesh.

PREPARING EGGPLANT

1. Slice away the ends of the eggplant. Use a paring knife or a vegetable peeler to remove the skin, if your recipe calls for this.

2. Cut the eggplant in half or into slices or cubes and transfer it to a large colander.

3. Sprinkle kosher salt liberally over the eggplant and then put the colander in a large bowl to catch the liquid that the eggplant will release as it drains.

4. If you wish, you may weight the eggplant while it drains as follows: Place a plate or similar flat object on top of the eggplant and press down to make an even, compact layer. Add a weight on top of the plate (such as a can or two of beans or tuna fish).

5. Leave the eggplant to drain for at least 1 hour, and then rinse well under cold running water. Let the eggplant drain again; to be sure that the eggplant is well dried, press it between a few layers of paper towels.

Blanching Greens

You can use this basic blanching technique to prepare spinach, kale, chard, escarole, arugula, and other greens. Once the greens are blanched and squeezed dry, you can simply sauté them with olive oil and garlic for a delicious side dish.

1. Trim the stems, and remove any split or bruised portions. Remove any wilted or bruised leaves.

2. Some greens, like collards or chard, may have stems that should be either cooked separately from the greens or started in the boiling water before the leaves. To prepare them, cut the stems away from the leaves, and keep them separate. Rinse the stems and cut them into pieces of the size required in your recipe.

3. Clean the leaves in plenty of cold water until there are no more traces of sand or grit. Drain them in a colander.

4. Fill a large pot with water and add enough salt to be able to barely taste it. Cover the pot and bring the water to a rolling boil over high heat.

5. If you are cooking greens with sturdy stems like chard, add them to the pot first and cook for 2 to 3 minutes before adding the leaves.

6. Add the cleaned greens all at once and stir to submerge them. Cook uncovered until tender and a deep color, 3 to 4 minutes. Lift the greens out of the water with a sieve or slotted spoon and transfer to a bowl of ice water. After the greens are chilled, drain in a colander for several minutes.

7. If necessary, squeeze the greens as follows: Drape a clean dish towel or a large piece of cheesecloth in a colander. Put the greens in the center of the cloth and gather the edges of the towel around the greens. Tighten the cloth by twisting the edges with one hand. Use the other hand to twist the ball of greens in the opposite direction. Once you have squeezed out the extra liquid, unwrap the greens and chop them as coarsely or finely as your recipe requires.

Working with Salted Ingredients: Capers and Anchovies

Capers and anchovies are best when salted; this preserves their natural flavor.

Salted anchovies are usually sold whole and headless, so you will need to scrape off the excess salt, butterfly the anchovy, and pull the bones out. Rinse under cold water or soak in a mixture of water and red vinegar for a few seconds, and pat dry.

To desalt capers, rinse them in cold water to remove the excess salt, put them in a pot, cover them with cold water, and bring to a simmer. As soon as the water is simmering, drain the capers and spread out on a dish to cool. Or, you can let the capers sit under running water for several minutes instead.

Brodi

Making a good broth, one like our mothers and grandmothers made, takes time but only a few simple ingredients. You need to have patience and the time to devote to tending to your broth. The rewards are a rich brodo that has incomparable depth and a satisfying fullness. A *brodo* can be made from a combination of meats or just a single meat. Capon (rooster), less widely used in the United States, is popular in Italy and makes a remarkable broth.

The Preparation of Brodo

A big pot of simmering brodo is a common sight in the Italian kitchen. The cook visits the brodo frequently, checking that it is simmering very gently and never approaches a boil. A skimmer is nearby to lift any debris on the surface. A spoon is handy to check the brodo while it simmers so that the cook is ready to add a bit of seasoning when it is needed.

Making Sachets and Bouquets Garni

Getting a hint of flavor into foods sometimes calls for special seasoning techniques. Broths simmer for a long time, but a sachet or a bouquet garni needs only 20 to 30 minutes to make a difference.

Even though they are somewhat interchangeable, sachets and bouquets are not exactly the same. A sachet is a bundle of aromatic ingredients—typically dried spices and herbs—tied up in a cheesecloth sack (or held in a tea ball, if you prefer). A bouquet garni is made from a selection of fresh herbs, wrapped in a leek leaf or inside a few pieces of celery. It is held together with cotton string. Once a sachet or bouquet has added the amount of flavor you like, remove it right away.

Meat Broth Brodo

MAKES 1½ GALLONS

One 3- to 4-lb chicken

3 lb beef (top blade chuck or shank)

3 medium Spanish onions

3 carrots, peeled and cut in half

3 celery stalks, cut in half

3 fresh or canned plum tomatoes

1 sachet containing 3 cloves, 8 black peppercorns, 2 bay leaves, a small bunch of flat-leaf parsley, and 3 thyme sprigs

Kosher salt, as needed

1. Pull out any pockets of fat from the chicken and rinse well. Trim the beef of any visible fat. Put the chicken and beef in a large pot and add enough cold water to completely cover the meats.

2. Put the pot over medium heat, cover, and bring the water to a simmer. As soon as it comes to a simmer, remove the lid and start skimming any foam that rises to the surface. Add the onions, carrots, celery, and tomatoes.

3. Partially cover the pot by setting the lid slightly ajar to leave an opening; that way, the pot won't be as likely to boil over and you can keep an eye on it more easily. Bring it back to a simmer and cook, periodically skimming the foam that rises to the surface, for about 2 hours. Add the sachet and cook for 30 minutes longer. Remove the meats from the broth, letting any broth inside the chicken drain back into the pot. Reserve the meat to use in other dishes. At this point, the broth should have a rich, deep flavor. If not, remove the sachet, but continue to simmer for 20 to 30 minutes longer. Add salt to taste.

4. Strain the broth through a wire-mesh sieve directly into a pot if you are planning to serve the broth right away. If made in advance, let the broth cool and then store in a covered container in the refrigerator for up to 6 days.

Fish Broth

MAKES 2 QUARTS

1 medium yellow onion, minced

2 tbsp extra-virgin olive oil

1 celery stalk, finely chopped

½ cup sliced leek

1½ lb fish heads (gills removed) and fish bones

¼ cup tomato paste

1 cup dry white wine

1 garlic clove, crushed

4 oz white mushrooms, finely chopped

1 tbsp sambuca or pastis (anise-flavored liqueur)

Zest from ½ orange (optional)

2 bay leaves

½ cup mixed herbs, such as thyme, fennel fronds, and flat-leaf parsley

Kosher salt and freshly ground black pepper, as needed

3 qt boiling water

1. In a large pot, sweat the onion in the oil over low heat until translucent. Add the celery and leek. Cut the fish heads into pieces and add them, along with the fish bones, and mix well. After 2 minutes, add the tomato paste and blend.

2. Add the wine and stir well. Add the garlic, mushrooms, sambuca, orange peel, bay leaves, herbs, salt, and pepper. Let everything cook down well, about 10 minutes, then add the boiling water and bring to a gentle simmer for about 20 minutes.

3. Strain the broth, discarding the solids. Before using, remove any fat that may be on top. You may also freeze the broth and use for other preparations.

Shellfish Broth

MAKES 2 QUARTS

2 tbsp extra-virgin olive oil

1 celery stalk, thinly sliced

¼ fennel bulb, thinly sliced

2 shallots, minced

2 garlic cloves, smashed

1 lb shells or bones reserved from cleaning seafood (optional)

½ cup dry white wine

2 whole canned tomatoes, crushed through a sieve or food mill

1 bouquet garni, containing 1 thyme sprig and 1 bay leaf

2 qt water

Kosher salt, as needed

1. Heat the oil in a deep the pot over medium heat Add the celery, fennel, shallots, and garlic. Cook, stirring frequently, until the celery is translucent, about 4 minutés. Add the shells and stir to coat them well with oil. Continue to cook until the shells turn color, about 3 minutes.

2. Add the wine and continue to cook until the wine is nearly cooked away, about 3 minutes. Add the tomatoes, the bouquet, and the water. Simmer for 30 to 40 minutes, then strain through a fine-mesh wire sieve. The broth is ready to use now or it can be cooled and stored in covered containers in the refrigerator for up to 5 days.

Langoustine Broth

MAKES 2 QUARTS

1 celery stalk

¼ fennel bulb, thinly sliced

2 shallots, minced

2 oz (¼ cup) unsalted butter

1 garlic clove smashed

Chopped shells and heads from 18 langoustines

½ cup dry white wine

2 ripe plum tomatoes, chopped

1 bouquet with thyme and bay leaf

2 qt Meat Broth (page 251) or Fish Broth (page 252)

In a large casserole sweat the celery, fennel and shallots in the butter over medium heat. Add the garlic and the langoustine shells and sauté at medium-high heat. Add the white wine, let it evaporate then add fresh chopped tomato, the bouquet and the broth. Simmer for 40 minutes then strain through a fine chinois, season with salt. The broth is ready to use now or it may be stored in a covered container in the refrigerator for up to 5 days.

Rabbit Broth

MAKES 2 QUARTS

¼ cup extra-virgin olive

Bones and head from trimmed rabbit

Kosher salt and freshly ground black pepper, as needed

1 medium yellow onion, chopped

1 garlic clove, smashed

¼ cup dry white wine

2 tbsp dry Marsala

1 tsp tomato paste

1 thyme sprig

1 bay leaf

In a large saucepan heat the oil. Season the bones and head with salt and pepper and brown them over medium-high heat. Once nice and brown, add half of the onions and one garlic clove and keep browning until onions are a rich, golden color. Deglaze with white wine, add the Marsala, and the tomato paste and cook for 2 to 3 minutes. Cover with water. Add the thyme sprig and bay leaf. Bring to a simmer, cover, and cook for a couple of hours until the liquid is reduced to a rich broth. Taste and adjust the seasoning, keeping in mind it will be reduce further. Strain and reserve. If made in advance, let the broth cool and then store in a covered container in the refrigerator for up to 6 days.

Dried Beans

Most beans, with the exception of lentils, need to be soaked before they are cooked. You'll find a variety of beans in our minestra recipes: borlotti, chickpea, and fava, to name a few.

PREPARING DRIED BEANS

1. The day before making a soup, or any other bean dish, pour the beans into a shallow pan, such as a baking sheet or roasting pan. Sort through the beans, removing any shriveled beans or other debris.

2. Rinse the beans well in a colander under cold running water and then transfer them to a bowl. Add enough cold water to cover the beans by at least 2 inches. Let the beans soak in the refrigerator for at least 8 and no more than 24 hours.

3. Drain the beans before cooking them in a pot of fresh water. Don't salt beans until they are almost completely cooked, or their skins can toughen.

Borlotti Beans

MAKES 3 TO 3½ CUPS

1 lb shelled fresh borlotti beans or ½ pound dry borlotti beans, soaked at least 8 hours in cold water

½ medium yellow onion

1 celery stalk, cut in half

2 bay leaves

2 garlic cloves, smashed

1 rosemary sprig

2 tbsp extra-virgin olive oil

1. Put the beans in a pan with enough water to cover them by about 2 inches. Add the onion, celery, bay leaves, garlic, rosemary sprig, and oil.

2. Bring to a simmer over medium heat and cook until the beans are very tender, about 20 minutes for fresh beans or 50 minutes for dry beans.

3. Strain the beans through a colander, catching the cooking liquid in a bowl. Remove and discard the onion, celery, bay leaves, garlic, and rosemary. Reserve the beans and the cooking liquid separately to use in sauces, soups, or stews (or you can keep the beans directly in the liquid if you are preparing them in advance).

Recipe note *If you can't find borlotti beans, substitute cranberry beans.*

White Beans Substitute dried white beans for the dried borlotti beans in this recipe.

Chestnuts

Chestnuts have sustained Italians over the centuries. They are a relatively starchy nut, perfect for cooking in thick creamy soups.

PREPARING CHESTNUTS

1. Cut an X on the flatter of the nut's two sides. Try to keep your cut shallow so that you don't cut into the nut meat.

2. Bring a pot of water to a boil and add the chestnuts. Let them boil just long enough for the shell around the crosshatch cut to start coming loose, about 2 minutes.

3. Remove the pot from the heat and take a few chestnuts at a time from the hot water. (Leave the rest in the water as you work.) Pull away the shell. The chestnuts are ready to use according to your recipe instructions.

Asparagus

If your asparagus is very tender, you may not want or need to peel the stem, but this added step has the advantage of evening out the cooking time so that you don't end up with undercooked stalks and overcooked tips.

PEELING ASPARAGUS

1. Slice away the dry ends of the asparagus. (This is actually much better than trying to bend and snap the stalk, especially if you are a fan of the more flavorful larger spears.)

2. Lay the asparagus flat on a work surface. It is ideal if you have a thick cutting board that raises the asparagus a few inches above your work surface. Otherwise, it is a little awkward to peel them without banging your knuckles into the counter. It also keeps the asparagus steady so that you won't accidentally snap the spear as you peel.

3. Use a vegetable peeler to remove a little of the peel from the stem, stopping 1 to 1½ inches short of the tip.

Fresh Artichokes

As artichokes age, they develop a tough "choke" in the center that needs to be removed before you cook them. (This is not true of small or baby artichokes; very small and tender artichokes may only need to be cut in half or quartered.)

PREPARING FRESH ARTICHOKES

1. Fill a large bowl halfway with cold water and add a bit of lemon juice.

2. Slice the end of the artichoke stem away with a paring knife. Pull away any leaves at the base of the artichoke that are bruised or shriveled.

3. Peel the stem. Slice the top third of the artichoke away. Remove any spines. Use scissors to clip any spines from the remaining leaves, if necessary.

4. Cut the artichoke in half and use a spoon (a grapefruit spoon is ideal) to scoop out the feathery, hairy choke in the center.

5. Put the trimmed artichoke halves into the lemon water to keep them from discoloring before you cook them.

Fresh Fava Beans

Italians consider fava beans their special province, as they have since ancient times. The word "fava" comes from the Italian *faba*, which means "bean." The fresh bean is usually available for only a short time in the spring. The pods look like gigantic, engorged green beans with some obvious bulges where the beans can be found.

If the fava beans are very young, the beans may be about the size of a pea. As the fava beans get larger, there may be a discernible stem that holds the bean to the pod; pull that from the bean. After you shell the beans, taste one to see if you like the flavor and the texture. If the beans are large, if the skins seem very tough, or if the beans taste a little bitter or starchy, you may want to blanch or parcook the beans for the best texture and flavor. There really aren't any shortcuts when it comes to peeling and skinning fava beans (unless you have a source for very tender young beans), but the payoff is worth the effort.

1. Slice off the ends of the pods and run your thumbnail down the seam in each pod, slicing it open as you go. Once each pod is opened, pop the beans out and collect them in a bowl.

2. Bring a pot of salted water to a boil over high heat. Add the shelled beans and cook for 30 seconds. (Taste one of the beans; if it still seems starchy, cook it for 10 to 15 seconds more.)

3. Immediately pour the beans into a colander and rinse them with cold running water to stop the cooking.

4. Use your thumbnail to slit open the outer skin of each bean and gently press the bean out of the skin or pull it away.

Fresh Garden Peas

Garden peas are one of the great treasures of springtime. When you find them in the market, feature them in a dish with fresh favas, which are in season at the same time.

PREPARING FRESH GARDEN PEAS

1. Look for bright green pods that are not shriveled or yellowed. Some experts say that if the peas are fresh, you will hear them squeak when you rub two pods together.

2. Hold the peapod between your thumb and forefinger so that the curved side is facing up and press the pod with your thumb to pop it open. Run your thumb down the inside of the pod to pop out the peas. Collect them in a bowl. A pound of peas in the pod will typically give you about ½ cup of shelled peas.

Choosing Fish and Seafood for Italian Dishes

Italy offers cooks an abundance of different types of fish: trout from the mountains, swordfish from the sea, along with tuna, mackerel, pike, mullet, and more. Squid, octopus, and cuttlefish are enjoyed all along the coasts. One of the most anticipated meals of the year is the famous feast of seven fishes, traditionally served on Christmas Eve.

Some types of fish familiar in Italy are difficult to find in this country, but if you know the appropriate quality of the fish—lean and delicate, meaty and firm, or rich and flaky—your fishmonger can help you find a suitable replacement. The flavors might differ a little from what you'd enjoy in Italy, but the dish will still be delicious.

LEAN WHITE FISH

Catfish

Pickerel

Pike

Alaskan pollock

Cod

Flounder

Haddock

Sole

FIRM, MODERATELY FATTY FISH

Trout

Salmon

Smelt

Anchovy

Sardine

Mackerel (kingfish)

Mullet

Red mullet

Snapper

Walleye pike

Shad

Fluke

Perch

Orange roughy

FIRM, MEATY FISH

Whitefish

Tuna

Swordfish

Grouper

Mahi mahi

Shark

Monkfish

Skate

Tilefish

Preparing Finfish

You can almost always ask your fishmonger to help with filleting, gutting, scaling, or trimming your fish. In some recipes, we suggest cooking the fish whole. The tradeoff for having to pick out the bones as you eat is the enhanced flavor in the dish.

Having said that, the basic techniques you need to know are not very difficult to master. Whole fish, sold with the head and fins in place, may need to be scaled. This is done by running a serving spoon against the grain. You can tell which way the scales lie by running your fingertips over the skin. This can be messy, so, if possible, work directly in a (very clean) kitchen sink.

Use a sharp knife or kitchen scissors to cut off the tail and fins, if you wish. To cut off the head, make a cut right behind the gills. A standard chef's knife is sturdy enough to cut through the bones of most fish. If you want to remove the bones from a round fish like a trout, a process known as filleting, you will need a thin knife with a sharp, narrow blade.

FILLETING FISH

1. Make a cut along the spine of the fish, cutting through the skin until you hit the bones.

2. Keep your knife angled so that the blade is pressed against the bones, and make short, stroking cuts to remove the fish from the bones.

3. Pull the fillet away from the fish and repeat on the second side.

Filleting a flatfish is a bit more difficult, since there are actually four fillets, two on the top (they are usually a little thicker) and two on the bottom of the fish.

Seafood

Whether you are selecting seafood for a *fritto misto*, to pan-roast and serve with caponata, or to include in one of Italy's many fish soups or stews, the most important advice we can give you is to buy very fresh ingredients from a reliable source and then cook them as soon as possible.

Shrimp

Shrimp come in a range of sizes. It really doesn't matter what size you choose. The smaller the shrimp, the shorter the cooking time, of course. Most shrimp are prepared for cooking by peeling and deveining.

PREPARING SHRIMP

1. Pull the shells off the shrimp, using the legs on the underside of the fish as a tab to start pulling. You can leave the little "fan" on at the tail, if you like.

2. Use a paring knife to devein shrimp before you cook them as follows: Run the blade along the outer curve of the shrimp, right down the center. You should cut into the shrimp about ½ inch. Then, open the flap you've created and scrape out the vein. Rinse the shrimp to remove any dirt, and then blot dry.

Salted and Dried Cod

Dried fish has been part of Italian culinary traditions for many generations. Dried fish keeps for a long time, making it ideal for the seasons or regions without a good supply of fresh fish. Also, the fact that Italy has a large Catholic population who traditionally abstain from meat on Fridays and throughout Lent also means that inventive Italian cooks have for centuries been at work devising delicious ways to serve fish.

Salt cod (*baccalà*) is salted and then dried. *Stoccafisso* (stockfish) is simply air-dried cod. Both types of cod require some specific handling before you can cook them. Salt cod is the easier of the two to find in the United States.

Salt Cod

Salt cod may be purchased in large pieces or chunks. You will find wooden boxes packed with salt cod in many Italian food shops. The salt cod must be soaked in cool water for at least 12 hours, or longer, depending upon how salty the cod is. You may need to let it soak for 2 or 3 days, so plan accordingly!

PREPARING SALT COD

1. Place the cod in a bowl and add enough cold water to cover the fish completely. Let it soak in the refrigerator for 12 to 72 hours, changing the water every 8 to 10 hours until a piece of the salt cod tastes the way you want it: salty, but not unbearably so.

2. Remove the fish from the water, and check the pieces for cartilage or skin and remove. Break the remaining cod into flakes and shreds.

If you would like to make your own salt cod, you'll need 1½ pounds cod fillet and 6 tablespoons kosher salt mixed with 1 tablespoon sugar. Place the cleaned cod (skin and bones removed) on a plate and sprinkle the salt mixture evenly over the top. Cover with plastic wrap and place another plate with a heavy weight (a can of vegetables or soup will do) on top, and let stand at room temperature at least 30 minutes. You may also refrigerate it for up to 24 hours. This creates a similar taste and texture to store-bought salt cod. Cod salted this way does not need to be soaked for a long period prior to use in a recipe. Just rinse off the salt on the surface before using.

Olives and Olive Oil

According to Greek mythology, Athena gave this luscious drupe to mankind as a gift—and, in gratitude, citizens of Attica were said to have named the city of Athens after her. Pliny described fifteen varieties of olive in his day. Today, there are many more varieties from Italy and around the world.

MANZANILLO: These large, rounded oval fruits with purple-green skin have a rich taste and thick pulp. Prolific bearers, they are grown around the world.

FRANTOIO AND LECCINO: These cultivars are the principal olives in Italian olive oils from Tuscany. Leccino has a mild, sweet flavor, while Frantoio is fruity, with a stronger aftertaste. Due to their sought-after flavor, these cultivars are also grown in other countries.

ARBEQUINA: This is a small brown olive grown in Catalonia, Spain, that is good for eating and for oil.

EMPELTRE: This is a medium black olive grown in Spain, good for eating and for oil.

KALAMATA (OR CALAMATA): This large, almond-shaped, black-purple olive comes from Greece. It has a smooth, meatlike taste and is used as a table olive. These olives are usually preserved in vinegar or olive oil. Kalamata olives have protected-designation status, and thus are only grown in Greece.

KORONEIKI: This small olive originates from the southern Peloponnese, around Kalamata and Mani in Greece.

PICHOLINE: This olive originated in the south of France. It is green, medium size, and elongated. The flavor is mild and nutty.

MISSION: This type originated in Baja and was cultivated on the lands of the California Missions. It is now grown throughout the state. They are black and generally used for table consumption.

SICILIAN-STYLE OLIVES: A medium green color, they are cured in brine and preserved with lactic acid. Made from the larger Seville variety, they are crisp and salty.

GREEK-STYLE OLIVES: This style is usually made from olives that have been allowed to ripen longer on the tree. They are dry salt–cured and rubbed with olive oil. They are strong-tasting, black, and wrinkled. Other Greek-style olives are brine-cured and packed with vinegar.

GAETA: From Italy, this olive is dry salt–cured, then rubbed with olive oil. It is black and wrinkled but surprisingly mild. Some styles with this name are brine-cured. They are often packed with rosemary and other herbs.

NIÇOISE: This brown to brown-green-black olive comes from France. It is a small, tasty olive with a large pit.

Olive Oil

Olive oil can be fruity, nutty, sweet, zesty, peppery, rich, intense, and assertive; mild, mellow, light or heavy, subtle, and delicate; opaque or clear, deep olive green, pale green, gold-green, golden, or pale yellow. Like wine, no two olive oils are exactly alike.

Frantoio olives grown in Tuscany and central regions of Italy are relatively big, and when ripe they are reddish purple. Oil extracted from this olive is of high quality with a fruity and aromatic flavor. Moraiolo olives, grown in Tuscany and Umbria, are small and round and black when ripe. This olive produces a very good-quality, fruity olive oil, with a green color. Carolea olives from Calabria, in the south of Italy, produce a medium-bodied fruity, golden oil.

The finest oil has the lowest free acidity. Virgin olive oil that has a free acidity of not more than 0.8 percent and has a noticeable fruitiness is classified as "extra-virgin olive oil." The most widely marketed grade of olive oil is simply labeled "olive oil." This oil is a blend of refined olive oil and virgin olive oil. The amount of virgin olive oil in a blended oil varies, depending on the flavor desired by the producer.

CHOOSING OLIVE OIL

Olive oils area at their best within the first year of their production, so choosing a fresh oil is important.The extra-virgin olive oils of small producers vary in taste from year to year, much like wines do. You can conduct an olive oil tasting the same way you would a "blind" wine tasting. Record your impressions as you taste your way through three or four oils.

Before you taste each olive oil, look at the color of the liquid. Next, smell each oil, noting any aroma—the smell of olives—and bouquet—the "nose" of the oil. Professional olive oil tasters often rub a small amount of olive oil on their wrists to get a full sense of the oil's bouquet.

Taste the oil, using either a nonreactive spoon or a piece of bread. Finally, and perhaps most importantly, ask yourself: Do I like this oil?

Cheeses

For the sake of discussion, this section presents several broad groups of cheese that have been loosely categorized according to texture.

Fresh Cheeses

Fresh cheeses are those cheeses that are unripened and generally have a fresh, clean, creamy flavor. These cheeses are typically the most perishable and include fresh goat cheese and Robiola.

Ricotta cheese, made from recooking whey, actually began in Italy as a by-product of the cheese-making industry (the name literally means "recooked"). When whey is heated, the proteins fuse together and create a new curd that, when drained, becomes a snowy white ricotta, which is high in moisture and naturally low in fat. It is commonly used in Italian cooking as a filling for pastas or as a base for cheesecakes. Today, some ricottas are made with added part-skim or whole milk for a richer flavor.

Soft Cheeses

Soft cheeses include a wide variety ranging from mild and buttery to very pungent and aromatic. They are allowed to ripen for a few days or up to several months, when they acquire a consistency typical for toma or caciotta.

This category also includes washed rind cheeses, periodically washed with brine, beer, cider, wine, or brandy during the ripening period. This remoistening encourages bacterial growth, sometimes known as a "smear," which allows the cheese to be ripened from the outside in. Popular examples of this type of cheese include Muenster and Taleggio.

Semihard Cheese

Semihard cheeses are made from curd that is cooked and often pressed and then and allowed to form a natural rind during ripening. This category includes many cheeses produced in the northern region of Italy. Some of the best known are Asiago, Montasio, Castelmagno, and Fontina.

Blue-Veined Cheeses

Blue or blue-veined cheeses are thought to have been among some of the first cheeses produced. Although there is no specific research to prove the theory, it is believed that the mold was first introduced to cheese from moldy bread that had come in contact with the cheese. In the modern production of blue cheeses, needles are used to form holes that allow gases to escape and oxygen to enter to support mold growth within the cheese. The cheese is then salted or brined and allowed to ripen in caves or under cavelike conditions.

Gorgonzola is the most widely known Italian blue cheese. Unlike its French counterpart, Roquefort, made from sheep's milk, Gorgonzola is made from cow's milk, and the mold used to inject the cheese comes from a completely different strain. Gorgonzola is made with evening milk and the following day's morning milk. There are two varieties available: "sweet," which is aged three months, and "naturale," which is aged further and has a fuller, more robust flavor.

Pasta Filata Cheeses

Pasta filata literally means "spun curds" or "spun paste." During manufacture, the curds are dipped into hot water and then stretched or spun until the proper consistency and texture is achieved. They are then kneaded and molded into the desired shapes.

This group of cheeses is related by the process used in their manufacture rather than by their texture. In fact, the textures of pasta filata cheeses run the gamut from soft to hard, depending upon how they are aged, if at all.

The most common cheese of this category is mozzarella. Today there are two types of mozzarella available: the traditional fresh style, which is available in a variety of shapes and sizes, and the newer American invention of low-moisture mozzarella, which has a longer shelf life than the fresh style. Both whole milk and part-skim varieties are available.

Provolone is another popular pasta filata cheese that is similarly handled but is made with a different culture. Once the curd is stretched and kneaded, it is rubbed with brine and tied into a shape. It is then hung and left to dry in sizes ranging from 250 grams to 200 pounds. Provolone is often smoked and/or aged for additional character and firmer texture.

Hard Cheeses

In Italy, these cheeses are most often grated or shaved, but they are also traditionally eaten in chunks broken off with a special knife. The most popular of these cheeses are Parmigiano-Reggiano and Grana Padano.

True Parmigiano-Reggiano is often referred to as the king of cheeses. It is believed that the formula for this cheese has not changed in more than 700 years, and its origins date back even farther. This legendary cheese is made slowly and carefully following strict guidelines that require it to be aged a minimum of 14 months, although most are aged for 24 months. *Stravecchio*, or extra aged, is ripened for as long as three years. The flavor of Parmigiano-Reggiano is complex and unique. Many hard cheeses from the central and southern parts of Italy are made with sheep's milk. Some of the most well known are Pecorino Romano, Pecorino Sardo, and Pecorino Toscano.

About Mozzarella

Good-quality mozzarella is crucial in our recipes. Mozzarella *"fior di latte"* is a mozzarella made of cow's milk. The original mozzarella (*mozzarella di bufala*), made in the south of Italy, is made from buffalo milk, and should be eaten before it is more than one day old, if you are a purist. The secret to any dish that calls for mozzarella is to have a good source. Choose the best you can find; don't even try to use one that is dry and hard. Make sure it is soft to the touch and moist, preferably one that you can buy at a specialty store that makes their mozzarella fresh weekly—or preferably daily.

Index

Page numbers in *italics* indicate illustrations

A

Agnolotti
  Filled with Braised Meat, Spinach, and Brown Butter, 146, *147*
  Veal, with Its Own Sauce, 84, *85*
Almond-Tomato Pesto, Maccheroncini with, 22
Amatriciana Sauce, 159
Anchovy(ies)
  desalting, 250
  Farfalle with Cauliflower, Hard-Cooked Egg, and, 6, *7*
  Linguine with Tuna and, 64, *65*
  Pasta Rolls with Fish, Broccoli, Capers, and, 32, *33*
  Ravioli with Mozzarella, Raw Tomato, Capers, Olives, and, 29
  Spaghetti with Wild Fennel, Toasted Bread Crumbs, and, 120, *121*
Arrabbiata Sauce, 114, *115*
Artichoke(s)
  Fava Bean, and Pea Ragù, Fresh Maccheroni with, 183
  fresh, preparing, 255
  Fried, Macaroni, Homemade, with Egg, Guanciale, and, 136, *137*
  Potato Gnocchi with Squid and, 154, *155*
  and Rabbit Ragù, Papppardelle with, 192
  in Rice Salad, 54, *55*
Arugula
  Pasta Salad with Grape Tomatoes and, 9
  Sausage and Bitter Greens, Fresh Spaghetti with, 72, *73*
Asparagus
  with Gnocchi, Smoked Salmon, Baked, 212, *213*
  Gratin of Crespelle Stuffed with Spring Vegetables, 206–208, *207*, *209*
  Lasagna with Fontina and, 211
  Potato Gnocchi with Rabbit, Liver, and, 216–218, *217*
  Ravioli, -Filled Half-Moon, with Truffle Butter, 193
  Risotto with Morels and, Wild, 226, *227*
  Tortelli with Ricotta, Crayfish, and, 196
  Vegetable Ragù, Spring, Whole Grain Black Risotto with, 230, *231*

B

Basil
  blanching, 247
  Herb Emulsion, 206
  Pesto, 247
  Pesto, Almond-Tomato, Maccheroncini with, 22
  and Tomato, Fresh, Penne with, 2, *3*
  -Tomato Sauce, 36, *37*
  Tomato Sauce, Herbed Fresh, 249
Batter, Crespelle, 242
Bavette with Walnut Sauce, 58
Bean(s). *See also* Chickpea; Fava Bean(s)
  Borlotti, 254

Bread Gnocchi with, 160, *161*
  dried, preparing, 254
  Green Beans, Pasta with Pesto, Potatoes, and, 40
  Handkerchief Pasta with Seafood and, 134, *135*
  Ravioli with Marjoram and Mussels, 138, *139*
  Risotto with Vegetables, Salame, Red Wine, and, 100, *101*
Beef
  Agnolotti Filled with Braised Meat, Spinach, and Brown Butter, 146, *147*
  Broth (Brodo), Meat, 251
  Offal and Mushroom (Finanziera) Sauce, Potato Dumplings with, 86, *87*
Besciamella, 249
Bitto
  Buckwheat Pasta with Potato, Cabbage, and, 132, *133*
  Buckwheat Polenta, 166
Black Pepper
  Bucatini with Cured Pork, Tomato, and, 60, *61*
  Spaghetti with Pecorino and, 117
Blueberries, Risotto with Porcini and, 105
Bouquets garni, making, 251
Bread Crumbs
  Pasta with Octopus and, 4
  Toasted, 247
  Toasted, Spaghetti with Anchovies, Wild Fennel, and, 120, *121*
Broccoli
  Orecchiette with Mussels and, 10, *11*
  Pasta Rolls with Fish, Capers, Anchovies, and, 32, *33*
Broccoli Rabe
  Orecchiette with, 122
  Pappardelle, Chestnut, with Ricotta and, 70, *71*
Broth (Brodo)
  Fish, 252
  Langoustine, 253
  Langoustine and Tomato, 202
  Meat, 251
  Rabbit, 253
  Saffron, 52
  Shellfish, 252
Bucatini
  with Eggs, Cheese, and Guanciale, 124, *125*
  Octopus and Bread Crumbs, Pasta with, 4
  with Pork, Cured, Onions, and Black Pepper, 60, *61*
  with Pork, Cured, Onions, and Tomato, 59
Butter
  Beets, and Poppy Seeds, Ravioli Filled with, 144, *145*
  Brown, Agnolotti Filled with Braised Meat, Spinach, and, 146, *147*
  Brown, Ravioli, Sausage-Filled, with Pancetta and, 141
  Ravioli with Nettles, Sage, and, 30, *31*
  Truffle, Asparagus-Filled Half-Moon Ravioli with, 193

C

Cabbage
  Buckwheat Pasta with Bitto, Potato, and, 132, *133*
  Risotto with, 104
Calamari. *See* Squid
Candied Tomatoes, Eggplant Ravioli with Olives and, 26–28, *27*
Cannelloni
  Monkfish, with Tuscan Kale Sauce, 78–80, *79*
  Pasta Sheets for, 235
  Pasta Sheets for, Squid Ink, 236
  Potato and Pecorino, with Tomato Sauce, 148, *149*
  with Swiss Chard and Fresh Goat Cheese, 34, *35*
Capers
  Cauliflower, Roasted, with Onions and, 6
  desalting, 250
  Maccheroncini with Swordfish, Olives, Pine Nuts, and, 176, *177*
  Pasta Rolls with Fish, Broccoli, Anchovies, and, 32, *33*
  Ravioli with Mozzarella, Raw Tomato, Olives, Anchovies, and, 29
Carbonara, Bucatini with Eggs, Cheese, and Guanciale, 124, *125*
Casonsei, Pasta Dough for, 236
Cauliflower
  Farfalle with Anchovy, Hard-Cooked Egg, and, 6, *7*
  Roasted, with Onions and Capers, 6
  Squid Ink Pasta with Lobster and, 66, *67*
Cavatelli with Fava Beans, Pancetta, and Pecorino, 180
Cavolo Nero Sauce, 78, *79*
Cheese. *See also specific cheeses*
  Bucatini with Eggs, Guanciale, and, 124, *125*
  Fondue, Truffled, Polenta Dumplings with, 156, *157*
  Polenta, and Truffle Timbales, 164, *165*
  Ravioli, Fresh Cheese, with Pesto and Pine Nuts, 24, *25*
  Ravioli with Raisins, Lemon Zest, and, 140
  Tube-Shaped Pasta Tossed with Four Cheeses, 116
  varieties of, 259–260
Chestnut(s)
  Fettuccine (Dough), 239
  Pappardelle (Dough), 239
  Pappardelle with Broccoli Rabe and Ricotta, 70, *71*
  preparing, 255
  Rolled Pasta with Pumpkin and, 76, *77*
  Tagliatelle (Dough), 239
Chicken
  Broth (Brodo), Meat, 251
  and Chanterelle Ragù, Farro with, 98, *99*
  Offal and Mushroom (Finanziera) Sauce, Potato Dumplings with, 86, *87*

Chickpea
Crespelle (Batter), 242
Crespelle with Bitter Greens, 150
Polenta, 94
Corzetti
with Marjoram and Pine Nuts, 194, *195*
Pasta Dough, 238
Crayfish
Pumpkin Dumplings with, 88–90, *89, 91*
Tortelli with Ricotta, Asparagus, and, 196
Crespelle, 242
Bundles Filled with Fresh Goat Cheese, Honey, and Marjoram, 205
Chickpea, 242
Chickpea, with Bitter Greens, 150
Gratin of, Stuffed with Spring Vegetables, 206–208, *207, 209*
Stuffed with Eggplant and Topped with Fresh Tomatoes and Ricotta, 41

D

Dandelion Greens
and Bread Dumplings, 214, *215*
Chickpea Crespelle with Bitter Greens, 150
Pansotti with Ricotta and Bitter Greens, 197
Duck Ragù, Pappardelle with, 69

E

Egg(s)
Bucatini with Cheese, Guanciale, and, 124, *125*
to hard cook, 6
Hard-Cooked, Farfalle with Cauliflower, Anchovy, and, 6, *7*
Hard-Cooked, in Rice Salad, 54, *55*
Macaroni, Homemade, with Guanciale, Fried Artichokes, and, 136, *137*
in pasta dough, 233
Eggplant
Crespelle Stuffed with, and Topped with Fresh Tomatoes and Ricotta, 41
Gnocchi with Fresh Tomato Sauce and Ricotta Salata, 42, *43*
Lasagna with Tomato, Mozzarella, and, 36, *37*
preparing, 250
Ravioli with Candied Tomatoes and Olives, 26–28, *27*

F

Farfalle with Cauliflower, Anchovy, and Hard-Cooked Egg, 6, *7*
Farfalline
Pasta Dough, 239
Pasta Sheets, Squid Ink, 236
Squid Ink, with Shrimp, Calamari, and Fava Beans, 186, *187*
Farro
with Chicken and Chanterelle Ragù, 98, *99*
Salad with Pesto, 174, *175*
soaking, 174
Fava Bean(s)
Cavatelli with Pancetta, Pecorino, and, 180
Farfalline, Squid Ink, with Shrimp, Calamari, and, 186, *187*
fresh, preparing, 255–256
Pea, and Artichoke Ragù, Fresh Maccheroni with, 183
Risotto with Peas, Mint, and, 228

Trofiette with Lobster, Leeks, Zucchini, and, 184, *185*
Fazzoletti
Basic Pasta for, 237
Handkerchief Pasta with Beans and Seafood, 134, *135*
Fennel
Wild, Ragù, Semolina Gnocchi with Sausage and, 151
Wild, Spaghetti with Anchovies, Toasted Bread Crumbs, and, 120, *121*
Fettuccine
Basic Pasta for, 237
Chestnut (Dough), 239
Red Wine (Dough), 238
Red Wine, with Wild Game, 129
Finanziera Sauce, 86, *87*
Fish. *See also* Anchovy(ies); Seafood
Bass, Striped (Branzino), Ravioli with Seafood Sauce, 198, *199*
Broth, 252
Cod, Salt
Polenta with, 163
preparing, 258
Cuttlefish, Marinated, Saffron-Scented Fregola with, 52, *53*
Cuttlefish, in Spaghetti with Squid Ink, 16
Monkfish Cannelloni with Tuscan Kale Sauce, 78, *79*
Pasta Rolls with Broccoli, Capers, Anchovies, and, 32, *33*
preparing/filleting, 257
Rockfish, Paccheri with Saffron, Grape Tomatoes, and, 14, *15*
Salmon, Smoked, Gnocchi with Asparagus, Baked, 212, *213*
Stew, Strozzapreti with, 126, *127*
Swordfish, Maccheroncini with Capers, Olives, Pine Nuts, and, 176, *177*
Tuna, Fresh, Spaghetti with Garlic, Tomato, Mint, and, 19
Tuna, Linguine with Anchovies and, 64, *65*
varieties of, for Italian dishes, 256–257
Fonduta Sauce, 156, 244
Fontina
Buckwheat Pasta with Potato, Cabbage, and, 132, *133*
Buckwheat Polenta, 166
Fonduta Sauce, 156
Lasagna with Asparagus and, 211
Polenta with Mushrooms, Sausage, and, 95
Risotto with Apple, Walnuts, Porcini Mushrooms, and, 106, *107*
Tube-Shaped Pasta Tossed with Four Cheeses, 116
Fregola, Saffron-Scented, with Marinated Cuttlefish, 52, *53*

G

Game, Wild
Boar Sauce, Cocoa Pappardelle with, 130, *131*
Red Wine Fettuccine with, 129
Garganelli
with Leeks and Morels, 181
with Red Onion, Pancetta, Olives, Pecorino, and Cream, 123

Garlic
Oil, and Hot Pepper, Spaghetti with, 118, *119*
in Pesto, 247
-Tomato Sauce, Spicy (Arrabbiata), Pennette with, 114, *115*
Gnocchi
about, 243–244
Baked, Smoked Salmon with Asparagus, 212, *213*
Bread, with Beans, 160, *161*
Bread Dumplings, and Dandelion, 214, *215*
Bread Dumplings, and Swiss Chard, 219
Buckwheat and Potato, with Mixed Root Vegetable Ragù, 92, *93*
Eggplant, with Fresh Tomato Sauce and Ricotta Salata, 42, *43*
gnudi (naked), 243
Oven-Puffed, with Truffle, 158, *159*
Polenta Dumplings with Truffled Cheese Fondue, 156, *157*
Potato
with Artichokes and Squid, 154, *155*
with Asparagus, Rabbit, and Liver, 216–218, *217*
Baked, with Tomato, Scamorza, and Oregano, 46
Dough, 245
Dumplings with Offal and Mushroom Sauce, 86, *87*
making, 243
and Prune, with Cinnamon and Smoked Prosciutto, 152
Pumpkin Dumplings with Crayfish, 88–90, *89, 91*
Ricotta and Spinach Dumplings (Gnudi), 44, *45*
Semolina, with Radicchio, 162
Semolina, Roman-Style, 153
Semolina, with Sausage and Wild Fennel Ragù, 151
soufflé., 244
Gnudi (naked gnocchi), 243
Ricotta and Spinach Dumplings, 44, *45*
Goat Cheese, 259
Fresh, Cannelloni with Swiss Chard and, 34, *35*
Fresh, Crespelle Bundles Filled with Honey, Marjoram, and, 205
Gorgonzola
about, 260
Ravioli with Cheese, Raisins, and Lemon Zest, 140
Risotto with Radicchio, Pear, and, 102, *103*
Tube-Shaped Pasta Tossed with Four Cheeses, 116
Gratin of Crespelle Stuffed with Spring Vegetables, 206–208, *207, 209*
Green Beans, Pesto, and Potatoes, Pasta with, 40
Green Pasta, Straw-and-Hay, 237
with Peas and Ham, 188, *189*
Greens, Bitter. *See also specific greens*
blanching, 250
Chickpea Crespelle with, 150
Pansotti with Ricotta and, 197
and Sausage, Fresh Spaghetti with, 72, *73*
Gricia Sauce, 160, *161*
Guanciale (Cured Pork)
Bucatini with Eggs, Cheese, and, 124, *125*
Bucatini with Onions, Black Pepper, and, 60, *61*

Bucatini with Onions, Tomato, and, 59
Macaroni, Homemade, with Egg, Fried
 Artichokes, and, 136, *137*

H

Ham
 Ravioli, Large, with Peas and Langoustines,
  202–204, *203*
 Rolled Pasta with Ricotta, Spinach, and, 210
 Straw-and-Hay Pasta with Peas and, 188, *189*
Handkerchief Pasta with Beans and Seafood,
  134, *135*
Herb(s). *See also specific herbs*
 bouquets garni/sachets, 251
 Emulsion, 206

K

Kale
 blanching, 250
 Sauce, Tuscan, Monkfish Cannelloni with,
  78–80, *79*

L

Lamb
 and Pepper Sauce, Troccoli with, 20, *21*
 Sauce, Fresh Spaghetti with, 74
Langoustine(s)
 Broth, 253
 Ravioli, Large, with Peas and, 202–204, *203*
 Risotto with Fresh Herbs and, 221
 Seafood Sauce, Striped Bass (Branzino)
  Ravioli with, 198, *199*
 and Tomato Broth, 202
Lasagna
 with Asparagus and Fontina, 211
 with Eggplant, Tomato, and Mozzarella,
  36, *37*
 Pasta Sheets for, 235
 Vegetable, with Fresh Tomato Sauce, 38, *39*
Leeks
 Garganelli with Morels and, 181
 Gratin of Crespelle Stuffed with Spring
  Vegetables, 206–208, *207*, *209*
 Trofiette with Lobster, Zucchini, Fava Beans,
  and, 184, *185*
Lemon Risotto, 47
Lemon Zest
 Orecchiette with Ricotta, Peas, and, 178, *179*
 Ravioli with Cheese, Raisins, and, 140
Linguine
 with Clams, Mussels, and Peppers, 12, *13*
 with Clams and Pancetta, 175
 Octopus and Bread Crumbs, Pasta with, 4
 with Tuna and Anchovies, 64, *65*
Liver
 Offal and Mushroom (Finanziera) Sauce,
  Potato Dumplings with, 86, *87*
 Potato Gnocchi with Asparagus, Rabbit, and,
  216–218, *217*
Lobster. *See also* Langoustine(s)
 cookimg/cutting up, 184
 Maccheroni with Seafood and Fresh Tomato, 5
 Squid Ink Pasta with Cauliflower and, 66, *67*
 Trofiette with Leeks, Zucchini, Fava Beans,
  and, 184, *185*

M

Macaroni, Homemade, with Egg, Guanciale, and
 Fried Artichokes, 136, *137*
Maccheroncini
 with Almond-Tomato Pesto, 22
 with Swordfish, Capers, Olives, and Pine
  Nuts, 176, *177*
Maccheroni
 alla Chitarra (Pasta Dough), 240
 Fresh, with Fava Bean, Pea, and Artichoke
  Ragù, 183
 Macaroni, Homemade, with Egg, Guanciale,
  and Fried Artichokes, 136, *137*
 with Seafood and Fresh Tomato, 5
 Spaghetti, Fresh, with Lamb Sauce, 74
 Spaghetti, Fresh, with Sausage and Bitter
  Greens, 72, *73*
Maltagliati, Basic Pasta for, 237
Marjoram
 Corzetti with Pine Nuts and, 194, *195*
 Crespelle Bundles Filled with Fresh Goat
  Cheese, Honey, and, 205
 Ravioli, Bean, with Mussels and, 138, *139*
Mascarpone
 Ravioli, Fresh Cheese, with Pesto and Pine
  Nuts, 24, *25*
 and Robiola Sauce, 208, *209*
Meat Broth (Brodo), 251
Mint
 Risotto with Fava Beans, Peas, and, 228
 Spaghetti, with Garlic, Tomato, Fresh Tuna,
  and, 19
Montasio, Risotto with Radicchio and, 168, *169*
Mozzarella
 about, 260
 Lasagna with Eggplant, Tomato, and, 36, *37*
 Ravioli with Raw Tomato, Capers, Olives,
  Anchovies, and, 29
Mushroom(s)
 Chanterelle and Chicken Ragù, Farro with,
  98, *99*
 Gratin of Crespelle Stuffed with Spring
  Vegetables, 206–208, *207*, *209*
 Marinated, in Rice Salad, 54, *55*
 Morels and Asparagus, Wild, Risotto with,
  226, *227*
 Morels and Leeks, Garganelli with, 181
 and Offal (Finanziera) Sauce, Potato
  Dumplings with, 86, *87*
 Polenta with Sausage, Fontina, and, 95
 Porcini
  Risotto with Apple, Walnuts, Fontina,
   and, 106, *107*
  Risotto with Blueberries and, 105
  with Spaghetti, Handmade, 75
  Tagliatelle with Shrimp and, 68
 Tortelli with Parsley Sauce, 82, *83*
 Vegetable Ragù, Spring, Whole Grain Black
  Risotto with, 230, *231*
Mussels
 Handkerchief Pasta with Beans and Seafood,
  134, *135*
 Linguine with Clams, Peppers, and, 12, *13*
 Maccheroni with Seafood and Fresh Tomato, 5
 Orecchiette with Broccoli and, 10, *11*
 Pan-Steamed, 12, 222
 Ravioli, Bean, with Marjoram and, 138, *139*
 Rice, Potato, and Oregano, 167

 Risotto with Saffron, Zucchini Blossoms, and,
  222, *223*
 Vermicelli with Pecorino Romano and, 18
Mustard, Fruit, Tortelli Filled with Pumpkin,
 Amaretti Cookies, and, 81

N

Nettles, Ravioli with Butter, Sage, and, 30, *31*

O

Octopus and Bread Crumbs, Pasta with, 4
Offal and Mushroom (Finanziera) Sauce, Potato
 Dumplings with, 86, *87*
Olive Oil
 Garlic, and Hot Pepper, Spaghetti with, 118,
  119
 selecting, 259
Olives
 Eggplant Ravioli with Candied Tomatoes
  and, 26–28, *27*
 Garganelli with Red Onion, Pancetta,
  Pecorino, Cream, and, 123
 Maccheroncini with Swordfish, Capers, Pine
  Nuts, and, 176, *177*
 Ravioli with Mozzarella, Raw Tomato, Capers,
  Anchovies, and, 29
 in Rice Salad, 54, *55*
 varieties of, 258–259
Onion(s)
 Cured Pork, and Black Pepper, Bucatini with,
  60, *61*
 Cured Pork, and Tomato, Bucatini with, 59
 Red Onion, Garganelli with Pancetta, Olives,
  Pecorino, Cream, and, 123
 Sauce, Spring, 230, *231*
 Trenette with Peppers and Spring Onions, 8
Orecchiette
 with Broccoli Rabe, 122
 with Mussels and Broccoli, 10, *11*
 with Ricotta, Peas, and Lemon Zest, 178, *179*

P

Paccheri with Rockfish, Saffron, and Grape
 Tomatoes, 14, *15*
Pancetta
 Cavatelli with Fava Beans, Pecorino, and, 180
 Garganelli with Red Onion, Olives, Pecorino,
  Cream, and, 123
 Linguine with Clams and, 175
 Ravioli, Sausage-Filled, with Brown Butter
  and, 141
 and Tomato Sauce with Borlotti Beans, 160,
  161
Pansotti with Ricotta and Bitter Greens, 197
Pappardelle
 Basic Pasta for, 237
 Chestnut, with Broccoli Rabe and Ricotta,
  70, *71*
 Cocoa (Dough), 240
 Cocoa, with Wild Boar Sauce, 130, *131*
 with Duck Ragù, 69
 with Rabbit and Artichoke Ragù, 192
Parmigiano-Reggiano
 about, 260
 in Pesto, 247
 Pumpkin, and Aged Balsamic Vinegar,
  Pennette Tossed with, 62

Parmigiano-Reggiano (continued)
    Ravioli with Cheese, Raisins, and Lemon Zest, 140
    Risotto with Pumpkin and, 110, *111*
Parsley Sauce, Mushroom Tortelli with, 82, *83*
Pasta. See also specific pasta
    cooking (dried), 233
    cooking (fresh), 241
    dough. See Pasta Dough; Pasta Sheets
    saucing, 241
    stuffed, making, 241
Pasta Dough. See also Pasta Sheets
    Casonsei, 236
    Corzetti, 238
    drying, 235
    Farfalline, 239
    Fazzoletti, 237
    Fettuccine, 237
    Fettuccine, Red Wine, 238
    handmade, 233, 234
    ingredients, 233–234
    machine made, 234–235
    Maltagliati, 237
    Pappardelle, 237
    Pappardelle, Chestnut, 239
    Pici, 238
    Pizzoccheri, 239
    Scialatielli, 240
    Stracci, 237
    Straw-and-Hay, 237
    Tagliatelle, 237
    Tagliatelle, Chestnut, 239
    Tajarin, 239
Pasta filata cheese, 260
Pasta machine, 234–235
Pasta Rolls with Fish, Broccoli, Capers, and Anchovies, 32, *33*
Pasta Salad with Arugula and Grape Tomatoes, 9
Pasta Sheets
    for Lasagna, Cannelloni, and Rotolo, 235
    Potato Ravioli, 236
    Ravioli, 235
    Squid Ink, 236
Pea(s)
    Fava Bean, and Artichoke Ragù, Fresh Maccheroni with, 183
    fresh, preparing, 256
    Orecchiette with Ricotta, Lemon Zest, and, 178, *179*
    Ravioli, Large, with Langoustines and, 202–204, *203*
    Rice and, 224, *225*
    Risotto with Calamari and Fresh Peas, 220
    Risotto with Fava Beans, Mint, and, 228
    Straw-and-Hay Pasta with Ham and, 188, *189*
    Vegetable Ragù, Spring, Whole Grain Black Risotto with, 230, *231*
Pear, Gorgonzola, and Radicchio, Risotto with, 102, *103*
Pecorino Romano
    Bucatini with Eggs, Cheese, Guanciale, and, 124, *125*
    Cannelloni, Potato and, with Tomato Sauce, 148, *149*
    Cavatelli with Fava Beans, Pancetta, and, 180
    Garganelli with Red Onion, Pancetta, Olives, Cream, and, 123
    in Orecchiette with Broccoli Rabe, 122
    in Pesto, 247

Spaghetti with Black Pepper and, 117
Tube-Shaped Pasta Tossed with Four Cheeses, 116
Vermicelli with Mussels and, 18
Penne
    with Tomato and Basil, Fresh, 2, *3*
    with Zucchini, Walnuts, and Provolone, 182
Pennette
    with Garlic-Tomato Sauce, Spicy, 114, *115*
    Pumpkin, Parmigiano, and Aged Balsamic Vinegar Tossed with, 62
Pepper
    Black, Cured Pork, and Tomato, Bucatini with, 60, *61*
    Black, and Pecorino, Spaghetti with, 117
    Hot, Garlic, and Oil, Spaghetti with, 118, *119*
    and Lamb Sauce, Troccoli with, 20, *21*
Peppers
    Linguine with Clams, Mussels, and, 12, *13*
    peeling, 50
    Risotto with Sweet Peppers and Scallops, 50, *51*
    Trenette with Spring Onions and, 8
Pesto, 247
    Almond-Tomato, Maccheroncini with, 22
    basil for, 246, *247*
    Farro Salad with, 174, *175*
    Green Beans, and Potatoes, Pasta with, 40
    making, 246–247
    and Pine Nuts, Fresh Cheese Ravioli with, 24, *25*
Pici, 238
    Spaghetti, Handmade, with Porcini Mushrooms, 75
Pine Nuts
    Corzetti with Marjoram and, 194, *195*
    Maccheroncini with Swordfish, Capers, Olives, and, 176, *177*
    in Pesto, 247
    and Pesto, Fresh Cheese Ravioli with, 24, *25*
Pizzoccheri, 239
    Buckwheat Pasta with Bitto, Potato, and Cabbage, 132, *133*
Polenta
    Buckwheat, 166
    Cheese, and Truffle Timbales, 164, *165*
    Chickpea, 94
    with Cod, Salt, 163
    Dumplings with Truffled Cheese Fondue, 156, *157*
    with Mushrooms, Sausage, and Fontina, 95
    with Sopressata and Vinegar Sauce, 87, *96*
Poppy Seeds, Beets, and Butter, Ravioli Filled with, 144, *145*
Porcini
    Risotto with Apple, Walnuts, Fontina, and, 106, *107*
    Risotto with Blueberries and, 105
    with Spaghetti, Homemade, 75
    Tagliatelle with Shrimp and, 68
Pork. See Ham; Pancetta; Prosciutto; Sausage
Potato(es)
    Buckwheat Pasta with Bitto, Cabbage, and, 132, *133*
    Cannelloni, and Pecorino, with Tomato Sauce, 148, *149*
    Gnocchi
        with Artichokes and Squid, 154, *155*

with Asparagus, Rabbit, and Liver, 216–218, *217*
    Baked, with Tomato, Scamorza, and Oregano, 46
    and Buckwheat, with Mixed Root Vegetable Ragù, 92, *93*
    Dough, 245
    making, 243
    and Prune, with Cinnamon and Smoked Prosciutto, 152
    Pesto, and Green Beans, Pasta with, 40
    Ravioli Sheets, 236
    Rice, Mussels, and Oregano, 167
Prosciutto
    Smoked, Prune and Potato Gnocchi with Cinnamon, 152
    Smoked, Radicchio and Speck, 162
Provolone, 260
    Penne with Zucchini, Walnuts, and, 182
Prune and Potato Gnocchi with Cinnamon and Smoked Prosciutto, 152
Pumpkin
    Dumplings with Crayfish, 88–90, *89, 91*
    Pennette Tossed with Parmigiano, Aged Balsamic Vinegar, and, 62
    Risotto with Parmigiano-Reggiano and, 110, *111*
    Rolled Pasta with Chestnut and, 76, *77*
    Tortelli Filled with Amaretti Cookies, Fruit Mustard, and, 81

Q

Quail, Roasted, Herbed Risotto with, 108, *109*

R

Rabbit
    and Artichoke Ragù, Papppardelle with, 192
    Broth, 252
    Potato Gnocchi with Asparagus, Liver, and, 216–218, *217*
Radicchio
    Risotto with Gorgonzola, Pear, and, 102, *103*
    Risotto with Montasio and, 168, *169*
    Sausage and Bitter Greens, Fresh Spaghetti with, 72, *73*
    Semolina Gnocchi with, 162
Ragù
    Boar, Wild, Cocoa Pappardelle with, 130, *131*
    Chicken and Chanterelles, Farro with, 98, *99*
    combining with pasta, 241
    Duck, Pappardelle with, 69
    Fava Bean, Pea, and Artichoke, Fresh Maccheroni with, 183
    Fennel, Wild, Semolina Gnocchi with Sausage and, 151
    Game, Braised, 129
    Lamb, Fresh Spaghetti with, 74
    Lamb and Pepper, Troccoli with, 20, *21*
    Mushroom, and Sausages, 95
    Rabbit and Artichoke, Papppardelle with, 192
    Rabbit, Potato Gnocchi with Asparagus, Liver, and, 216–218, *217*
    Veal, White, Tagliatelle with, 190, *191*
    Vegetable, Root, Mixed, Buckwheat and Potato Gnocchi with, 92, *93*
    Vegetable, Spring, Whole Grain Black Risotto with, 230, *231*
Raisins, Ravioli with Cheese, Lemon Zest, and, 140

Ravioli
    Asparagus-Filled Half-Moon, with Truffle
        Butter, 193
    Bass, Striped (Branzino), with Seafood Sauce,
        198, *199*
    Bean, with Marjoram and Mussels, 138, *139*
    Beets, Butter, and Poppy Seeds, Filled with,
        144, *145*
    Cheese, Fresh, with Pesto and Pine Nuts,
        24, *25*
    with Cheese, Raisins, and Lemon Zest, 140
    Eggplant, with Candied Tomatoes and
        Olives, 26–28, *27*
    forming, 241
    Large, with Peas and Langoustines, 202–204,
        203
    with Mozzarella, Raw Tomato, Capers, Olives,
        and Anchovies, 29
    with Nettles, Butter, and Sage, 30, *31*
    Pasta Sheets for, 235
    Potato Sheets, 236
    Sausage-Filled, with Brown Butter and
        Pancetta, 141
Red Onion, Garganelli with Pancetta, Olives,
    Pecorino, Cream, and, 123
Red Wine
    Fettuccine (Dough), 238
    Fettuccine with Wild Game, 129
    Risotto with Salami, 170, *171*
    Risotto with Vegetables, Beans, Salame, and,
        100, *101*
Rice. *See also* Risotto
    and Peas, 224, *225*
    Potato, Mussels, and Oregano, 167
    Salad, 54, *55*
    varieties of, 245
Ricotta
    about, 259
    Crespelle, Chickpea, with Bitter Greens, 150
    Crespelle Stuffed with Eggplant and Topped
        with Fresh Tomatoes and, 41
    Orecchiette with Peas, Lemon Zest, and,
        178, *179*
    Pansotti with Bitter Greens and, 197
    Pappardelle, Chestnut, with Broccoli Rabe
        and, 70, *71*
    Ravioli with Cheese, Raisins, and Lemon
        Zest, 140
    Ravioli Filled with Beets, Butter, and Poppy
        Seeds, 144, *145*
    Ravioli, Fresh Cheese, with Pesto and Pine
        Nuts, 24, *25*
    Rolled Pasta with Spinach, Ham, and, 210
    and Spinach Dumplings (Gnudi), 44, *45*
    -Spinach Filling, in Egg-Filled Tortelli with
        White Truffle, 142, *143*
    Tortelli, with Asparagus, Crayfish, and, 196
Ricotta Salata, Eggplant Gnocchi with Fresh
    Tomato Sauce and, 42, *43*
Rigatoni with Sausage and a Touch of Cream, 128
Risotto
    with Apple, Walnuts, Porcini Mushrooms, and
        Fontina, 106, *107*
    with Asparagus and Morels, Wild, 226, *227*
    Black, Whole Grain, with Spring Vegetable
        Ragù, 230, *231*
    with Cabbage, 104
    with Calamari and Fresh Peas, 220
    cooking pan, 245

cooking/serving, 246
with Fava Beans, Peas, and Mint, 228
with Gorgonzola, Radicchio, and Pear, 102,
    103
Herbed, with Roasted Quail, 108, *109*
with Langoustines and Fresh Herbs, 221
Lemon, 47
with Mussels, Saffron, and Zucchini Blossoms,
    222, *223*
with Porcini and Blueberries, 105
with Pumpkin and Parmigiano-Reggiano,
    110, *111*
with Radicchio and Montasio, 168, *169*
Red Wine, with Salame, 170, *171*
rice for, 245
with Seafood, 48, *49*
with Sweet Peppers and Scallops, 50, *51*
with Vegetables, Beans, Salame, and Red
    Wine, 100, *101*
with Zucchini Blossoms and Truffles, 229
Robiola, 259
    and Mascarpone Sauce, 208, *209*
    Ravioli, Fresh Cheese, with Pesto and Pine
        Nuts, 24, *25*
Rolled Pasta. *See also* Cannelloni
    with Pumpkin and Chestnut, 76, *77*
    with Ricotta, Spinach, and Ham, 210
Roman-Style Semolina Gnocchi, 153
Root Vegetable Ragù, Mixed, Buckwheat and
    Potato Gnocchi with, 92, *93*
Rotolini Pasta Sheets, Squid Ink, 236
Rotolo Pasta Sheets, 235

S

Saffron
    Fregola, -Scented, with Marinated Cuttlefish,
        52, *53*
    Risotto with Mussels, Zucchini Blossoms, and,
        222, *223*
    Rockfish, and Grape Tomatoes, Paccheri with,
        14, *15*
Salad(s)
    Farro, with Pesto, 174
    Pasta, with Arugula and Grape Tomatoes, 9
    Rice, 54, *55*
Salami (Salame)
    Red Wine Risotto with, 170, *171*
    Risotto with Vegetables, Beans, Red Wine,
        and, 100, *101*
    Sopressata and Vinegar Sauce, Polenta with,
        96, *97*
Sauce(s). *See also* Pesto; Ragù; Tomato Sauce
    Amatriciana, 159
    Artichoke and Squid, 154, *155*
    Besciamella, 249
    Besciamella, in Lasagna with Asparagus and
        Fontina, 211
    Cavolo Nero, 78, *79*
    Cod, Salt, 163
    combining with pasta, 241
    Crayfish, 196
    Fonduta, 156
    Gricia, 160, *161*
    Leek and Morel, 181
    Lobster, Leek, Zucchini, and Fava, 184, *185*
    Lobster and Cauliflower, 66, *67*
    Offal and Mushroom (Finanziera), Potato
        Dumplings with, 86, *87*
    Onion, Spring, 230, *231*

Parsley, Mushroom Tortelli with, 82, *83*
Porcini and Shrimp, 68
Pumpkin, 62
Robiola and Mascarpone, 208, *209*
Seafood, with Beans and Tomatoes, 134, *135*
Seafood and Fresh Tomato, 5
Seafood, Striped Bass (Branzino), Ravioli with,
    198, *199*
Shrimp, Calamari, and Fava Bean, 186, *187*
Sopressata and Vinegar, Polenta with, 96, *97*
Truffle Butter, Asparagus-Filled Half-Moon
    Ravioli with, 193
Tuna and Anchovy, 64, *65*
Walnut, Bavette with, 58
Sausage
    and Bitter Greens, Fresh Spaghetti with, 72, *73*
    Offal and Mushroom (Finanziera) Sauce,
        Potato Dumplings with, 86, *87*
    Polenta with Mushrooms, Fontina, and, 95
    Ravioli, -Filled, with Brown Butter and
        Pancetta, 141
    Rigatoni with a Touch of Cream and, 128
    Semolina Gnocchi with Wild Fennel Ragù
        and, 151
Scallops
    Handkerchief Pasta with Beans and Seafood,
        134, *135*
    Maccheroni with Seafood and Fresh Tomato, 5
    Risotto with Sweet Peppers and, 50, *51*
Scamorza, Tomato, and Oregano, Baked Potato
    Gnocchi with, 46
Scialatielli, 240
    with Baby Squid and Fresh Tomatoes, 23
Sea Bass, Pasta Rolls with Fish, Broccoli, Capers,
    and Anchovies, 32, *33*
Seafood. *See also* Fish; Mussels; Shrimp; Squid
    Broth, Shellfish, 252
    Clams, Linguine with Mussels, Peppers, and,
        12, *13*
    Clams, Linguine with Pancetta and, 175
    Crayfish, Pumpkin Dumplings with, 88–90,
        89, 91
    Crayfish, Tortelli with Ricotta, Asparagus,
        and, 196
    Handkerchief Pasta with Beans and, 134, *135*
    Langoustines, Large Ravioli with Peas and,
        202–204, *203*
    Langoustines, Risotto with Fresh Herbs and,
        221
    Linguine with Clams, Mussels, and Peppers,
        12, *13*
    Lobster, Squid Ink Pasta with Cauliflower and,
        66, *67*
    Lobster, Trofiette with Leeks, Zucchini, Fava
        Beans, and, 184, *185*
    Maccheroni with Fresh Tomato and, 5
    Octopus and Bread Crumbs, Pasta with, 4
    Risotto with, 48, *49*
    Sauce with Beans and Tomatoes, 134, *135*
    Sauce, Fresh Tomato and, 5
    Sauce, Striped Bass (Branzino), Ravioli with,
        198, *199*
    Scallops, Risotto with Sweet Peppers and,
        50, *51*
    Stew, Fish, Strozzapreti with, 126, *127*
Sedanini Tossed with Four Cheeses, 116
Semolina Gnocchi
    with Radicchio, 162
    Ricotta and Spinach Dumplings, 44, *45*

Semolina Gnocchi (continued)
    Roman-Style, 153
    with Sausage and Wild Fennel Ragù, 151
Shellfish. See Seafood
Shrimp
    Farfalline, Squid Ink, with Calamari, Fava
        Beans, and, 186, 187
    Handkerchief Pasta with Beans and Seafood,
        134, 135
    Maccheroni with Seafood and Fresh Tomato, 5
    peeling/deveining, 257
    Seafood Sauce, Striped Bass (Branzino)
        Ravioli with, 198, 199
    Tagliatelle with Porcini and, 68
Sopressata and Vinegar Sauce, Polenta with, 96, 97
Souffléd gnocchi, 244
Spaghetti
    with Anchovies, Wild Fennel, and Toasted
        Bread Crumbs, 120, 121
    with Black Pepper and Pecorino, 117
    Fresh, with Lamb Sauce, 74
    Fresh, with Sausage and Bitter Greens, 72, 73
    with Garlic, Oil, and Hot Pepper, 118, 119
    with Garlic, Tomato, Mint, and Fresh Tuna, 19
    Handmade, with Porcini Mushrooms, 75
    Octopus and Bread Crumbs, Pasta with, 4
    Porcini Mushrooms with Handmade
        Spaghetti, 75
    with Squid Ink, 16, 17
Spinach
    Agnolotti Filled with Braised Meat, Brown
        Butter, and, 146, 147
    blanching, 250
    Green Pasta, Straw-and-Hay, 237
    and Ricotta Dumplings (Gnudi), 44, 45
    -Ricotta Filling, in Egg-Filled Tortelli with
        White Truffle, 142, 143
    Rolled Pasta with Ricotta, Ham, and, 210
Squid
    Baby, Scialatielli with Fresh Tomatoes and, 23
    Farfalline, Squid Ink, with Shrimp, Calamari,
        and Fava Beans, 186, 187
    Maccheroni with Seafood and Fresh Tomato, 5
    Potato Gnocchi with Artichokes and, 154, 155
    Risotto with Calamari and Fresh Peas, 220
Squid Ink
    Farfalline with Shrimp, Calamari, and Fava
        Beans, 186, 187
    Pasta with Lobster and Cauliflower, 66, 67
    Pasta Sheets, 236
    Spaghetti with, 16, 17
Stew, Fish, Strozzapreti with, 126, 127
Stock. See Broth
Stracchino Cheese, Tortelli with Zucchini and,
        200, 201
Stracci
    Basic Pasta for, 237
    with Pesto, Green Beans, and Potatoes, 40
Straw-and-Hay Pasta, 237
    with Peas and Ham, 188, 189
Strozzapreti with Fish Stew, 126, 127
Sweetbreads, Veal, in Offal and Mushroom
        (Finanziera) Sauce, Potato
        Dumplings with, 86, 87
Swiss Chard
    blanching, 250
    and Bread Dumplings, 219
    Cannelloni with Fresh Goat Cheese and, 34, 35
    Pansotti with Ricotta and Bitter Greens, 197

T
Tagliatelle
    Basic Pasta for, 237
    Pasta Dough for, 237
    with Porcini and Shrimp, 68
    with White Veal Ragù, 190, 191
Tagliolini, Squid Ink Pasta Sheets, 236
Tajarin
    Pasta Dough, 239
    with White Truffle, 63
Taleggio, Ravioli with Cheese, Raisins, and
        Lemon Zest, 140
Timbales, Polenta, Cheese, and Truffle, 164, 165
Tomato(es)
    -Almond Pesto, Maccheroncini with, 22
    Broth, Langoustine and, 202
    Bucatini with Cured Pork, Onions, and, 59
    Candied, Eggplant Ravioli with Olives and,
        26–28, 27
    canned, crushing/sieving, 248
    Crespelle Stuffed with Eggplant and Topped
        with Fresh Tomatoes and Ricotta, 41
    Grape, Paccheri with Rockfish, Saffron, and,
        14, 15
    Grape, Pasta Salad with Arugula and, 9
    Lasagna with Eggplant, Mozzarella, and,
        36, 37
    Maccheroni with Seafood and Fresh Tomato, 5
    Pasta Salad with Arugula and, 9
    peeling/seeding, 248
    Penne with Fresh Tomato and Basil, 2, 3
    Potato Gnocchi, Baked, with Scamorza,
        Oregano, and, 46
    Ravioli with Mozzarella, Raw Tomato, Capers,
        Olives, and Anchovies, 29
    Scialatielli with Baby Squid and Fresh
        Tomatoes, 23
    Seafood Sauce with Beans and, 134, 135
    Spaghetti, with Garlic, Mint, Fresh Tuna,
        and, 19
Tomato Sauce, 248
    -Basil, 36, 37
    with Cannelloni, Potato, and Pecorino, 148,
        149
    Fresh, 249
        and Baby Squid, 23
        and Basil, 2, 3
        Eggplant Gnocchi with Ricotta Salata
            and, 42, 43
        Herbed, 249
        and Mussels, Pan-Steamed, 18
        Saffron-, 14, 15
        and Seafood, 5
        Vegetable Lasagna with, 38, 39
    Garlic-, Spicy (Arrabbiata), Pennette with,
        114, 115
    and Octopus, 4
    and Pancetta, with Borlotti Beans, 160, 161
Tortelli
    Egg-Filled, with White Truffle, 142, 143
    Mushroom, with Parsley Sauce, 82, 83
    Pumpkin, Amaretti Cookies, and Fruit
        Mustard, Filled with, 81
    with Ricotta, Asparagus, and Crayfish, 196
    with Stracchino Cheese and Zucchini, 200, 201
Tortellini, forming, 241
Trenette with Peppers and Spring Onions, 8

Troccoli
    with Lamb and Pepper Sauce, 20, 21
    Pasta Dough, 240
Trofiette with Lobster, Leeks, Zucchini, and Fava
        Beans, 184, 185
Truffle(s)
    Butter, Asparagus-Filled Half-Moon Ravioli
        with, 193
    Cheese Fondue, Truffled, Polenta Dumplings
        with, 156, 157
    with Gnocchi, Oven-Puffed, 158, 159
    Polenta, and Cheese Timbales, 164, 165
    Risotto with Zucchini Blossoms and, 229
    Tajarin with White Truffle, 63
    Tortelli, Egg-Filled, with White Truffle, 142, 143
Tube-Shaped Pasta Tossed with Four Cheeses,
        116
Tuna
    Linguine with Anchovies and, 64, 65
    Spaghetti, with Garlic, Tomato, Mint, and
        Fresh Tuna, 19

V
Veal
    Agnolotti with Its Own Sauce, 84, 85
    Ragù, White, Tagliatelle with, 190, 191
    Sweetbreads, in Offal and Mushroom
        (Finanziera) Sauce, Potato
        Dumplings with, 86, 87
Vegetable(s). See also specific vegetables
    Gratin of Crespelle Stuffed with Spring
        Vegetables, 206–208, 207, 209
    Lasagna with Fresh Tomato Sauce, 38, 39
    Ragù, Root, Mixed, Buckwheat and Potato
        Gnocchi with, 92, 93
    Ragù, Spring, Whole Grain Black Risotto with,
        230, 231
    Risotto with Beans, Salame, Red Wine, and,
        100, 101
    Roasted, 38
Vermicelli with Mussels and Pecorino Romano, 18
Vinegar
    Balsamic, Aged, Pennette Tossed with
        Pumpkin, Parmigiano, and, 62
    and Sopressata Sauce, Polenta with, 96, 97

W
Walnut(s)
    Apple, Porcini Mushrooms, and Fontina,
        Risotto with, 106, 107
    Penne with Zucchini, Provolone, and, 182
    Sauce, Bavette with, 58
White Pasta, Straw-and-Hay, 237
    with Peas and Ham, 188, 189

Z
Zucchini
    Gratin of Crespelle Stuffed with Spring
        Vegetables, 206–208, 207, 209
    Penne with Walnuts, Provolone, and, 182
    Purée, 229
    Tortelli with Stracchino Cheese and, 200, 201
    Trofiette with Lobster, Leeks, Fava Beans,
        and, 184, 185
    Vegetable Ragù, Spring, Whole Grain Black
        Risotto with, 230, 231
Zucchini Blossoms
    Risotto with Mussels, Saffron, and, 222, 223
    Risotto with Truffles and, 229